D1215059

VENTURE INTO GREECE

VENTURE INTO GREECE

With the Guerrillas
1943–44

Nicholas Hammond

WILLIAM KIMBER · LONDON

First published in 1983 by
WILLIAM KIMBER & CO. LIMITED
Godolphin House, 22a Queen Anne's Gate,
London, SW1H 9AE

© Nicholas Hammond, 1983
ISBN 0-7183-0299-0

Photoset by Jubal Multiwrite Limited
Printed in Great Britain by
Garden City Press Limited,
Pixmore Avenue, Letchworth, Herts.

TO GREEK FRIENDS
IN WAR AND PEACE

Contents

List of Illustrations

List of Maps

*Acknowledgements: to wartime companions, especially Ronald
Prentice, Arthur Wickstead and Vincent Desborough, and to
Richard Clogg of King's College, London.*

Preface

After my return to England in September 1944, I was in and out of hospital for some months and it was then that I wrote down the account which is published here. My aim was to get my experiences in Greece out of my head and out of my blood. Since I brought home only the draft of my last long signal, my writing throughout was from memory. The views which I held *then*, in 1944, are given here unaltered; for they were part of the scene — a time of war within an occupied country, when one saw things in distinct colours and had to make firm decisions. The manuscript was read by the Hon C.M. Woodhouse, DSO, OBE, Allen Sotiracopoulos and R.R. Prentice, who were with me at various times in Greece. Monty Woodhouse, whose *Apple of Discord* (London, 1948) is the classical book on this period, saved me from error in some points of fact, and I express my gratitude to him for that and for a great deal else in Greece.

In 1981 I added the Introduction, the Retrospect and the Appendix. The importance of this period in contemporary Greek politics was brought home to me by taking part in a conference in 1978 which was reported in the book *Greece: From Resistance to Civil War* (ed. M. Sarafis, Nottingham 1980), and by being in Macedonia during the elections of 1981. It was always my intention to publish these reminiscences in my retirement, when the chances of harming any other participants in these affairs will be minimal and when at least some of the facts need to be saved from the veneer of partisan writing. I am particularly grateful to my wife who helped me throughout and made the final typescript and to Mrs Howlett and other members of Kimber's staff who have been kindness itself.

Clare College
Cambridge.

N.G.L. Hammond.
December 1982

List of Abbreviations

ALO	Allied Liaison Officer
AMM	Allied Military Mission
BLO	British Liaison Officer
BMM	British Military Mission
CO	Commanding Officer
EAM	National Liberation Front
EDES	National Republican Greek League
EKKA	National and Social Liberation
ELAS	People's National Liberation Army
ELAN	People's National Liberation Navy
EOM	National Organisation of Magnetes
FO	Foreign Office
GHQ	General Headquarters
GOC	General Officer Commanding
HQ	Headquarters
IMRO	Internal Macedonian Revolutionary Organisation
KKE	Communist Party of Greece
MG	Machine Gun
OSS	Officer of Strategic Services
PAO	Panhellenic Liberation Organisation
PEEA	Political Committee of Greek Resistance
RE	Royal Engineers
RSR	Raiding Support Regiment
SOE	Special Operations Executive
UNRRA	United Nations Relief and Rehabilitation Administration
WT	Wireless Telegraphy
YBE	Defenders of Northern Greece

Introduction

In 1938 the War Office asked all dons whether they had any special qualification in the event of war. I replied that I spoke Greek and some Albanian and knew north-west Greece and southern Albania very fully, because I had been making an archaeological survey of those regions since 1930. The call came in May 1940, and after a minimal training in the use of explosives I was flown out to Athens on 7 June, only to be refused admission by the Greek authorities. They probably had some suspicion of my mission, which was to enter Albania secretly and instigate a rising against the Italians (they had seized Albania on Good Friday 1939). The Greeks were maintaining a strict neutrality at that time. It was the Italians who moved first. They joined Germany on 10 June, and any mission to Albania was in abeyance.

In October 1940 Greece rejected an ultimatum by Italy and entered into alliance with us against Italy. During that winter the Greek army drove the Italians back into Albania by amazing feats of courage and endurance. I came to Athens on 15 March 1941, when the Greek army was about to launch a spring offensive against the Italians. The department which I joined, Special Operations Executive, was attached to the British Embassy. Its function was not to help in the Greek offensive but secretly to train Greeks as wireless operators and as saboteurs who would act if Greece were ever occupied by the Axis powers. The Greeks who had been selected hitherto for this training were opponents of the Greek Government: a few elderly Venizelists (liberal democrats) and a considerable number of Communists, who since the banning of the Communist Party in 1936 by Metaxas had maintained their underground organisation. The latter were the tougher characters, but their allegiance was to Russia, then at peace with Germany and her partner in the partitioning of Poland. The whole business was conducted without the knowledge of the Greek Government, although Greece was then our only ally. The rationale behind this policy was that the Greek King and the Government, headed by the dictator Metaxas, who had been trained as an officer in Germany, would side with the Germans, who had cleverly remained neutral and were disregarding the war of their ally, Italy, with Greece.

The policy of SOE seemed to me misguided, and I persuaded the staff officers at Athens to widen the field of recruitment. But it was too late. Germany delivered her ultimatum to Greece, the successor of Metaxas, Koryzis, rejected it and a German army invaded on 6 April. Meanwhile in Athens there was a fervour of enthusiasm. Crowds collected outside the British Embassy and sang 'God save the King' and 'Tipperary.' Morale was very high, but more than morale was needed. On 21 April the Greek army of the Albanian front laid down its arms. It had been completely outmanoeuvred by a German mechanised column. The soldiers, undefeated in battle, began the long march home.

The British expeditionary force had no alternative but to retreat. SOE made its final arrangements, and at night in Athens I delivered wireless sets and sabotage materials to agents I had trained and to others unknown to me. During the retreat I undertook to destroy the cotton stocks of the Lake Copais Company at Haliartus. This was successfully achieved at night while the last troops were withdrawing, and with them I drove south at a snail's pace between lines of proud Greek soldiers who were marching homewards. They called out to me, 'Come back and we shall fight alongside you.' Just before dawn I passed through Athens. The streets were deserted and the blinds were drawn, and they remained so when the Germans drove into the city later that day and ordered the sentry on the Acropolis to take down the Greek flag. He did so, wrapped himself in it and committed suicide over the cliff. Koryzis as Prime Minister stayed in Athens, signed the surrender and committed suicide.

The King, the Government and such forces as had not been serving on the Albanian front continued the war by fighting in Crete and then in the Middle East. They expressed no criticism of our part in Greece, and probably they felt none; it was rather we who felt guilty that we had failed to hold Crete for them. Some of the Greek troops volunteered to go back to Greece. They were trained at Haifa in wireless operating, demolition (my speciality) and guerrilla warfare, and of their first instructors three spoke Greek: Monty Woodhouse, Paddy Leigh-Fermor and myself, my nickname then being Captain Vamvakopyrites, 'Captain Guncotton'. The holding camp for those who had been trained was at Athlit in a ruined Crusader castle, where we danced Greek dances and sang Greek songs together. It was from these men that we chose our companions for the return to Greece.

In occupied Greece a new Government was formed but only with the approval of the Germans and the Italians. To us and to most Greeks it was labelled 'collaborationist.' News of Greek affairs came to SOE in Cairo from the wireless sets in Athens at first of both groups and then only of the Communists; for the Venizelist operators were caught. Other information was brought out by escapees. They talked of incipient resistance movements and especially of one called ELAS. I heard one escapee, Sophia Vembo, sing to a wildly enthusiastic audience in Alexandria the Rigas song of the Greek War of Independence against the Turks, 'Better one day of freedom than forty years of slavery and prison'.

The first attempt to link up with the resistance movements of the Greek mainland came in October 1942, when a group of volunteers, officers and men, were dropped by parachute into the mountains of Central Greece. Their target was the Gorgopotamos railway bridge, and they had been told through the wireless set in Athens to expect the assistance of the local ELAS forces and their commander 'Ares'. However, there was no sign whatsoever of ELAS. Monty Woodhouse, who had already been on a mission in occupied Crete, made his way to north-west Greece, found Napoleon Zervas, the leader of another resistance movement, EDES, and brought him and a group of his men back towards the target. At this moment Ares and a group of his men surfaced. All three — British, Edesites and Elasites — combined in the attack and destroyed the Gorgopotamos bridge on the night of 25 November.

With the exception of Monty Woodhouse, who was to stay on, the British group was to be evacuated by submarine from the coast of north-west Greece. All of them spent a harassed winter there in the territory of EDES, where they owed their survival to Zervas and his men. The submarine never came. They realised they were there indefinitely. Meanwhile SOE in Cairo decided to send an independent mission into north-west Greece in order to establish contact with this mysterious ELAS, which had failed to live up to the fine achievements which were still being reported through the wireless set in Athens. The staff officers of 'the Greek desk' were those who had directed affairs in Athens, and their sympathies were less with EDES than with ELAS, because their contacts in Athens had been with the left wing in politics and they believed the reports that ELAS was militarily efficient. But they had very little information indeed when they briefed the first two volunteers for this mission, Rufus Sheppard and myself.

Rufus was probably about my age, which was thirty-five. He was a bachelor who had taught English at Cairo University for some years, and he had taken part in the guerrilla war which led to the liberation of Abyssinia from the Italians. He spoke no Greek and had no special knowledge of the country. He was a friendly man, and we enjoyed one another's company in Cairo. My own past was imbued with Greece: off and on for ten years in peace-time; then through the campaign on the Greek mainland and the campaign in Crete; and afterwards in training Greek soldiers. I had also been engaged in the clandestine training of Jewish youths selected by the Zionist Agency (Moshe Dayan led the first group); and in the planting of agents in Syria, and the selection of a secret caique base in Cyprus and the training of the first group of Dodecanesian Greeks in the applying of explosive 'limpets' (metal containers with a magnetised thin plate which cling to the hull of an enemy ship). I was perhaps the only married BLO (British Liaison Officer, as we came to be called officially), and Monty Woodhouse, being in his twenties like most of the BLOs, once referred to me as 'a fatherly old gentleman' (I had an infant daughter I had not seen).

Each of us had to pick three companions. Rufus took an English wireless operator, an English-speaking Egyptian Greek as his interpreter, and a Greek soldier whose home was in Thessaly, the area Rufus was bound for. I selected three Greeks from those I had trained at Haifa. Yanni, a regular army officer, commissioned in 1940, had seen some action in Albania and had escaped from Athens. Alekko, a regular NCO of the Air Force, had served on a mission in occupied Crete. Palaeologus, an Egyptian Greek, had served on a mission in occupied Samos as a wireless operator. We were trained together on a variety of courses and ended up with a truncated parachute course at Kibrit in Egypt.

My task was to be a military one. The target which had been chosen was the railway bridge over the Peneus river in the Tempe Pass of Thessaly, and the officer who briefed me for this undertaking was a regular brigadier in whom I had little confidence. However, captains cannot be choosers. The main thing was to get away from Cairo as quickly as possible. Rufus and his three dropped onto Mount Olympus with the full moon of the New Year 1943. We were to go in February.

First Experiences in Thessaly

This chapter covers the period February to May 1943. At the beginning of February the Russian victory at Stalingrad ended Hitler's attempt to destroy the heart of Russia. In their turn the Russians advanced, and the Anglo-American forces drove the Germans out of North Africa. The Japanese were in occupation of Burma, but their advance was halted at Guadalcanal and in New Guinea.

The first attempt to get us off during the February moon was a failure. We were keyed up for hours before the news came through: 'Not tonight.' The following day, the 20th, a sudden change of plan put us in the top position. We were kitted up with parachute equipment. I was given a crash-cap of solid rubber, although I had asked for one with solid sides and a canvas top to which I had become accustomed at Kibrit. The despatching officer took us down to the plane, a four-engined bomber. It was still daylight when the engines started up and we were off on the way to Mount Kissavo (the ancient Mount Ossa) in north-eastern Thessaly.

As soon as we began to climb, the warmth of Egypt turned to a cold which became more and more numbing. In our part of the plane the heating had broken down, and we flew very high over Crete, where there were said to be German night-fighters. We were miserable with cold, and ate lots of chocolate to warm our stomachs. Nothing was to be seen, as we were in cloud or above the clouds, until we suddenly saw land far below. One of the crew told us it was Thessaly. The snowfields on its ring of mountains, the rivers and the sea glinted in the moonlight, and we could spot Mount Olympus.

We were told to make final preparations and obey the system of lights, green to get ready and orange to go. The escape hatch in the floor was not circular but rectangular. We sat round its top. I was to go first, and the others as soon as possible after me. We were so numb with cold that none of us had the usual panicky feeling. Suddenly the green light, then the orange, and I shot

out into the wind-slip of the four engines. I gasped for breath as
I fell free. Then the heart-filling pull of the parachute. I was
floating thousands of feet up, higher than I had ever been in
practice. I looked down and saw a fire glittering. I looked up,
and saw that almost half of my parachute was caved in. There
must be the most terrific wind. I looked down again. The welcom-
ing fire had disappeared. The wind was drifting me rapidly, and I
was oscillating like the pendulum of a clock.

Features of the ground were becoming dimly visible in the
moonlight; fields of snow, black patches of trees and grey patches
with darker lumps which were probably rocks. I got myself into
the sideways position I preferred for landing and waited for the
bump ... something was pulling hard at my leg. I opened my
eyes and saw my parachute flapping in the wind with my right
leg entangled in the shrouds. I slapped the release-buckle, freed
myself, crawled out of the prickly shrub in which I lay, and
freed my leg. I felt dazed and dizzy, and I realized I had been
knocked out. The top of my head was painful, and a knob of
swelling was developing on it, even beneath the thick-crowned
cap. Had I worn the cap I preferred without the padded crown,
I might not have survived. But I was excited and warm.

I fired a Very light, as had been arranged, and after an interval a
Very light replied. I went towards it and met Yanni and Palaeologus,
who had fallen into trees. They were scratched and torn, but
unhurt. They had found each other with Very lights, but there was
no sign of Alekko. We set off up-wind, which was also uphill, on
the ground that the wind had drifted us away from the fire, and
before long we were greeted by shouts in Greek and shouted in
reply. Dim, ragged figures appeared out of the moonlight, embraced
us, and led us on uphill, singing the Rigas song 'Better one day of
freedom than forty years of slavery'. We came over a ridge, and
down to where a fire burned. More men embraced us. We had
arrived.

Dawn found us huddled round the brushwood fire in a small
dell. There were pockets of snow on the sides of the dell, and
the cold wind was still blowing strongly. Our new friends looked
more ragged and more dirty by daylight than they had by moonlight. The leader, Kissavos, wore an old Greek army tunic, stained
and buttonless, which covered several layers of dirty sweater,
shirt, and vest; a pair of rough brown trousers, of which the legs
were pushed into high cavalryman's boots, and a khaki side-cap
bearing a strip of white cloth with the Greek letters ΕΛΑΣ sewn

on it. He also wore three belts of various sizes, one carrying a holster and revolver, another ammunition and another an old map-case into which he put his papers. Kissavos was a short, stocky man of middle age. He struck me from the outset as rather grudging in his welcome, and very un-Greek in his lack of spontaneous hospitality and of garrulity. The other men were in rags of various hues and materials, some with one or more bandoliers of ammunition slung across their chests, with dilapidated army greatcoats, and others with nothing khaki at all. Kissavos alone had boots. The others wore either Vlach shoes, shaped like a small gondola, or thin hide tied round the ankle, or simply rags bundled round their feet.

Apart from Kissavos, they showed the usual loquacity and curiosity of the Greek peasant. They regarded us with the utmost interest. Huge ungainly Yanni with his thick-soled crepe-rubbered jumping boots, and the all-enveloping dark-brown 'sirensuit', with zips and silk cover; Palaeologus, stocky, swarthy and boastful in a childish way, proud of his Luger pistol, Commando knife, compass and gadgets; myself with a face covered with frozen blood and deep scratches, and so swollen that only partial vision with one eye was possible. My foot and ankle, too, were so swollen that they could not get into a boot. As Yanni said later, it was a queer-looking Englishman who had dropped to them from Heaven.

The section of Andartes* scattered to look for Alekko and the canisters, which had dropped after us. Alekko turned up several hours after dawn, having been knocked unconscious like myself by hitting his head on a rock. On coming round, he decided to lie doggo until dawn and see where he was before he began moving. He arrived carrying his parachute and flying-suit neatly folded. The canisters came in gradually. Some were never recovered, having been drifted miles away by the wind, which was the worst of that winter, we were told. The last package, the charging-engine for the wireless-set, was brought up by a tough peasant who had found it low down the mountain and transported it on his back. He waved our thanks aside, delighted at the thought of an Englishman returned to Greece.

With Alekko the party was complete. Kissavos, who had been restless since dawn, insisted that we should move at once up the mountain; he spoke with alarm of Italian patrols and of Italian aircraft. Some mules in sorry condition were produced, and we

* The Greek name for resistance fighters.

moved slowly through the groups of pine trees into the snow belt. Before we started, Kissavos told me that he wished to conceal our identity, and that the Italians would chase us if they got to know that an Englishman was with them. He suggested we should all wear the ELAS strip and pass as Elasites. It would then be supposed, he said, that the plane had dropped stores only and not bodies. I agreed with some reluctance; but as I was unable to walk, I would clearly be a hindrance if any pursuit ensued, and I might, as an Englishman, invite one. The conditions anyhow were strange to me, and I let Kissavos take the lead at first.

At midday we had out first meal, boiled lentils and some maize bread (*boubota*). We continued on up the mountain in the afternoon. The going had been bad, and my mule had fallen several times, so that I began to learn how to be thrown off without hurting my injured leg. When the snow deepened, I had to get off and hop along supported on one side by a Greek. Finally, the mules were off-loaded and sent down the mountain. We slept high up in the snow, inside a low windbreak of scrub and branches, with a huge fire of pine trunks in the centre of the circle. Lying fully clothed inside a kapok sleeping-bag, and with a greatcoat over me, I slept like a log, and awoke in the morning feeling very cold and contracted about the head. I put up my hand and found my hair was frozen. Unlike the others, I had slept with my head outside my greatcoat. During the night the snow and frost had congealed on my hair, which was stiff with icicles and hoar frost. I slept the next night with my head inside.

The others felt the cold intensely, in fact more than I did, after the warmth of Egypt. Yanni, in particular, crowded on every garment he could. We spent several days and nights in the snow; and Kissavos insisted on moving camp each day to evade possible pursuers. The cold by day and night was bitter. Moreover, during the day we had no fire, lest the smoke should betray our position. As I could not walk unaided in snow, I had great difficulty in keeping warm, and even in removing myself a reasonable distance to obey nature's calls. We had left our store lower down and we fed as the Andartes, that is, twice a day, at noon and at nightfall, on either lentils or boiled beans and a little maize bread. Our avid hunger counter-balanced the monotony of the diet.

Meanwhile, Palaeologus was trying in vain to make contact with Cairo. He maintained that his set and his batteries were in order, and he insisted repeatedly that he would certainly contact Cairo soon. The charging engine had been damaged, and would not work, but the batteries were in order, and should have sufficed for some time. His twice-daily failure to make contact, our dismal and inadequate food, the feeling of running away from hypothetical dangers, and the fact that my ankle was still huge, had a depressing effect. The cold, too, was intense, the *Vardharis* blowing steadily from the north.

One evening Kissavos told us he had found a tent for us. After the evening meal of lentils and maize bread, I crawled into it first. The tent was two-sided, open at each end; it formed a natural funnel for the *Vardharis*. Lying on the windward side, I called to Yanni, who lay down alongside me, and the other two fitted in beyond him, so that we lay all four like sardines inside the tent. I was woken up in the small hours by the tremors of Yanni, who was shivering all over. He soon rose and left me, and I saw that the others had already gone to the usual camp-fire outside. On losing the protection and warmth of Yanni's large frame, I was soon shivering, and joined the others squatting round the fire.

These fruitless and chilling days were not wasted. Kissavos remained impenetrable, but we got to know the six or seven Andartes who lived with us. Kissavos himself proved to be a doctor; he examined my ankle, and pronounced no bones broken. The only other educated man in the group was Clearchus, a thin, gentle-looking man of wide interests. Before the war he had worked in the Greek Patent Office, and he had been a con-scientious objector in the war in Albania against Italy. The winter of 1941/2 in Athens changed his attitude. His wife and children survived the famine, but he had watched children and adults dying in the streets, spurned not only by Germans and Italians but also by those Greeks who had wealth and thereby the means of saving their starving fellow-countrymen. Leaving his wife and children with friends in Volos, he joined the first resistance group, which happened to be ELAS in Thessaly, in order to gain revenge and to liberate Greece.

When I asked him what his role was in the group, he told me he was the man who executed prisoners and collaborators with an axe. His victims, he said, were almost always fellow-Greeks, and their crime was 'collaboration'. He told me he had a thrill of pleasure in hacking off the head of a fellow-Greek who had shared in the guilt of the Germans in starving Greeks to death. Clearchus was clearly unbalanced in this one respect. Otherwise he was a gentle and cultured man, and we became quite close friends. Yanni, too, found him congenial as a fellow Athenian of cultured background.

The other members of the party were Thessalian peasants and shepherds, whose motives were mixed, part patriotism, part love of adventure, part vainglory as would-be heroes; and it was also a way of being fed. They were rough and illiterate fellows. Most of them had had fighting experience in Albania, and they put up with real hardship in a cheerful way. We liked them and got to know them all.

As February drew to a close my leg got no better. Kissavos absented himself more often, Palaeologus ended by ascending almost to the top of Mount Ossa in a vain effort to establish radio contact, and two of his batteries split with the intense frost. I told Kissavos we must change our plan. I should move into a house until my leg mended, Yanni should tour the groups of Andartes in Mavrovouni and Pelion, and the other two should stay with him and his group. I gave him a number of boot-soles and blankets from our stores, and offered him some gold sovereigns. At first he was offended, muttering the words *e kitrine lepra* (the yellow leprosy), and refused to take any, almost as if I were trying to corrupt him. Eventually he accepted one hundred sovereigns expressly to buy boots for his forces.

Next day he took me after dark into a village called Spilia and left me in what appeared to be the poorest house. My host was a rough fellow and dirty, his wife was suspicious, and the baby of three was filthy. The room was devoid of furniture and so was the house, apart from an occasional rickety chair. The food was worse than I had been having, in that there was even less of it, and I had no company and nothing to read except Jannaris' English-Greek dictionary. But the swelling of my ankle began to go down a bit after a few days, and Kissavos had me moved to a *kalivi* or turf-hut on a wooded hillside. In the village no one had called to see me except one man, a friend of my host, and he was equally crude and suspicious. On leaving the village, I did speak to a better-dressed man, but he obviously wanted to avoid conversation with me because my host was with me.

At the *kalivi* Alekko and Palaeologus joined me. We now obtained car batteries from Larissa, and Alekko repaired the charging engine with an axe and a commando knife as his tools. At last Palaeologus managed to make contact with Cairo. By now Yanni was with us, and I could give Cairo some picture of ELAS as we had found it. In military organisation ELAS consisted of groups of fifteen or so men, each called an *omadha*. A varying number of these groups made up a *synkrotema*, the group covering a canton such as Ossa or Olympus. The *synkrotema* was directed from above by a centralising command, with which I was not then acquainted. The vital element was the *omadha*, or group of fifteen men, who in this first winter of the resistance movement lived a hard and sometimes dangerous life, ill-armed with Greek or Italian army rifles, few machine-guns and little ammunition. Ill-clad for the rigours of camping out in winter weather on the mountain-sides, they had developed a corporate morale and some esprit de corps. They had attacked small posts and alarmed the Italians. In our area, the *omadhes* were on Ossa, Mavrovouni, Pelion and Tsangli (inland of Volos).

The whole complex was commanded by Kissavos, who put the total number of his armed guerrillas at four hundred. The individual groups were fed by the hill villages, either voluntarily or by force, and there was a requisitioning system, under which the ELAS commander issued a chit payable by the future Greek Government after the liberation. The miserable rations of the guerrillas in February 1943 showed that there was little spontaneous support from the local villagers.

In addition to the armed guerrillas, there were the village guerrillas or militia who had some weapons, and were expected to defend their villages. These latter were organised village by village and formed 'reserve troops' in ELAS jargon. Their leader was usually the ELAS agent or 'responsible' (*ypefthynos*) in the village. Intercommunication between *omadhes* and *synkrotemata* was maintained largely by village runners, drawn from the militia, and the collecting of news and stores from towns was arranged in a similar way wherever an ELAS militia could be organised.

This organisation suited the facts and the geographical conditions of guerrilla warfare in its infancy. It left the initiative almost completely in the hands of the leader of an *omadha* or of a *synkrotema*. Its demands on the villages and on man-power were small, and it could exist in small mobile units capable of pin-pricking Italian morale, which was always weak. The members of the ELAS *omadhes* were mainly trained men of mature age who had seen service in Albania, simple and rough characters who were genuinely eager to attack Italians in their country's cause. On the surface, ELAS had military possibilities. Given arms and clothing, it could expand and embarrass the occupying forces.

The more serious problem, however, was the nature of its command. Kissavos, the doctor, was clearly a competent organiser and disciplinarian, but he was morose and suspicious. Why was he secretive, afraid of accepting sovereigns, anxious to conceal my presence with his force? It might be a personal idiosyncrasy; yet the query remained, why was a doctor of this sullen type selected to command an area? He had no military experience at all. When I asked him about the political affinities of the movement, he told me of the oath which all members of ELAS took, namely, to resist the occupying powers, liberate Greece, and resist the return of the King unless and until a plebiscite was taken. As Kissavos pointed out, this oath admitted all patriotic Greeks and even Royalists, if they agreed that a plebiscite should be held.

He explained that ELAS was the armed force of a civilian organisation, EAM, which organised resistance in the cities and villages. To this EAM all republican parties belonged; in so far as ELAS had a political background, it was republican of a moderate kind. On the face of it, Kissavos appeared to be telling the truth, and the *omadhes* I knew (for by now we had trained several in the use of explosives at the *kalivi*) consisted of people with such political views. But the selection of Kissavos as CO and of my host at Spilia as the 'responsible' remained strange, as did the reaction of the villagers so unlike what I had known in prewar and pre-occupation days.

At this point, my choice of Greeks instead of Englishmen as my companions bore fruit. Yanni, as an Athenian and a regular officer, was a student of politics. He was not a violent partisan, although his sympathies were Royalist. He had been struck almost at once by the terminology of ELAS, and as he travelled through the villages to Pelion, he heard more of the ELAS propaganda terms. These, he assured me, were mainly of Communist origin. Yanni brought back with him some examples of EAM literature, which showed the same characteristics. This peculiar quality, a matter of diction and not of content, was not apparent to a Greek-speaking Englishman, or even to a Greek peasant unless he was conversant with Athenian political jargon. For example, it was not apparent to Palaeologus, a Greek of Cairo origin, and was only occasionally apparent to Alekko, a Corinthian with little formal education.

Yanni also brought back a good deal of information which he had got from an ELAS commander on Mavrovouni, a young

Greek officer and a regular like Yanni. He told Yanni that he had
at first been an officer in a rival guerrilla movement called EOM,
or National Organisation of Magnetes, a local movement originat-
ing in Volos, operating on Pelion, and willing to co-operate with
ELAS, then also in its infancy. ELAS had soon refused to co-
operate. Then with EAM support from Volos, it had succeeded
in frightening EOM into liquidation. Yanni's friend Christos had
gone over to ELAS as a military commander. Christos thought
that some of his former associates in EOM had been assassinated,
and he was quite certain that the ultimate control of ELAS was
in Communist hands. Yanni had also heard of an EAM youth
movement in Volos, which had an unhealthy precedent in the
'Neolaia' or young Fascist group of the Metaxas regime. On the
other hand, Alekko, whose sympathies were republican and
leftist, was reticent about the political colour of the EAM-ELAS
movement. He concentrated on its ability to attack the occupying troops. He was scornful of men like Kissavos; but he was
equally scornful of any Greek officer. Palaeologus had no clues
at all, partly because he was slightly imperceptive, but mainly
because he was an Egyptian Greek. For instance, he went one
day to a Church Festival, and came back saying everyone had
been shouting 'Long live Russia!' (*Zeeto e Rosseea!*). Yanni
thought this most significant; but when I questioned Palaeologus,
I found that he himself had been the first to raise the cry!

In this way we had gained some idea of EAM-ELAS and some
conception of the doubts and questions still outstanding, before
Palaeologus made contact with Cairo. As I had been ordered
to concentrate on military matters and to leave Rufus Sheppard
to deal with political affairs, I sent strictly military information
about ELAS and Italian posts and positions. The only political
question which Cairo asked of me was about the real nature of
EAM-ELAS. I gave the opinion which I had formed on the evidence
we had, and I added that only acquaintance with the ELAS
command at a higher level and with EAM committees could enable
me to give a confident diagnosis.

During the last days in the house at Spilia Rufus Sheppard
walked over from his station on Mount Olympus, in order to see
how I was getting on. He had dropped in January onto Olympus,
where the ELAS movement in Thessaly had its military HQ,
the total force under its command being called a *soma*. Here
Rufus had met the military commanders and the principal EAM
agent in Thessaly. His impressions were entirely favourable to

EAM-ELAS. He believed their reports of frequent large-scale and successful operations against the enemy, and he accepted their picture of a broad political movement which was essentially non-party. The queries which Yanni and I had evolved were not within his ken at all. In many ways this was not surprising. Rufus knew no Greek. He had no idea of Greek politics, his operator was English, and his Greek sergeant Papadhakis came from Cairo. The fourth member of his party, Papayannis, a Thessalian villager, had been killed in dropping, when his parachute failed to open. As Rufus had stayed mostly with the ELAS commanders and as Papadhakis had broken his ankle in dropping, they had had little chance of checking the truth of the official accounts.

The question, who controlled the policy of EAM-ELAS, was an important one for us. We were serving as British Liaison Officers between GHQ Middle East and irregular Greek troops in a war which we regarded as a continuation of the 1940–41 war conducted by the British Government and the Greek Government against Italy and Germany. The political affiliations of GHQ Middle East were of course to the Governments of the Western Allies; and one of them was the Greek Government in Exile of King George. However, *if* the irregular troops of ELAS were ultimately controlled by the Greek Communist party, it was clear that their allegiance would be directed neither to GHQ Middle East nor to any Government among the Western Allies but to Moscow alone. In that event the duties of liaison which we were carrying out as representatives of GHQ Middle East would be unwelcome to ELAS sooner or later. It might be that the immediate aim of the Greek Communist party and of Moscow was the same as ours, namely to attack the occupying forces; but this did not assure us of any continuing community of interest.

In those days we did not think of Russia as a gallant ally; for the memory of her pact with Germany, her bombing of Helsinki and her partitioning of Poland and the Baltic states was too vivid in our minds. The Spanish Civil War, too, had taught us the lesson that any Communist party in touch with Moscow was out to seize power and then conform with Russia's policy. The days when the Russian system of Communism had been regarded as a paradise of egalitarian liberty had passed long since, and the majority of us shared the view which was expressed by Churchill in his *Second World War*, Volume II. 117: 'Hitler and Stalin had much in common as totalitarians, and their systems of government were akin.' In short ELAS could not serve two masters. If its loyalty was to Russia, the sooner we became aware of it the better.

The days at the *kalivi* were rather tiresome, because my ankle was slow to mend. In early March, the weather suddenly changed from snow, sleet and cold mist to a sunny spring. My ankle began to improve as the first aconites came out. Our food remained extremely meagre, so much so that one midday one of our number, who shall be nameless, stole the loaf of maize bread and ate some, to the indignation of the rest of the party, when the crime was discovered. Our beans or lentils were cooked for us by an old shepherd, who lived with his grandson and his dogs in a nearby *kalivi* where his sheep were penned. The old man was known to us as Grandpa (*papous*) and he had all the common sense of the aged. We sat with him most evenings and talked. During a conversation about religion and fasting, when I had mentioned the Ramadan fasts in Egypt and the unwillingness of the English to fast, he produced the epigram '*nestevoune e Arapadhes kai trone e Angle*' (the Arabs fast and the English feast). It was his definition of Imperialism. The old man had a remarkable cry which he would suddenly emit in mid-conversation to frighten the wolves; and Alekko (his favourite) and the dogs would rush out into the night howling and barking. They were always successful; at least he lost no sheep.

We were sorry to leave the old grandfather in late March, when my ankle was fit to hobble on and the weather was warmer. By then we had done our best for Kissavos. I had chosen a dropping-ground high on the mountain, being carted up by mule and on the shoulders of an Andarte through the snow-drifts. At last an aeroplane came and dropped stores, light machine-guns, ammunition, boots, and rations for us. The roar of the plane reached me and Palaeologus at the *kalivi*, just as Palaeologus came off the air to Cairo. When the plane flashed the expected signals with its lights, Palaeologus danced for joy and we experienced the thrill of contact with the outer world.

Alekko was then away on a reconnaissance of the coast. I had sent him off to find suitable coves for a caique base, whence crossings could be made to the Turkish coast. He returned one evening with a haversack full of *soupyes* (cuttle-fish), which made a wonderful change from our diet of beans and lentils. He had made an excellent reconnaissance, and two of his coves were later used for this purpose. He was able to confirm that ELAS groups had attacked some Italian posts south of the Peneios river mouth, and he had heard of a caique laid up for the winter there, which might be commissioned for a trip to Turkey.

At this stage an ELAS doctor called Skoufas, who was a cheerful and hearty fellow and a general factotum, came to see my leg. He told me that he was from the island of Sciathos. I discussed with him my plan of chartering a caique and opening communication with Turkey and the Middle East. Skoufas was enthusiastic. He admitted that there were few caiques available, but he mentioned the sum of 250 gold sovereigns as the purchase-price of a small caique. On the other hand he suggested that it would be best to requisition a caique without more ado. He told me later that he knew of some possible boats.

Our other task before we left Mount Kissavo was to train men in demolition and in small arms. This Yanni and I did. We sent some Andartes to make a reconnaissance of the Tempe pass, and in particular of the Peneus railway bridge, which, I had been told before leaving Cairo, might be my first major target. Yanni and Alekko made a full reconnaissance later, while I went by mule and approved a dropping-ground on a plateau in the hills above the Peneus bridge. Alekko took a group of ELAS trained in demolition by us to the line near the Thessalian end of the Tempe pass. There they laid a charge with a pressure-point detonator on a bend of the line, and the first train to come along set off the charge and was derailed. But it was not going fast enough for the engines and the carriages to be seriously damaged.

Another point of interest in this area of Thessaly was the chrome, which was mined at Tsangli. The Middle East authorities wanted any information I could get about chrome, an important ore for war purposes. ELAS told me they had captured a German engineer and his wife during a raid on a mine at Tsangli, but they had no one capable of interrogating them in German. I visited them in a house at Spilia when they were being taken to the HQ of ELAS on Olympus. They were both terrified of the Andartes. They were amazed and slightly incredulous at the presence of an Englishman, and they were willing to give me any information I wanted. The man was middle-aged, unwell, and harmless. He was the chief mining engineer in North Greece, and he gave me the production figures and the numbers of workers in all the mines of Macedonia and Thessaly. His role had been to step up production as much as possible. He admitted to a lack of success in this respect which, he said, was at least partly due to guerrilla action. His wife was very frightened. She protested a great deal about her diet (the same as that of the Andartes), but she had been as well treated as guerrilla conditions allowed.

In late March I walked out of the *kalivi* without help for the first time, some six weeks after we had dropped, and ascended the ridge above the small valley in which the *kalivi* lay. Below me stretched the flat plain of Thessaly as far as I could see, with Larissa clearly visible, and beyond Larissa the Pindus range. The main road from Larissa, the Italian HQ in Thessaly, ran clear below us and ascended towards Spilia. We were, in fact, not far from the Italians, but they had not moved at all during the winter and spring. We had a feeling of complete security on our mountain. We buried most of our stuff near the *kalivi* of the Grandpa, who alone knew its precise location, and we set off on the mules. Many months later, I sent Alekko to the *kalivi*, and the Grandpa had kept the secret. I walked with a guide provided by the village of Spilia, a stupid youth who lost the way. We were benighted in thick scrub among snow-pockets. A rough cross-country walk in the dark renewed the pain in my ankle, but it wore off in the next few days.

We were on the way to Olympus. This involved crossing the Peneus railway-line, the main road and the river, an area guarded by German troops. We came down one afternoon to a village on the edge of the plain. There I left Palaeologus in the house of the 'Responsible', while I went up the hill to see the ELAS section which had carried out the demolitions on the railway line under Alekko. They were a good section with a regular subaltern, who was known to Yanni. I left Alekko with them for another exploit (p. 33 below). At dusk I returned to Palaeologus. He had been bundled into a back room, when two German soldiers had called and been admitted to the front room. They had come to buy eggs. We were told that Germans often came up in twos and threes from the railway guard-points and from road-posts. It did not pay either them or us to cause trouble.

During the night we crossed the road and the railway line, myself on a mule as my ankle was of little use in the dark. The Germans appeared to be nervous after the recent derailment. Many Very lights were fired, and we crossed the line in their glow just before a slow train passed. As the moon was going down, we reached the ferry point on our side of the Peneus. Just before dawn an old ferryman came over in a small boat and took us across. The ELAS guard which had come with us from Kissavo said goodbye, and we found an ELAS section of the Olympus group across the river. With them we climbed up the hillside above the river in the first rays of the rising sun.

Next day, as my ankle felt better, I walked on my own ahead of the mules, and reached Rufus Sheppard's HQ in the evening. On the way I made friends with some Greek Government gendarmes who had joined ELAS. One walked alone with me. He warned me that the ELAS command and control were Communist, and that they were committing many crimes. He and his colleagues had joined, because they had no option; for ELAS had raided a post they were manning, and they had had to come over to them. Rufus lived in a village house at Karyta on Olympus. His wireless-operator, Evans, was first-rate at his job, but the room was a pigsty. They lived mainly on the rations dropped to them by the planes which had come to them several times. Yanni and Palaeologus envied them their style of living, as I had kept our small stock of tinned food unopened in case of a crisis.

Since our meeting in early March Rufus and I had travelled further apart in our views about ELAS. As Cairo had ordered him to deal primarily with the political side, I did not labour the point, and he was not open to argument or persuasion. He told me the claims of ELAS, and their estimates of what they could achieve if properly armed. The doubts I expressed fell from him like water off a duck's back.

A climax came when the two of us met the ELAS commander of Thessaly, Karayeoryis, an amiable and charming diplomat who was a lawyer by training, not a soldier. As Rufus had told Karayeoryis that my concern was only with demolition and with the caique project, I did not share in their general discussion, but I came in on the matter of a caique route. Rufus had told me that Karayeoryis did not talk any English. I did not talk any Greek at first. Papadhakis acted as our interpreter.

From the outset Karayeoryis was sceptical about inter-communication by caique. He set out to win Rufus's approval and he tended to treat my remarks as those of a junior officer (Rufus and I were both majors, but he was senior in Thessaly). Despite his objections, I persisted and asked him his view about a purchase-price for a caique. He suggested up to 2,000 sovereigns. Remembering Skoufas' price of 250 sovereigns, I told Rufus in English that this was a fantastic sum, and mentioned figures of caique prices in Crete in 1941. Although none of this was translated, Karayeoryis went on to defend the high price, which showed he had understood. I realised then that Karayeoryis knew English well but was concealing the fact, and I guessed that he did not want to open contact by caique with the Middle East. Later I told Rufus this, but he did not agree. He regarded me as cynical, but there seemed to me to be no other rational explanation. For the moment Karayeoryis had his way. The first caique came later in the year from the Middle East to one of Alekko's coves on the coast of Thessaly; we did not at that stage open communication from our end.

On the same occasion the secretary of all Thessaly EAM joined us. He was introduced as Demos. His face was familiar to me. During the discussion I remembered that he was a brother of one of my prewar friends at Ioannina, and that I had once met him at a village called Khouliaradhes. Demos clearly did not recognise me in uniform, with my long reddish moustaches. At the end of the discussion I said I had met him in Ioannina, but he denied it. Only later, when we were alone, he admitted his identity and asked me not to give it away. Like all members of EAM-ELAS, specially the key men, he used a pseudonym and carefully concealed his real name. I too had a pseudonym 'Eggs' (being a schoolboy pun on Hammond-eggs), and Sheppard had the pseudonym 'Hills'. My penetration of Demos's pseudonym was not of much help as evidence about the political nature of EAM, because I only knew him as a capable lawyer in Athens, whose brother had been a Venizelist.

At this meeting I brought up the conduct of Kissavos as a commander, and I said I thought he was exploiting his position to make political propaganda. Karayeoryis agreed this was most improper. He put on a still more indignant manner when I said that the propaganda was for the Communist party. As a matter of fact, I had little evidence and was simply trying out Karayeoryis's reaction. I thought he over-acted, but Rufus held him to be sincere. Karayeoryis said Kissavos would be removed from his command. He was, but I met him later in September holding a higher command elsewhere.

Life at Karyta was in some ways more comfortable than it had been in our *kalivi* on Mount Kissavo, but the presence of a British Mission was public knowledge in the vicinity. German planes had been over recently, and at dawn on the day after our arrival they came again and bombed the village rather inefficiently. But the villagers did not like it, and we were alarmed for our wireless sets. Next day at noon we were told that a German drive had begun from several sides of Mount Olympus, and the ELAS command told us to get ready to move. Mules were requisitioned and loaded up by late afternoon. As we moved uphill from the village, we could hear firing not far off on the hillside towards Elassona. We withdrew all night in the direction from which the Germans were coming, but at a higher level. As we left Karyta, we had heard some shots near the village. I was told that the Elasites were executing their prisoners, including the mining engineer and his wife.*

By dawn, we were up on the flank of Olympus high above the main road which runs north of Elassona. Our mules straggled slowly in, and I found we were one mule short. The missing mule had been loaded with a container of gold sovereigns, 800 of them. I sent Yanni back to find them. During these enquiries, I noticed plumes of smoke rising from the horizon, and identified one centre of the fires as Karyta, which was being burnt to the ground by the Germans. This was the first of many instances where the Andartes withdrew and the villagers suffered.

Before evening we moved towards the lower ground, and we spent all night in crossing two main roads and reaching the first village off the road. All ELAS forces were now retiring from Olympus, and we were a motley crew, more than a hundred strong, with our strings of mules and donkeys. We crossed each main road in groups, letting an occasional German convoy pass by, while we lay low. As usual all precautions lapsed as soon as we were across the road and had reached the first village. Every-one off-loaded and lay in the sun, and no sentries were posted, although a side road led to our village. A convoy of German troops passing along the main road caused a scare.

About noon we moved on into the thick country of Hasia. We continued at the pace of the slowest mule all that night. Sleep nearly overcame us on the way. Indeed Rufus seemed to have the power of sleeping on his feet, as he lumbered slowly along in the dim moonlight. Nightingales sang throughout the night, and we passed sometimes through the acrid smoke of fires which had been started deliberately to burn down the oak scrub. Next day we kept on past Akri, where I spotted a good dropping ground,

---

*   The Germans and the Italians shot all Andarte prisoners. ELAS shot their prisoners on this occasion because they knew too much about the movement, and they were likely to escape or be re-captured by the enemy.

Training of future guerrillas by Jumbo Steele at Haifa in 1942.

ELAS guerrilla with shepherd's cloak and crook.

ΕΛΛΗΝΙΚΗ ΠΟΛΙΤΕΙΑ   ΔΕΛΤΙΟΝ ΤΑΥΤΟΤΗΤΟΣ

'Επώνυμον *Μπακας*
"Ονομα *Σωτήριος*
'Ονομα Πατρός *Γιάννης*
« Μητρός *Μαρία*
'Επάγγελμα *Κλωστήρας*
'Εγγεγραμμένος εἰς τὰ Μητρῷα τοῦ Δήμου ἤ Κοινότητος *Κοζάνης*
ὑπ' αὔξ, ἀριθ. *35* καὶ ἔτος γεννήσεως *1901*
'Εν *Κοζάνῃ* τῇ *23 Μαΐου* 1943
Ο ΔΙΟΙΚΗΤΗΣ

The author's forged id card for entering Salon Sotirios Bakas

Karatsas (left) and Diplas (right)

Old villagers (right) watch mustering of mules for Mission and ELAS

and around midday we reached Ayiofyllo, a dirty village with swarms of rather small pigs. There we rested at last for a few days. I bathed in a rock pool to the surprise of the Greeks. It was my first immersion since leaving Egypt.

The withdrawal, organised by Karayeoryis and Smolikas, a younger and more military man, had gone well. There had been no casualties and no strain, except on the goodwill of the villagers. One result of this withdrawal was that several hundred Andartes found themselves together, whereas they had acted hitherto in groups of fifteen. They now felt themselves to be part of an important movement, and Karayeoryis and Smolikas did all they could to build up this feeling. The withdrawal was depicted as a fine strategic movement of evasive action. In terms of guerrilla warfare the withdrawal was prudent, but in terms of civilian suffering it was a tragedy, as we learnt later, if one had any feeling for the sufferings of the villagers.

Another party had dropped in to reinforce Rufus, just before we left Olympus. It was headed by Jim Power, known as 'Horse', a hearty and forthright RE officer. From Ayiofyllo, Karayeoryis retreated still further into the Pindus range, and to the annoyance of Power and myself Rufus followed suit. We were then rejoined by Yanni, who had found the canister of sovereigns on a fallen mule and crossed the main road later than us, and by Alekko, who had completed his last attempt on the railway in the Peneus valley. Alekko had had an exciting time. Because the line had been blown up recently, German trains were travelling at a very slow speed, so that, if an engine set off an explosive charge, the whole train was not derailed. Having laid his charge on the track at a curve, Alekko planned to board an engine, put it at full speed ahead and jump off before it came to the curve. He and an Elasite waited by a railway halt, while an ELAS group lay hidden on the hill above the halt, prepared to intervene if things went wrong.

When a train drew in, Alekko and the Elasite dashed into the driver's cabin. By good luck, the driver and his fireman were unarmed Greeks. The Elasite covered them with his Sten gun and took them on to the track. Alekko reckoned he would make a thorough job of it by putting a time-delay bomb in the locomotive's smoke-box. As he went forward to plant it, the ELAS group opened fire prematurely. The volume of fire in reply showed that the train was full of troops. Alekko had to take cover from the ELAS bullets behind the locomotive. Suddenly it began to

move out, and Alekko realised that some Germans must have
manned the engine. As the train moved slowly out, he fired
magazine after magazine of ammunition with his Sten gun into
the carriages from his own side, from which the Germans were not
expecting any fire. When the train reached the curve, the charge
went off. It damaged the locomotive, but the train was not derailed.
The German troops on the train were some of those who were
conducting the drive on Olympus. During the drive Alekko lay
low. Afterwards he crossed Olympus on his own and talked to
the villagers. From them he learnt that the Germans had burnt
down a number of villages, and had shot some villagers at Karyta
in reprisal for the killing of the captured Germans by ELAS.

At this time it was decided that I should go to Macedonia and
act with the resistance there. But my departure was delayed
because I was instructed to make an immediate enquiry into the
rights and wrongs of an affray between ELAS and an independent
force under Sarafis and Kostopoulos.

The general position at this stage was rather complicated. The
original mission, commanded by Brigadier Eddie Myers, with
Chris (as Monty Woodhouse was now known) as his second-in-
command, was all in the north-west or in Roumeli (central Greece
south of Thessaly) and mainly in non-ELAS zones. Rufus himself, together with me and Power, were independent and not
under Eddie's command, and we had experience of ELAS but
not of Zervas (leader of EDES). Rufus thought Eddie was unduly
pro-Zervas and anti-ELAS. In my opinion, but probably not in
Cairo's, Rufus was unduly anti-Zervas and pro-ELAS. His views
were known to Karayeoryis, who played up the successes of
ELAS and exaggerated the failings of Zervas and EDES. In view
of this, I had suggested to Rufus that he or I, or both, should
visit Eddie in an attempt to co-ordinate our policy in the field.
Rufus would not do this, and I felt his aim was to discredit both
Eddie and Zervas.

Friction had arisen between Rufus and Eddie and between
ELAS and EDES over the affray of Sarafis and Kostopoulos, two
officers who had led an independent band out of Trikkala and had
tried to establish a new movement on the foothills of West Thessaly. There ELAS had attacked the band and wiped it out. Their
prisoners included Sarafis, a Greek colonel with a good military
reputation and a revolutionary of Venizelist (i.e. liberal democratic) sympathies. The argument of ELAS was that Sarafis and
others were in the pay of the Germans and intended to act as a

fifth column. Karayeoryis told me that he had written evidence
in support of this view, but I neither saw it nor wished to see it;
for no one could tell whether it was a forgery or not. My enquiries
had to be made independently in the area where the slaughter had
occurred. So I walked by myself up the Peneus valley from Kalabaka to above Malakasi.

On the way I met Denys Hamson, an officer of Eddie's mission,
who was in an embittered state of mind, very anti-Eddie and
indeed anti-Greek. Having volunteered only for the Gorgopotamos
operation, he felt he had been kept in by a breach of faith. We had
met in Cairo, and we now exchanged friendly greetings. I told
him what I was up to, but he did not return the compliment.*
He rode on down to Kalabaka. I also met Kozakas, a fiery ELAS
commander who had been fighting the forces of the Germans in
the area west of the Zygos pass. He said he had been attacked by
some EDES men. I spent Easter Day with him and his group at
Malakasi. There was much firing of small arms and machine-guns
and much roasting of requisitioned lambs, all in honour of the
Risen Christ and of an ELAS hero killed in the fighting below the
Zygos.

Kozakas himself was a young, handsome fellow who had
served as a muleteer in the war in Albania and boasted of his
humble position then. He had the natural bravado which sits
well on a guerrilla leader. The villagers of Malakasi were terrified
of him and of the ELAS men. I had had friends in Malakasi in
1939 and in earlier years, but my attempts to thaw out any of
the villagers apart from the 'Responsible' and his friends failed
completely.

On my return journey via Kalabaka, I stopped in a village
where the ELAS troops showed their hostility by turning their
backs on me when I walked into the village square, but not before
I had noticed a man with a pair of fair-sized moustaches. By now
my red moustaches were so enormous that the ends were visible
from behind me. So I went up to the man, and said in Greek,
'Poor fellow, what's that stuff you have under your nose?' The
others looked round and laughed. We were soon on good terms.
They said they had cold-shouldered me because they thought I
had come from EDES, as Hamson had done.

One night I slept in a village where hostility to ELAS was very

* See D. Hamson, *We fell among Greeks* (London, 1946) 150 f. and
E.C.W. Myers, *Greek Entanglement* (London, 1955) 114 f. and 125 f.

marked. Here my host was very reticent, because an ELAS 'responsible' had parked me with him, but late in the night a widow came in and told me with hysterical weeping that the ELAS police had tortured and murdered her husband on a charge of collaboration, which she swore was false. She herself had been turned out of her house and was wandering from friend to friend. I had no means of establishing the facts, and I could do nothing to help.

My investigations had been in a sense a wild-goose chase. I had not been able to see and question Sarafis. No one could disentangle the facts from the fiction in the different accounts of the villagers, Kozakas, Karayeoryis, and others. It was probable that ELAS had taken steps to prevent any rival band from establishing itself in Thessaly, as it had evidently done in the case of EOM earlier (see p. 25 above). But this did not mean either that Sarafis' band was above suspicion of having an understanding with the Germans or the Italians, or that ELAS was unjustified, from the point of view of wartime, in trying to centralise all organised resistance in this area under one flag, namely its own, to which British officers were accredited. Whatever the motives or the grounds of ELAS action, they were not clear yet. One thing was obvious, that in this region, where ELAS, Sarafis, and EDES had clashed, the villagers were frightened and terrorised. The widow's story gave me my first insight into civilian reprisals by guerrilla bands.

From Kalabaka I walked to Rufus's new and remote HQ west of Ayiofyllo. I made a report on the Sarafis business, but I found Rufus (predictably) unduly credulous of the Karayeoryis version. Rufus was even more indignant with the British command than with the Greeks. He regarded Eddie Myers as responsible in some way for the Sarafis episode and he resented the appearance of Denys Hamson in Thessaly, which he regarded as his own preserve. Rufus sat down to concoct an angry signal to Cairo. He was aiming at a show-down over the matter of the command in Greece. I was not willing to support Rufus in his views either of ELAS or of Eddie Myers (I did not know Eddie at this stage, but I knew Chris, his second-in-command), and it was with relief that I prepared to move to Macedonia.

It was now the beginning of May 1943. I had lived almost entirely with groups of ELAS men in the open or in village hovels or huts, and I had been infested with lice and fleas. As the summer began, the bed bugs opened their season. Our food had been of the scantiest, for we had fed with the Andartes and we had often got the worst of their rations. Yanni, being the biggest man, had felt this most, but I had often sent him off on jobs on his own when he had obtained better food. At this time he was at Akri, organising a dropping-ground for receiving planes. I sent orders to him to join me at Grevena. I set off ahead of Palaeologus and Alekko, who were to bring the wireless set and other gear on mules. Karayeoryis, the sleek lawyer, having been told of my appointment to Macedonia, remarked that he was himself in command of all Northern Greece, including ELAS in Macedonia.

CHAPTER TWO

The Growth of ELAS in Macedonia

The next three chapters cover the period May to July 1943. Anglo-American forces landed in Sicily on 10 July, and the German armies in Russia delivered a counter-attack which failed.

Being on ground which was familiar from prewar days, I walked on my own to Kipouryio, where an ELAS unit was stationed. The commander telephoned to Grevena, saying I was on the way. I took a short cut and reached Grevena in the heat of the afternoon. I had no military cap, and was bare-headed; I carried my battle-dress tunic, and I wore dark blue breeches, blue puttees and heavily-nailed army boots. In this attire, and in a muck sweat, I walked unnoticed into the square of Grevena, the market town of a large area, and went to the local ELAS Headquarters.

When they grasped that I was the expected Major Eggs, they were obviously surprised and rather put out. After some delay I was taken into a large building (a bank), where I was welcomed effusively by the Mayor of Grevena (a thinly disguised 'responsible'), the Bishop of Kozani, an impressive figure in purple robes with a long beard and tall hat, the local ELAS commander and the leading citizens of Grevena. They offered me a bath; but I declined, because a bath might have meant anything from being sluiced with cupfuls of water to immersion in a hip-bath, and because I had no change of clothes. However, all was cordiality. I was asked to attend a parade in my honour, at which I would be expected to speak. The Bishop asked to see my speech, but I had none prepared. So I asked what he thought should be said. He suggested I should begin with the words 'Members of EAM and fellow-fighters of ELAS!' I then withdrew and had something to eat.

The parade was in the evening. The Bishop, the ELAS commander — a rather dissolute-looking character who had been on the famous 'withdrawal' from Olympus — and I mounted a raised fountain in the centre of the square. The ELAS troops and the EAM supporters then paraded round the square with much trumpeting and uproar. The Bishop spoke first in my honour. He spoke at length and in the most fulsome style, drawing the attention of the assembled people of Grevena to the fact that the 'Great Allies' in my person showed their support of ELAS and EAM. I made a short speech, emphasising our support of all Greeks fighting in the Allied cause, whatever their organisation. Finally, the ELAS commander ended with a violent onslaught on the actions of EDES and Zervas, whom he called a drunken traitor, and also on the bands of Kostopoulos and Sarafis, which had, of course, been liquidated. This speech may have owed something to the personal idiosyncrasies of the speaker, but the occasion was ill-chosen. It revealed that here too ELAS was out to blacken any possible rival.

A complete rally of all EAM in South-West Macedonia was billed for the next day in a large hall at Grevena. The Bishop declared it would be considered discourteous of me not to attend. So I did so, and made a short speech on the lines that it was the villagers who suffered in guerrilla warfare, but that their aid was essential to us; and that the Greeks were always hoping for a speedy victory, but the English went 'slow but sure'. I expressed this in an epigrammatic form, which was often quoted back to me later by villagers: '*trekhoune e Ellenes, alla vadhizoun e Angle siga siga ma sigoura.*' The rally lasted from dawn till dark, and I had to endure endless speeches, including three fiery ones from the Bishop. The capacity of the audience to listen was amazing to me. But politics is the stuff of life for Greeks, and they had been without political speeches for two years and more.

Months later the 'responsible' of Grevena (who had more humour than most) told me that my arrival had caused consternation. A car and trumpeters had been sent out to meet me and to escort me into the town in triumph. A dapper English officer, mounted and escorted, was what they had expected. Instead, a sweaty, dirty fellow with huge red moustaches and dark breeches like a Vlach shepherd turned up, refused a bath, and made a speech without an interpreter and in a Greek which might have been spoken by a Vlach. The EAM-ELAS command imagined that people might think I was not an Englishman at all, but an EAM stooge dressed up and passed off as an Englishman. But my speech had removed that possibility; for I had expressed a willingness to approve Greek resistance under any organisation, and this was the last thing EAM wanted.

In Grevena I had talks with many EAM leaders who called to see me. They were men of different backgrounds and outlooks.

The Bishop of Kozani proclaimed himself 'the spiritual leader of EAM'. He was a conceited and foolish man, and he had a weird-looking attendant priest, armed with a huge knife, whom he called 'Mickey Mouse'.

The EAM secretary for South-West Macedonia, Andreas, a man of fanatical features and eyes, commanded my respect. He was much more open than any other EAM official. For instance, he told me how many members of the Communist Party in Macedonia were members of EAM; they were certainly a very small proportion of the membership of EAM. Another leader was a journalist, Dhimitriadhis, a keen liberal of the Venizelist school. I met a competent doctor called Kokkinos, who ran a surgery and a clinic. These were all leading men in Grevena and its environs. They assured me that ELAS and EAM were broad in their political outlook, included men of all parties, and organised a real and effective resistance to the occupying powers.

There was no doubt about the effective resistance. An Italian battalion, complete with its equipment, had recently been beaten into surrender, and the Italian command had then evacuated Grevena. This really was an achievement, unlike the many so-called 'battles' to which ELAS laid claim (for instance, I had seen a 'battle' near Kalabaka, which was nothing more than a skirmish when some Italians were withdrawing). This and other successes had 'liberated' the foothills of South-West Macedonia. ELAS had repaired a couple of cars and motor-cycles, and was using the roads in the 'liberated' area, which had a front facing the enemy in Macedonia of some fifty miles.

Yanni and the other two now joined me — Yanni with his tit-bit of news: ELAS had given him a letter of introduction which, when he steamed it open, described him as 'a traitor sold to the British'. These sinister words were significant. They showed, as I had suspected, that the ELAS command was hostile to the British, and they warned me that my Greek companions were in serious danger; for a traitor (*prodhotes* in Greek), if he fell into the hands of ELAS, was executed without trial. It was essential that we BLOs should protect them as soldiers serving under the orders of GHQ, Middle East, and that we should make this clear to ELAS time and again.

While Alekko and Palaeologus stayed in Grevena to set up the wireless, I took Yanni with me on an extensive tour of the area in the hope of finding one or more dropping-grounds. This tour gave me the impression that ELAS in Macedonia had drawn on a

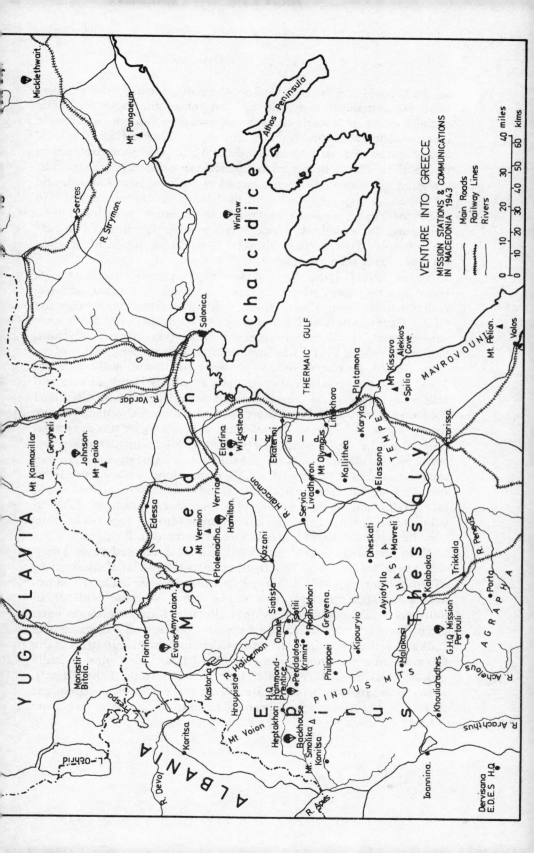

VENTURE INTO GREECE

MISSION STATIONS & COMMUNICATIONS
IN MACEDONIA 1943

——— Main Roads
++++++ Railway Lines
——— Rivers

0 10 20 30 40 miles
0 10 20 30 40 50 60 klms

YUGOSLAVIA

ALBANIA

Monastir-Bitola.

R. Devol

R. Prespa

Koritsa

Florina

Kastoria

Hroupiste

R. Haliacmon

Heptakhori

Mt Voion

H.Q. Hammond-Prentice

Pendalofos

Krimini

Backhouse

Mt Smolika

Konitsa

Ioannina.

R. Aoos.

Dervisana
E.D.E.S H.Q

Mt Kaimaxillar

Gevgheli

Johnson.

Mt Paiko

Micklethwait.

Serres

R. Strymon.

Mt Pangaeum

Athos Peninsula

Chalcidice

Winlaw

Salonica.

R. Vardar

Macedonia

Edessa

Mt Vermion

Verria
Hamilton.

Ptolemaidha.

Kozani

Evans
Amyntaion

Siatista

Omale

Tsotili

Rodhokhori

Grevena.

Philippaei

Kipouryio

Elafina
Wickstead

Ekaterini

Servia.
Livadheron.

Mt Olympus

Litokhoro

Karyia

Kallithea

Platamona

Elassona

TEMPE

Mt Kissavo
Alekko's
Cove.

Spilia

Larissa.

MAVROVOUNI

Mt Pelion.

Volos

THERMAIC GULF

THESSALY

Dheskati

Mavreli

HASIA

Ayiofyllo

Kalabaka.

Trikkala

R. Peneus

Porta

AGRAPHA

G.H.Q Mission
Pertouli

R. Acheloous

R. Arachthus

Khouliaradhes

PINDUS MTS

PIDO-42L

better type of man than ELAS in Thessaly, and that the villagers were not terrorised, but genuinely supported the movement. The initial success in Macedonia was due partly to there being separate command-areas of the Italians and the Germans, (the Germans' area commenced at Kozani), and partly to the good material in ELAS there, both men and officers. One officer was Yiannakis, a regular subaltern who commanded at Siatista, near Kozani, and who had a high reputation with ELAS. A contemporary and friend of Yanni, he was comparable to Christos on Pelion and to Evangelos, an excellent Greek engineer officer, whom I had met on Olympus. His presence showed that ELAS appealed to some capable young regulars at least.

Yanni and I found a suitable dropping-ground near Omale, some twenty miles north of Grevena. While we made arrangements for receiving planes there, I kept in close touch with the ELAS Headquarters which happened to be nearby. Relations were very cordial, and I found out some interesting things. Communication between units was maintained by runners, who often took verbal messages and were therefore quite well-informed. I got into conversation with a man at ELAS Headquarters and asked him which was his village. He named Labovë in Albania. I told him that I had been there and mentioned the name of the priest. He was delighted. When I asked him why he was at Omale, he told me he was a runner between the Albanian guerrilla movement and ELAS in Macedonia. From his description the Albanian movement was a replica of ELAS in its name, policy, system of *omadhes* and *syncrotemata*. It was now expanding its numbers, like ELAS, and it had an organisation corresponding to EAM in villages and towns. I met another runner who told me his brother 'ran' between ELAS and a resistance movement in Bulgaria.

Rumours also reached me that ELAS had allowed some Yugoslav guerrillas to cross the frontier into Greece at Kaliniki near Florina; later, but still in May, I met one of their leaders, Tempo, at ELAS Headquarters. The explanation of these widespread contacts was almost certainly that all these resistance movements were inspired and organised by the Communist parties in the Balkans rather than by Russia, which had been cut off by the German invasion since summer 1941. I heard also of a guerrilla group on Mount Kaïmatsala, led by one 'Aetos' ('the Eagle'), close to the frontier with Yugoslavia. It was evidently independent of ELAS. Otherwise ELAS seemed to hold the field in Macedonia west of the river Vardar.

As soon as the dropping-ground was organised, I left Yanni in charge of it, and returned on my own to Grevena. I sent off a series of reports on the movement to Cairo. These included all the political pointers mentioned in the preceding paragraph (see also p. 49 below). Thus in May 1943 Cairo and the Foreign Office had strong evidence for believing that EAM-ELAS was part of a general organisation inspired by the Balkan Communist parties.

My reports were concerned primarily with the military situation. Macedonia was not only the most important area strategically in Greece, but also the heart of the German occupation of the Balkans. It seemed desirable to foster in Macedonia a strong guerrilla movement which was showing itself willing to co-operate with neighbouring movements both in Albania and Yugoslavia. ELAS in Macedonia was certainly a popular and rapidly developing force, organised in *omadhes* and *syncrotemata* and commanded by capable men. It had been unusually successful so far, its commanders were co-operative with me, and the rank and file covered a wide range of political opinions. Cairo decided to build up ELAS in Macedonia. I was told that a party headed by a major and a considerable quantity of supplies would be dropped at Omale.

There were two commanders, apparently of equal authority, in ELAS at this time. One, called Vangeli, was a vigorous, blustering fellow who claimed that he was a cavalry officer. He swaggered around in riding breeches, booted and spurred, and was often on a horse. I thought he was a Macedonian of mixed Greek and Yugoslav blood. I distrusted him from what I had seen of him so far. On one occasion he challenged me to go riding with him on some captured Italian chargers. An enormous beast was brought to my house, and I got on to its back from a balcony, being no rider, before he appeared on his horse. He charged off at speed. My beast broke into a gallop in pursuit, which made it easier for me to stay on. We flew down a stony track till his mount stumbled and threw him. Mine then stopped, and I slipped off it. Leading it back with considerable relief I consoled Vangeli. But his sense of honour (*philotimo*) was hurt, and we did not ride together again.

The other commander was a little, dapper, neat-featured man of thirty-five or forty, who had a lively sense of humour, a dashing style, and black moustachios. He called himself Kikitsas after a leader in the Greek War of Independence, and he modelled himself on the traditions of that period. He struck me as a genuine guerrilla, a fighter and a good leader of men, with no false pretensions. In many ways he was a man after my own heart.

At Grevena Alekko, Palaeologus and I lived in a small house on the western side of the town. Our only light after dark was a wick in a saucer of olive-oil, and it was very tiring on the eyes to encode and decode messages to and from Cairo daily. We were grateful when we received an unexpected accession to our party. The ELAS commander in Grevena asked me to examine a man who was pretending to be an escaped English prisoner-of-war but who, he thought, was really a German sent to kill me. Such a trick had been tried elsewhere. The man was sent under escort to me, and he proved to be bald-headed, puffy-eyed and in considerable discomfort, as his skin had been sunburnt and was peeling and blistered. He limped along with his feet on the uppers of his burst boots.

At first he could hardly utter any words that even sounded like English. When I told the ELAS escort that he appeared not to be English at all, they wanted to shoot him. But I took him home and I sat him down on a bench to share our evening lentils. He gradually found the use of his tongue. He began to speak English with a Welsh accent, and unfolded his story. He told me he had been taken prisoner at Chania in Crete where he was serving as a hospital orderly. I happened to know the hospital. So I asked him whether he remembered any naval men there. He mentioned some survivors of the *Wryneck*; these were the men we had brought from the Anana islands in escaping from the Greek mainland to Souda Bay. This answer established his bona fides.

It was almost two years since Alfred Booth, as he was called, and a younger man named Atkins had been travelling north through Macedonia on a prisoner-of-war train, when they managed to cut some of the wire on the truck window. They fell out head-first, rejoined one another, and took to the hills. They did not know where they were, they had no food, and it was cold. After tramping for some days, Atkins stopped, intending to give himself up. Booth went on. Just before dark he went down to a village to ask for food, and met a small boy who took him to his grandfather's house. He was fed there that evening. As he was about to go, they indicated that he was to stay the night. He stayed for almost two years, living in the space between the roof and the ceiling, and going out only in the dark, because there were Germans billeted in the village and the loyalties of the villagers were divided. During these two years he learnt Lazika (a Turkish-Greek dialect), the games and the proverbial wisdom of the village, and all the songs; for he had a fine Welsh singing voice. This was an example of a man's lively interest keeping him sane.

After a few days Booth settled down with me as if he had never been anywhere else. He had come out of hiding in order to find me, because one of the family had heard my speech on that first day at Grevena and had reported it to Booth. The old grandfather came later to visit him and embraced him as his own son. Booth like me was a married man with a daughter, and we became fast friends.* Booth's younger companion, Atkins, was found in 1944 and joined the Mission in Macedonia when I was no longer there. He had gone to ground in the same way.

Another escaped prisoner-of-war was an Australian who, after many adventures and privations, joined an early band of ELAS on Olympus. When Rufus arrived, he reported to him, but Rufus decided that he had better continue to serve with ELAS. The Australian had spoken to me during the retreat from Olympus, and he now came to spend a day or two's leave at Grevena. He had really come to warn me about ELAS. Having joined it at the beginning, he had been subjected to a good deal of Communist propaganda, and he had seen people tortured and killed for purely political reasons. He knew that many of the leading men were anti-British.

This Australian's account did little more than confirm the suspicions which I had formed on other evidence; taken by itself, his account might not have carried conviction (it did not with Rufus), because he had suffered a great deal and was obviously unbalanced in mind and temperament. Some time later he was one of the first party which was evacuated from Alekko's cove on the Ossa-Pelion range. He was sent out because he had become unstable and then shot a Greek with his revolver.

The next arrivals were Major Johnson and his party. Like Rufus, he had been in guerrilla warfare in Abyssinia, where he had won the DSO and bar. He was a bluff and direct man, with pale blue eyes and a taciturn manner. He hated fuss, but he was out of luck. He came in for the reception that I had side-stepped. The morning after he had dropped at Omale, he and his party

---

* In September, I had him flown home with the rank of sergeant. He died at home, as the result of falling from his bicycle; he proved to have an unusually thin skull.

were driven to Grevena in a degutted butcher's van, which was the ceremonial ELAS vehicle. On debussing, they were kissed and wreathed with flowers, blessed and harangued by the Bishop of Kozani, and escorted by cheering crowds to the bank, where the Mayor and other citizens gave them an honorary luncheon, which compared well with our lentils, beans and *boubota* diet but badly with the gourmet delights of Cairo. Johnson was glad to be rescued by me from the party. I liked him very much, but I found it difficult to train him as a liaison officer. His lack of interest in local affairs and his intolerance of Greek tortuousness made him uncongenial to the Elasites, and I gave him mainly commando operations.

All this happened at Grevena in South-West Macedonia during a week or two. Meanwhile, in Thessaly, the ELAS units had not returned to Olympus, and Rufus was still at Ayiofyllo. The local ELAS commanders had begun sending messages to me that the Germans were massing in Macedonia for a great drive through Grevena to Kalabaka (i.e. via Ayiofyllo), and they asked me to move westwards and go with them into the Pindus range. By this time, I had Johnson running a rear station with his WT set at Rodhokhori near Omale, and I found Grevena as a market town a good centre for obtaining information from civilian sources. Since there seemed to be no sure evidence of an impending drive, I refused to move. ELAS gradually withdrew, and a few civilians also left Grevena. Meanwhile, Cairo was relaying to me signals from Rufus and other officers in Thessaly, repeating the same information of a threatened German drive, to which I replied telling Cairo that it was probably an ELAS stunt and had no foundation.

When all ELAS had left, life was pleasant in Grevena, and no news of any German moves came in at all. But I could not stay as long as I wished. Cairo ordered me to go and see Rufus at Kipouryio, where I found him and Karayeoryis both full of the impending German drive and demanding my withdrawal from Grevena. As Rufus was particularly anxious, I gave way and joined Johnson at Rodhokhori. There was, in fact, no German move at all. My obstinacy had achieved one object; it had shown Cairo how much our information tended to derive from the ELAS command and could be coloured as ELAS chose. In fact, ELAS had withdrawn for quite another reason. Once they had concentrated their forces in a safe area of Pindus, they organised some so-called elections, the first since the outbreak of war in

October 1940. The Andartes realised their own power and numbers for the first time. It was the first clear indication of the political purpose of the whole movement and of the skill with which it was organised.

In late May, before I left Grevena, I sent a long report on the situation to Cairo. The decision to use the forces of ELAS in Macedonia had already been taken in Cairo. Operations were required in June, and there was no active force there other than ELAS. From the military point of view, the Macedonian Elasites were of better value than those in Thessaly for several reasons. They were composed of all types. They were not yet riddled with political differences, and there had been no fighting against other Greeks (as had happened near Kalambaka and in other places) to upset their morale. They had been very successful in capturing an Italian battalion with its equipment and in liberating Grevena and Siatista. During my first friendly days with ELAS I had obtained details of the weapons and ammunition which ELAS held in Macedonia. They gave the information in order that I might estimate what they should receive from Cairo. The expansion of their forces was now going ahead rapidly.

As in Thessaly, the winter months had been hard and the numbers had been few, because it was a tough life, and because supplies were not organised for large numbers of men. But with the spring men and beasts moved into the open, and in May the shepherds and their sheep were migrating from the occupied lowlands into the 'liberated' highlands. The life of a guerrilla was now much easier; food was improving, and experience had shown it was a comparatively safe occupation with plenty of glory. In consequence, recruiting was easy. ELAS now recruited young boys in preference to grown men. In the early summer their strength in Macedonia stood at about 3,000, of whom the bulk were in the south-west. One of my tasks was to equip this force up to a useful point. In fact, equipment by air-drop could never be on a large scale, and I tended to discourage ELAS from recruiting any more men.

One problem was the question of relief for the villages that had been burnt to ashes. In withdrawing from Siatista and Grevena the Italians had burnt a string of villages along the main road, and had destroyed all the livestock. Some of these villages I had already visited. The people were on the brink of starvation. Moreover, there was danger of disease, as they were all crowded together in lean-to hovels. The Bishop of Kozani emphasised the moral right of such villagers to the help of the 'Great Allies'. In practice, the only help we could give was in the form of gold sovereigns, which would enable the villagers to buy grain in the German-occupied plains. The problem was how to ensure that the money stayed in the hands of the villagers and was not diverted into those of EAM-ELAS.

My answer was to form a committee of three in each village, consisting of the headman of 1941, the priest, and the school-master. This committee was to be in charge of the whole matter, and the British would distribute the sovereigns to individuals in the presence of the committee. This method was approved by Cairo. At first it cost comparatively little in relation to the allevi-ation of suffering it brought and the goodwill it earned us.

I had also to report on the need for medical supplies of all kinds, especially for malaria. The health of the villagers was surprisingly good, although below peacetime standards. The main need was for drugs and for surgical gloves. I had to go on asking for several months before the gloves came, because they were in short supply. Here again, it was difficult to ensure that EAM-ELAS did not tap the supply of drugs in order to benefit them-selves. The other problem was how to feed the guerrillas. Cairo proposed to pay as a fee for maintenance a gold sovereign a month for each man. I was opposed to this, because it was important from many points of view, including efficiency, to keep the numbers down. To pay a gold sovereign per head, it seemed to me, would lead ELAS to increase its numbers by leaps and bounds and to divert more food from the mouths of the hill villagers. Despite my opposition (and independently that of Chris), the system of paying a sovereign a man was introduced for all guer-rillas in Greece after I left Grevena.

In building up the strength of ELAS we had to consider how far the Communist element controlled the EAM-ELAS complex, and how far it would be able to do so, if ELAS expanded. The evidence for a centralised control was strong. The subordination of military command to political command was strict; indeed most of the high-up commanders had no qualifications for holding military posts, e.g. Kissavos, Vangeli and Karayeoryis. The 'withdrawal' in May on the pretext of an impending German drive had been a political move. There were also signs of Communist propaganda being cautiously conducted in individual *omadhes*, and we learnt occasionally of atrocities committed for political reasons. Each unit had its own executioner, like Clearchus on Mount Ossa,

Satellite view of North Pindus with Corfu (lower left), Lake of Ioannina (lower centre),
NW Thessalian plain (lower right) and Lake Kastoria (upper centre).

Rock pinnacles above Kalabaka
(some of them are crowned
by the Meteora monasteries).

Dawn view of the Mezilo valley

and the executioner at Grevena was an ELAS officer, Aoutis, whom I strongly disliked. He was later assassinated.

It was equally clear that EAM had an efficient method of organising the villages and towns. In each village a 'responsible' was appointed. He acted as liaison with ELAS for billeting, requisitioning, and recruiting; for by now ELAS was living mostly in the villages and demanded various services from the civilians. The 'responsible', nominated by EAM-ELAS, had replaced the elected president (*proedhros*) of the village, who had been a leading man by conventional standards. Now the 'responsible' was often the roughest member of the village. The change was certainly indicative of a left-wing tendency in the organisation. On the other hand, as Andreas had told me at Grevena, the actual number of Communists in EAM-ELAS in Macedonia was relatively small, although it was the Communists who were most active. The great bulk of ELAS and even many of the EAM leaders, like Dhimitriadhis, held moderate political views. There was a very real hope that, if ELAS expanded, it might swamp the Communist control. Both Andreas and the Bishop had argued that all patriotic Greeks should join ELAS, although they had given different reasons.

When I was with Rufus and Karayeoryis at Kipouryio, I was introduced to the newly-appointed commander of ELAS in Macedonia, one Karatsas, so named after a hero of the Greek War of Independence. He was extremely nervous, rather boorish, and at first ingratiating; I suspected he was one of Karayeoryis' nominees and not a Macedonian. He followed me to Rodhokhori and pitched his HQ nearby at Omale, from which Vangeli disappeared, for good as far as I ever knew. While I was at Rodhokhori the nature of ELAS became somewhat clearer. Its affinities with other Balkan movements became more obvious. One of Johnson's men, who went under the pseudonym 'Heracles', came from this part of Macedonia. He was a dashing, brilliant officer who had done well in Albania. He was some thirty years of age, and like most regular officers of that age he was a Royalist. He arrived in Greece almost on the very day that his father was beaten to death by an ELAS group, because, according to Heracles, he was of a different political persuasion.

Hroupista, his birthplace, lies in an area where there are villages of both Greek and Bulgarian speech. The Italians had a garrison in this area and they had armed some Komitaji, that is Bulgarian-speaking guerrillas, to fight against ELAS. This put

ELAS in an awkward position, because the EAM doctrine — which I had heard preached at the Grevena rally — was that all Balkan peoples, even Bulgars, were brothers. If they quarrelled it was only because they had been misled by Fascist monsters. This internationalist thinking was upset by the conflict of nationalisms which had now broken out between the Komitaji and the Elasites.

I came across the Komitaji in a personal way on two occasions. I interrogated a couple of them who had been captured. They were simple, indeed stupid, men who had taken arms and ammunition from the Italians. When asked why, they said to defend their villages from the Greeks, who, according to the Italians, were about to burn them down. When I said the Italians were more likely to burn their villages, these two were equally happy to fight for ELAS.

The other occasion was one evening when I was riding pillion with an ELAS despatch rider on a motor-cycle. Some Komitaji took pot-shots at us, but fortunately their aim was poor. At first ELAS, led by Vangeli, burnt the Komitaji villages.

Then ELAS changed its policy (and changed its commander, who was now Karatsas) and began to recruit Bulgars into its own force. ELAS now avoided any clash with the Komitaji, and in fact their units quickly died out. The new attitude revealed the policy of EAM-ELAS headquarters as opposed to that of a local commander, and there was no doubt that it sprang from Communist doctrine and policy. For it had always been a declared aim of Stalinist Russia to create an independent Macedonian state, in which Greek, Serb, Albanian and Bulgarian would be fused together into a non-national community.

CHAPTER THREE

The Mission Expands

The arrival of Bill Johnson and his party and the withdrawal from Grevena to Rodhokhori marked the end for me of the first phase in Greece. Hitherto I had worked on my own, using my three Greeks for particular jobs. Palaeologus was a slow but competent wireless operator, but he had not learnt to encode or decode with any speed. I did almost all this dull work in the evening by the dim light of a wick burning in olive-oil. The arrival of Booth was a great help to me; for he soon learnt to handle the coding. I often sent Yanni in advance of me to make the first contacts with ELAS commanders, and he had opened and organised the dropping-ground at Omale with great efficiency. I had sent Alekko back to our first base on Mount Kissavo near Spilia in order to dispose of the explosive which we had left there, and to make further reconnaissance of the coast for the establishment of a caique base.

Ever since we left Kissavo we had all been going at full stretch. Having had no time to organise a separate store of food, we had fed on Andarte rations, which were very poor. For four months we had existed mainly on bread and beans and lentils. This was partly my fault, because I preferred to live like the rank and file of Andartes and give the lie to the stories which were rife of British luxury.

When Johnson, his English wireless operator Mike, his English Commando Sergeant Kite, and the Greek officer Heracles joined us, a more organised and comfortable headquarters became possible and even necessary. I had sent Johnson ahead to choose a HQ in Rodhokhori, an attractive hill village, some eight hours on foot from Grevena, and I now moved my HQ to join him. We took rooms in several houses, and we built up a stock of stores, including food, from the drops at Omale. Thus from May onwards, we always had a base HQ (although it moved fairly often later), to which we could return for a rest and for better food. Shortly after the establishment of this HQ, an RAF wireless operator, Leo Voller, was dropped at Omale. He took over my wireless set and gave Palaeologus a much-needed rest.

Our main task was to organise and develop the military side

of ELAS in Macedonia to its highest potential for the intended operations in June. As the ELAS commanders had the same aim, although with a further objective in mind, their co-operation was exemplary. They even kept their hands off the sovereigns we were distributing to the *pyropatheis*, the victims in the burnt villages. They had between 3,000 and 4,000 men, armed mainly with Greek and Italian rifles and only a few machine-guns. Most of the men had joined for patriotic and not political reasons and, being Macedonians, they were sturdy fighters, and less excitable than the Greeks of the southern provinces.

In late May and early June, a large number of planes dropped rifles, machine-guns, ammunition and explosives at Omale and Philippaei, our subsidiary dropping-ground. When German planes intervened and bombed the fires we had lit to bring in our own planes, I arranged to start fires early on a dummy dropping-ground and these fires drew the bombs of the German planes. Once they had gone, we waited for an agreed signal from our planes and then lit the fires on the proper dropping-ground. It amused Leo Voller and me to listen to the Germans bombing a barren hillside to blazes. Johnson, Kite and Heracles trained selected groups of ELAS men as Commando teams and demolition squads for joint operations in the future.

I visited advanced ELAS units near Kastoria and at Siatista. The Italian forces in Macedonia were now confined to Kastoria, for they had lost all the country west and south of the Haliakmon river. The new ELAS Commander, Karatsas, organised a night attack on Kastoria, but it failed badly. This did not surprise me. I had always opposed attacks on towns by ELAS. There was practically no chance of taking a town held by regular troops in any strength, and there was little or no point, if one did succeed, in committing guerrilla troops to the defence of a town. There was, I thought, a particular reason for ELAS trying to capture Kastoria. From it there is an easy route over the hills to Koritsa in Albania, and with Kastoria in ELAS hands communications with the left-wing Albanian movement of Enver Hoxha would have been greatly eased.

The advanced unit at Siatista was doing a useful job. It was able to block the main route into the Haliakmon valley from Kozani, the nearest German base, and to bring supplies from the German-occupied area to a main road which served the Haliakmon valley. A small number of lorries and motor-cycles were smuggled from the occupied area into ELAS territory, and these eased the problems of communications and supplies so long as Siatista was held.

The commander of the ELAS unit at Siatista, Yanni Lamiotis, was a young regular officer who had great qualities of leadership and courage. We struck up a close friendship, but he never revealed to me his views on the political trend of ELAS and EAM. He claimed that he had no interest in politics, and that he lived for war and liberation. I think he was sincere. He took me round Siatista on one occasion, and I gave some sovereigns and made a speech to the next-of-kin of men killed in the capture of Siatista from the Italians. The women were in deep black and wept bitterly, but they and the people of Siatista were proud of their achievement and of the ELAS movement. With the usual Greek optimism they failed to realise their danger. The road between Kozani and Siatista was open, and the Germans could carry the pass or capture the town any day they liked.

On this occasion, Yanni and I had what was to be our last meal together. We drank each other's health in the excellent Siatista wine before he saw me off on my walk back to Rodhokhori. He lost his life soon afterwards, when he led a night attack on a German armoured force, which came on to capture and burn Siatista. He was the only ELAS officer in Macedonia whom I recommended for the Military Cross. He was one of the few regular Greek officers who had joined the ELAS forces in the early days.

The bulk of the ELAS forces in Macedonia were now concentrated in the mountains west and south of the Haliakmon, between the two market towns Kastoria and Grevena. The withdrawal in Thessaly from Kissavo and Olympus to Pindus, in which we had participated, had been paralleled by withdrawals from Pieria and Mount Vermion into the mountains of north-east Pindus. The whole countryside there was dominated by ELAS. Rumours reached me that full-scale elections in 'Free Greece' were being planned, and the 'responsible' in the villages became exceedingly officious. Rallies were frequently held, and at these the support of ELAS by the 'Great Allies' was much emphasised. This term, of course, included Russia. An odd manifestation of Russian sympathies occurred at Omale, where I noticed some men wearing not the Greek letters ELAS on their caps, but a five-pointed star. I sent for Karatsas and asked him to explain the significance of this change. He said that the men came from Northern Macedonia, where the first guerrilla forces of the movement had worn such a star, and he undertook to have them discard the symbol.

At the end of May Eddie Myers came to see me. He was now the Brigadier in command of the British Military Mission, and Rufus Sheppard and I had been placed under his orders. When I met him, in a village house near Rodhokhori, he took me to the light and had a good look at me.

'It is Nick Hammond,' he said.

We had been at Caius College, Cambridge together, he as a Royal Engineer officer, and I as an undergraduate. We had a long talk about the situation in Macedonia. He agreed with me that there were greater potentialities in the Macedonian ELAS, and that Macedonia was the area of greatest strategic value in Greece. He agreed with Cairo's policy of developing ELAS in Macedonia, although he was alive to the danger of the Communist element taking control. He was interested in our method of giving relief to the *pyropatheis*, and he told me of a proposal to subsidise ELAS with gold in order that they might lay in stores for the winter. I was all against this proposal. I told him that ELAS would obtain the stores in any case by confiscation and by requisition, and that the gold would go into the coffers of EAM. It seemed to me that he did not have sufficient distrust of EAM-ELAS at that stage.

During June we received orders to prepare for attacks on the enemy's lines of communication. These attacks were to be the latest in a series which would start farther south and be staggered in time. The GHQ of ELAS and the GHQ of EDES had both agreed to accept the orders of GHQ Middle East for these operations, and the British Liaison Officer in each area was to work out a scheme of co-operation with his opposite number in ELAS or EDES. I drew up plans with Johnson at Rodhokhori and then went into consultation with ELAS HQ. My first request was that Kikitsas should be appointed commander of any ELAS force that was to co-operate with me, and to my delight the request was granted. Kikitsas was enthusiastic and eager for action. However, ELAS HQ said that their own GHQ had not yet sent them any orders about these operations, and that no ELAS force could move until the orders were received.

The plans at least were mutually agreed. Johnson was to attack a number of points on the main road which led from Kozani to Elassona; his targets included a temporary road-bridge over the Haliakmon river at Servia and a number of smaller bridges and culverts. I was to attack points on the railway line which runs along the coast from Platamona to south of the Haliakmon.

As it would take almost a week to walk from Rodhokhori to the railway line, I was anxious to set off. But Karatsas and his colleagues insisted that they had not yet received any orders. As their attitude since the great 'withdrawal' had been entirely defensive, so far as the enemy were concerned, it was difficult not to become suspicious. We waited for several days. Meanwhile I arranged a rendezvous for a fluid date with Horse (Jim Power), near the place where we had crossed the Elassona-Kozani road in April, in order that we could co-ordinate the timing of our attacks on the railway-line. As ELAS HQ still procrastinated and denied having received any orders from its own HQ, I sent Johnson ahead. He was to follow the bend of the Haliakmon river and take up a position near Livadheron above Servia. I then persuaded ELAS to let me set off together with Kikitsas and a small force, consisting of some three hundred men. We caught Johnson up before he reached Livadheron, and we arranged for some of our ELAS troops to support him. Kikitsas and I moved on to our rendezvous with Horse. He was there, accompanied by some ELAS men from Thessaly.

His story was the same as mine; ELAS had not received any orders to act even yet. Time was now short, for we had to synchronise our attacks on the morning of a fixed day, of which we had been informed by GHQ Middle East. Even if we started now, we could reach our objectives only with difficulty. Power and I discussed the situation frankly and forcibly with Kikitsas and the Thessalian ELAS commander, and in the end I said we would go without them. They then decided to come with us; they declared the next morning that orders to act had just reached them.

Kikitsas and I moved across the main Kozani-Elassona road that night, and we were high on the north-western flank of Mount Olympus by dawn. By midday we reached a high point above the Katerini-Elassona road and in the clear air we could see the coast and the railway-line. Here Palaeologus set up his wireless station. At nightfall we set off again. It was essential now not to be observed. We moved all night on forest paths, aiming for a point some five hours distant from the railway line. At dawn we were in thick oak-scrub, and Kikitsas said we had reached the point. I sent Alekko on in plain clothes to make a preliminary reconnaissance of the two targets we had in mind, and Kikitsas gave him some ELAS men. We arranged to meet them at midnight at an agreed place in the plain, where a small church stood on a mound.

The rest of us stayed put for twelve hours. Heavy drizzle fell all day. We were hungry and wet. The only food we had was some maize-bread, cheese and goat's milk, commandeered from a shepherd. I sat all day under a *kapa* (a heavy goatskin cape), which was heavy and dank with the rain, and the taste of the goat's milk kept recurring from my empty stomach. At 7 pm we had another scanty meal. Then we moved down first in the dusk and then through the darkness to the edge of the plain. It was a moonless but luminous night with a clear sky and bright stars. About midnight we found Alekko and some ELAS men in plain clothes at the church on the mound. He described the two targets. He had seen one which was unguarded; the other was guarded by Greek police in German service. I sent him to the former target with a section of fifteen ELAS men, who carried their share of the explosive which we had brought on one mule, and I undertook the latter target. The hour set for the demolitions on which Power and I had agreed was 2 am.

I took my section of fifteen ELAS men and the mule with my explosives along the main coastal road, and then struck across the fields east of Litokhoro. As there was a German guard post at Litokhoro station, about a mile from my target, it was essential that the Greek police at the target should be disposed of in silence. This particular ELAS section had been allocated to me three days earlier, and I had got to know its members individually. The leader was a shrewd old peasant, and most of the others were young lads who had not been in action. The leader and his men went on over the fields while I stayed with the mule. After a long silence I moved forward to find out what was happening, and met the section leader and his men with the Greek police, who had agreed to desert, when faced by the two machine-guns of the section.

I posted the section in the fields on the western side of the track with orders to cover the approaches to the bridge until I came back. A young Andarte and I off-loaded the mule and I carried the explosive to the bridge, a girder suspension bridge of which the king girder ran along the top and was heavily riveted. I calculated that I had just about enough explosive for the job, and began to lay the charges, using several limpets with magnetic studs on the under-side. I had filled these with explosive during the halt in the scrub. The Andarte was nervous because lights were showing down the line where the German post was, and I sent him off to join the other Andartes.

I had to work carefully on the open girders between which I could see the water down below in the deep-cut river-bed. Before all the charges were laid and before the cordtex was fixed for simultaneous firing, I heard a train approaching from Salonica. It was some ten minutes before 2 am. I realised that I could not get my charges laid in time to blow the bridge when the train was on it; so I left the bridge and sat on the embankment, looking up at the passing train outlined against the luminous sky. Motor transport and armoured cars were visible on the trucks, and there was a sentry on each fifth truck. It was a great disappointment that it had to pass in safety. To blow the bridge under the train would have served two purposes: destroy the train and ensure the collapse of the bridge. As soon as it had passed, I went back on to the bridge, completed laying my charges, linked them with the cordtex and lit my slow bickford fuse.

I hastened back to warn the ELAS men, but I found none there. So I hid behind a bank. Then came the tremendous explosion with a heart-lifting bang and the singing of flying metal. I ran back to the bridge and saw that it was twisted and collapsed. Sounds of shouting came from the German post, as I ran through the fields towards the road, which ran parallel to the railway. I almost tripped over an Andarte who had been terrified by the bang and was lying low. He came with me, and we caught up with the others some ten minutes later. They had evidently left their posts when the train was heard approaching.

We now set off at full speed over the plain. By dawn we were in the fields north of Litokhoro town, in which some German troops were said to be stationed. Two hours later we reached the scrub and could slacken our pace. We were now on the low foot-hills, where it was extremely hot, but we dragged on at our best pace until noon, when we reached a crystal-clear torrent, rushing out of a gorge on Mount Olympus. Here we found the others as pre-arranged. Alekko had been successful in blowing his bridge, which consisted of two sections; he, too, had watched that desirable train pass by in safety.

At last we could take off our boots, and I bathed in the icy stream. Then I lay in the shade, but even so the skin on my ankles became tight drawn. Many of the Andartes blistered badly through lying in the sun. After a meal, the first since the evening in the oak-scrub, we all climbed up the escarpment of Olympus into a corrie among some pines, which had been used by Kikitsas as a hide-out in his early days in Pieria. It was so well hidden that we made a camp-fire and slept round it that night.

At dawn Alekko and I went on ahead of the others to reach Palaeologus and the wireless set that evening. We passed through beautiful oak, pine and beech forest, saw red squirrels and ate ripe cherries from the trees. We stayed a day with Palaeologus in his hut on the high ridge. From our eyrie we saw a train standing still all day north of the bridge I had blown up below Litokhoro. We were also thrilled to see some thirty large bombers, glistening in the sun, which passed over us towards Salonica and the north-east. They were evidently American planes.

The Andartes, who had now rejoined us, were tremendously excited. At this time, late in June 1943, they knew that the coast of Africa had been cleared of the enemy, and that an invasion of Europe was impending. They were confident that these planes were a sign that an Allied landing by sea on the plain of Salonica was about to be made. Liberation, they shouted, was at hand. Ironically, the very purpose of our own operations was to create in the minds of the Germans the impression that we were preparing the way for such a landing. Indeed, the purpose was achieved.* Some squadrons of the Luftwaffe were transferred from Italy to Macedonia just before the Allied landings in Sicily. But we knew nothing of this at the time; nor did we know that the American planes passing overhead were on their way to Ploesti in Rumania, the Germans' chief source for petroleum. We heard later about the bridge at Litokhoro. When the German guards came up from the station, they found an unexploded 'limpet'. Because they connected limpets with the sabotage of ships, they deduced that the demolition was the work of British troops landed from a submarine; so they and the troops from Litokhoro hastened down to the coast at the time when we were hurrying inland. The great advantage of the Germans' misconception was that they did not carry out reprisals against the Greek population.

The explosion had twisted the bridge, which then collapsed into the river and pulled away the foundations on one side.

---

*   See Churchill's *Second World War* V, 31 and 472 f. 'The result was that two German divisions were moved into Greece which might have been used in Sicily.'

There was a delay of four or five days before a temporary bridge was laid, and trains could pass over the river again. Both parts of Alekko's bridge were wrecked, and farther south Power just missed the train, which passed before he cut the line, and blew up the embankment in several places.

Next day Alekko and I set off on a more northerly route. We wanted to cross the main Servia-Elassona road at a narrow defile south of Servia by daylight. When we reached the eastern side of the pass, we could see a stationary convoy of vehicles in the defile. Observing them through glasses, we saw that they were deserted. We realised that one of Power's detachments had caught this convoy in the defile. We went down and saw that they had been looted, some had been burnt, and all the tyres had been ripped or removed.

We climbed up the western side of the defile, and found Johnson that evening near Livadheron. He had destroyed all his targets at 2 am without loss, except for the temporary bridge at Servia, which was too heavily guarded, but he had had a ticklish time, as the road was in considerable use. All said and done, it had been a successful operation. Although the ELAS men had not been much use in action, their co-operation had been essential to us in getting us to our targets. In particular we were grateful to Kikitsas who had chosen excellent routes and had timed our moves well.

I now pushed ahead on the long trek back to Rodhokhori where I had left Phillips, a young officer recently arrived, in charge of the station. He and Johnson had established themselves at Krimini, a neighbouring village, famous as *To Mikro Parisio* (the little Paris), where they stayed in the fine house of a 'Hullo Boy', an American Greek, who possessed the only bath in the area. When I went over to have a bath, I found John Stevens there. He had been head of the Greek Section in Cairo, when I left in February, and he was completing a tour of the mission stations north of the Peloponnese. He was unduly favourable in his opinion of ELAS, partly as a result of an initial prejudice gained in Cairo, and mainly from the very brief experience he had had in Greece. I tried to correct his view, but without success at this stage. He was a clever, quick-witted man of eager temperament and quick enthusiasms.

My orders were to pass him on to Chalcidice, where there was an intelligence team working for Cairo. They would then send him by sea to Turkey. ELAS undertook to take him to

Chalcidice but by a route to the north of Salonica. He set off in great confidence. A few days later he returned in a rage. He had narrowly escaped capture and had lost one of his guides in a village where there was a German post. His view of ELAS was now at the other extreme. In the end I sent him and Alekko to the caique base which was now established on the coast north of Volos in Thessaly, and he crossed safely from there to Turkey.

It was natural to wonder what had prompted this visit. There had hitherto been a clear division between those at the office end and those in the field not only in the present context but also in my experience in Greece in 1941 and in Palestine. It was right that there should be; for the understanding of the ways of the resistance movements (and indeed of the Zionist Agency's groups of young Jews) depended on sharing their ways, discussing their problems and knowing their leaders over a considerable time. There was no short cut, however brilliant the visitor from the office end might be. Indeed we had seen this with Stevens; for it was due to his inexperience that he swivelled from one extreme to another in his judgement of ELAS. It seemed at the time that the visit might be due to a serious distrust of the policy which was being advocated from the field and implemented by the BLOs. If so, I did all I could to support that policy which seemed to me completely right under the circumstances which we had found in Greece. Such a visit did not happen again until Force 133 (as our Mission came to be called) had almost run its course.

CHAPTER FOUR

Journey to Salonica

In July a plan which I had originated came suddenly to a head.
It meant going into German-occupied Salonica in some disguise.
As the idea was born when I first came to Grevena, a sketch of
the background is needed. ELAS at this time was very short of
capable officers, and this impaired their military efficiency and
their political image. They constantly claimed that they were
an all-party non-partisan movement, but despite this they could
not show more than a sprinkling of regular or reserve Army
officers. I always expressed agreement with their claim, and I
said I should do my best to attract officers of high quality, if
only I could go into Salonica and convince them that the Allies
were co-operating with ELAS. In this way I accustomed the
ELAS commanders to the idea that I might go into Salonica.
There was of course some deception on both sides. ELAS wanted
such officers merely to improve their façade and not to change
their policy, whereas I hoped that influential officers might wean
ELAS from its political partner EAM.

If I went into Salonica, I should be in the hands and at the
mercy of EAM. It would be only too easy to get rid of me by
betrayal or assassination. I had therefore to calculate their attitude
towards me. On the personal level, as I spoke Greek fluently and
enjoyed joking with any Greeks, we were good friends, except for
Karatsas, who was nervous and tense. But this friendship was
entirely superficial. I had always apparently accepted their claims
at their face value, and never hinted that I thought that they were
under Communist control. I had concentrated on the efficient
administration of the military and financial aid which they wanted,
and although I was more strict than other liaison officers in
checking their military numbers and materials, and in controlling
the direction in which sovereigns went, they had obtained a
great deal through my services. The odds were that they thought
of me as rather a simple military type and politically naive. If so,
they would have no particular desire to remove me from the
scene.

Another reason for going to Salonica emerged while we were

waiting to go off on our operations with ELAS. The collection
of intelligence in Greece was managed not by SOE but by a
different organisation, called ISLD which had no contact with
EAM-ELAS. Salonica was a particularly important centre for
ISLD but getting their agents into Salonica presented great difficulties. Cairo asked if I could pass ISLD agents into Salonica,
and it seemed to me that this could be done only if I had my
own contacts there, because the agents were Greeks and would
certainly be detected if they went in through EAM-ELAS, which
preferred to supply its own version of the news. I therefore
arranged to send Yanni into Salonica. I was to follow, if he thought
it possible to recruit officers of quality. ELAS HQ was willing
for him to go, and he departed with an EAM runner. It was a
brave decision on his part to put his life in the hands of EAM
which had labelled him 'a traitor' and might choose to dispose
of him.

Yanni now sent me a message in code, which an EAM runner
brought from Salonica. He himself, he said, could make little
progress, but he thought I might be successful. I then told ELAS
HQ that Yanni's report was favourable, and that I would set
off for Salonica with the same EAM runner. Karatsas and the
others did not take me seriously. I then deployed to them all
the arguments which they had so often used in favour of recruiting distinguished officers and maintaining the broad non-party
nature of their movement, etc., etc. They agreed reluctantly and
emphasised that I went at my own risk. I was off before they
could change their minds, leaving Johnson in charge and telling
him to inform Cairo.

A Balkan-type suit which I had bought in Cairo was too smart
for the job. So on my way I hired an old suit off the back of an
acquaintance in Tsotili. I trained my flowing moustaches down
over my mouth, cut the centre straight along the line of the upper
lip, and left the ends trailing down beyond the corners of my
mouth. I looked now not unlike a Vlach shepherd on a trip to
town. We crossed the Haliakmon river, and waited for dusk before
entering the no man's land between 'Free Greece' and the German
zone. It was a hilly and broken area which ELAS patrolled more
frequently than did the German forces. As we were crossing over,
we were stopped by an ELAS unit. The officer in command of it
was known to me, but he gave me only a passing glance and did
not recognise me. Our EAM runner had a general pass which
covered his companions.

So on we went, and before dawn the runner left me in a peasant's hut, while he arranged for the fabrication of a forged identity card for me under the name of Soterios Bakas. The peasant's wife was inquisitive and asked many questions about the 'free Greeks'. Representing myself as a Vlach shepherd I managed to reply without giving myself away. But when she asked me about the methods of making various cheeses, I silenced her decisively by saying, 'Shut up, granny' (*skasou, yaya*). An ISLD agent, whom Cairo had sent to me for infiltration into Salonica, was also with me. He was an unpleasant and over-confident young Greek officer, who distrusted EAM.

In the evening the peasant took us into the fields to sleep, in case the German patrols visited the huts. There were swarms of mosquitoes, and I got badly bitten. We set off before dawn, and reached the outskirts of Kozani, which had a large German garrison. At a pre-arranged rendezvous, our peasant passed us to a youth, who took us through the outlying streets of Kozani towards a monastery. In the first of these streets a troop of German cavalry trotted towards us and went past. When we reached the monastery, we sat and waited, and the youth said there was some hitch, as another man should have met us. The ISLD agent lost his temper and strafed the youth.

'You fool,' I said, 'you are in the hands of EAM, and if you criticise EAM's arrangements again, I shall abandon you at once.' He caused no more trouble.

After a long delay another man appeared and took us over, and we went to a disused warehouse on the outskirts of Kozani, where some youths joined us. The identity cards, they said, were not yet ready. While we waited, they brought us some food. As my shoes were too good for my part as a Vlach shepherd, I left them with one of the youths and put his shoes on. They were tattered enough, but they did not fit at all well. Later, our EAM runner arrived with the identity cards, and we walked out of Kozani and entered a sparse wood beside the main road. A lorry stopped for a moment, and we jumped up behind and sat on some sacks of grain.

We were now on the main road to Salonica. The lorry ground its way up the flank of Mount Vermion, and came to a halt near the head of the pass beside a wayside café and a strong-flowing fountain (the Zoodokos Pege). We all got down, and I went to the fountain, where two men drank before me. When I had had my drink, I turned round and found two German soldiers at my elbow. That gave me a surprise, but I moved aside and they washed. A German convoy had just pulled up, and there were a lot of soldiers on the road. I went up above the fountain, and lay face down in the shade beside a small shrine. The EAM runner came up and said we were going on our way. As we climbed into the lorry, a German officer sitting at a table watched us, as one naturally does over one's coffee. I had to appear more calm than I felt as we drove off past the convoy.

When we came to the edge of Verria, we got off the lorry and into the town and sat in a coffee shop, while the runner made his contact. He came back to say that we had missed our next lorry because of the delay at Kozani; we must go on by bus. We fought our way on to a crowded bus. I was last in, and sat down on the front seat, but not for long. The driver came with his friends, and chased me out with streams of abuse, much to the amusement of the passengers. I sat on the floor as no other seat was available, and after a considerable delay, we set off on our bumpy journey. A small girl of ten or so talked to me for some time. Then she suddenly said to her mother, 'He is different.' The mother told her to be quiet and paid no attention. All went well at the check posts, and we reached Salonica in the evening.

When we got out of the bus, the runner told us to follow him at intervals. We walked uphill towards the old part of the town, which had been burnt in the war of 1914–1918 and had been only partly rebuilt. At a bend in a small street we turned into a house with two rooms and a kitchen. This was occupied by a married pair with a baby boy about three years old. Our runner left us there for the night. We stayed the next day and the next night in one room. The man of the house was a lorry-driver. He and his wife belonged to families of refugees from Asia Minor, who had settled in Thrace, and they had recently fled from Thrace to Salonica when the Bulgarians were given control of Thrace by the Axis powers. They told us of Bulgarian atrocities, in which they had lost close relatives. They were both Communist in sympathy and keen members of EAM, and they hated the Axis. They had even taught their little son to throw stones at the German soldiers. I thanked them for sheltering us when we left, but they made nothing of the risk of death which they had run, being devoted to the downfall of the enemy.

My next conductor was a small dark-skinned man, who handled me for the rest of my stay. He was a leading member of EAM, had been an officer in the Greek army, and was a type I disliked, but he knew his job. He took me into a large ramshackle tenement in the Ghetto, where we shared a room with some youths of the gangster type. The room was filthy, and the food was badly cooked by a girl of student age. The ISLD agent had been taken off by another conductor. My man explained the merits of the Ghetto to me. The Germans had recently deported the 35,000 or so Jews of Salonica (they were of Spanish origin), and they had no check on who was now living in the Ghetto, which swarmed with squatters and refugees. He gave me cheap smoked glasses to conceal my blue eyes, and we went out to meet Yanni who was living in one room of a ramshackle house.

Yanni told me that EAM and ELAS were widely distrusted by the officer class in Salonica, and that several rival organizations existed there. These were 'YBE' (Defenders of Northern Greece) led by four colonels, Avgerinos, Avdelas, Mousterakis and Demaratos, which was right-wing in sympathy; EDES under a Captain Hadziyannis; and a League of Officers of the Reserve, which was Republican-Venizelist in sympathy. None of these trusted either each other or EAM. Next day I was moved from one runner to another, each falling into step beside me at a prearranged place and time in the street, and I was taken to a quarter on the outskirts of Salonica, which had better housing. Here I stayed several days.

My host was Vasilios, the Chief Engineer of Salonica, who was serving under the Germans, but had already passed seven Englishmen through his house on the way out via Chalcidice to Turkey. He talked good English. His wife was a French-speaking Swiss. They had a nice ground-floor flat. My presence was known to their married daughter who lived above, but not to her husband (for the fewer who knew the better); so they kept the bottom flat locked off from the one above. They had two grandchildren who had the run of the house, a girl of fifteen and a boy of thirteen. At night, I slept in Mrs Vasilios' bed, one of twin beds, under a mosquito net, and Mr Vasilios slept alongside me. She slept elsewhere. The idea was that if the Germans came at night to search the flat, I might pass as Mrs Vasilios under the mosquito net. During the daytime, when Mr and Mrs Vasilios were out, they used to lock the flat. There was no easy exit, except by the front door. When I was out in the streets, it was interesting and amusing to pass Germans in the road, but sitting for any length of time in a closed house made me nervous. One morning when I was sitting in a side room which had a window overlooking the street, I noticed a German steel helmet pass under the window-sill. The man stopped and knocked hard on the door several times. This threw me into a cold fear, but after a few more knocks he went away.

I went out during the siesta hour, usually with my regular conductor and sometimes with another EAM man. We chose that time because fewer policemen were around. My first meeting with Colonel Avgerinos was a chilly one, because the EAM officer was with me, and he and Avgerinos were hostile to each other. On the second occasion I refused to let the EAM officer come in with me, much to his annoyance, and Avgerinos spoke more freely. It was clear that he hated EAM and ELAS. Earlier in the year, he said, ELAS had attacked some YBE men who had tried to start their own guerrilla movement. He himself was anxious to start a guerrilla movement in Pieria, if he could do so under British protection.

I also saw the head of the EDES organisation in Salonica. He was less hostile to EAM, but he mistrusted YBE. On another occasion, I saw the head of the League of Officers of the Reserve, to whom Yanni introduced me without the knowledge of EAM. The members of this League were anxious to know what their duty was and to execute any orders which the Greek Government in exile might give, but they were afraid to act on their own initiative in case they did the wrong thing. They distrusted ELAS and YBE equally, the former on the grounds that the Communists controlled it, and the latter because it was headed by regular officers of the Metaxas regime. As they had no group of men ready to take the field as guerrillas, I could do little for them. Each man had to decide for himself, whether to join one of the organisations already in existence, or whether to sit idle under the occupation. It was clear that most of them would sit still, at least until liberation was near.

Although it was forbidden by the German police for more than three people to assemble together, we held two conferences in private houses during the siesta hour. YBE sent two represent-atives, Avgerinos and Avdelas; EAM had two, the little dark officer and a more senior EAM man whom I had met before; EDES had Hadziyannis and Papachristodoulou; Yanni and I made up the list.

The first conference was spent mainly in recriminations and quarrels, but it gradually became clear that both YBE and EDES were unwilling to come out and enter the ranks of ELAS. They wanted to establish themselves separately in the field, if ELAS would permit them to do so. The EAM representatives accused YBE and, to a lesser degree, EDES of collaborating with the quisling Greek government or at least of acquiescing in the German occupation. The first meeting broke up after a great deal of bickering, but I persuaded them all to meet again.

Before the second meeting I pressed the EAM representatives to clarify their attitude. They said they had no authority to conclude any agreement without consulting the EAM General Committee in Athens and the ELAS HQ. It was clear that they wanted to prevent YBE and EDES from getting established in the field, but they did not want to say so openly, and thus belie their propaganda that they wanted all men to join in 'the struggle'. I spoke to Avgerinos before the meeting, and told him that ELAS held the initiative and that he must be more conciliatory.

The upshot of the second conference was an agreement which Yanni and I drafted, and which they all signed, but with the proviso on EAM's side that the EAM signatories did not have full powers to sign, and that their signatures were subject to confirmation by ELAS HQ. Under this agreement the three movements undertook to collaborate in the field under the command of GHQ Middle East. YBE and EDES were to make their preparations now and to send out armed bands as soon as ELAS HQ confirmed the agreement. This was a considerable achievement, and I was well satisfied. But there was a price. The EAM representatives were now uneasy and suspicious of my motives, for they had signed under a moral persuasion which they resented. They were also afraid that they might get into trouble with their own bosses.

I had now been more than a week in Salonica. My host, Vasilios, had given me useful information about the German aerodromes, which he knew through his work as chief engineer. In moving about Salonica I had had to be particularly careful when I was with a companion. Vasilios was apt to speak English to me. Yanni was over-anxious and showed it, especially on trams. I had resisted the temptation to bathe. I knew that Englishmen had been detected when bathing, because their untanned skin was much fairer than that of the average Greek.

One day I noticed that the EAM man who was with me changed over to my left side whenever we crossed a street or turned round. When I asked him why he did so, he said it was out of respect for me. Since I was dressed as a poor shepherd and he was well-to-do, I told him this might draw attention to us. My Greek had not let me down since my conversation with the little girl in the bus, but unfamiliarity with conditions in an occupied city could give me away. When I was waiting one afternoon in a café for a new conductor to collect me, I thought a neighbour who kept asking me questions might become a nuisance, and I went outside and stood against a wall in the sun. I was holding an open carton of cigarettes in my hand. A man suddenly stopped and said, 'How much?'

I said at once, '*Par to, then polao*', 'Take one, I am not selling', because I had no idea at all how much a cigarette would have cost at that time.

The EAM officer thought we should be on the move. Yanni was sure that the presence of a British officer in Salonica had been leaked to the Germans. So on the evening after the second conference, Yanni and I moved to the house at which I had first stayed, and the EAM runner who had brought us into Salonica arranged for transport in a lorry. Soon after dawn we walked out of Salonica. We went through a poor quarter, and proceeded to a rendezvous several miles out on the main road to Verria.

The rendezvous proved to be at a crossroads. By an unhappy chance a German pioneer unit was encamped there. The troops were working at a newly improvised siding on the railway just beside the road, and magnetic mines and ammunition were being stacked there. The runner, Yanni and I sat in the shade under the wall of the only house at the crossroads. Its owner was selling coffee, and he had a tap of running water, to which the Germans kept coming to drink. It was a most unsuitable rendezvous. It became more and more unsuitable, as hour after hour passed without a sign of our lorry.

Towards noon a German sergeant and two corporals came to the tap and then walked round us as we lay reclining on the ground. I overheard them talking about us. My knowledge of German came in useful; for they talked of arresting us as suspects, but they decided that they should first report our presence to an officer. As they moved off, I told Yanni and the runner, who knew no German. When they were some way off, we got up and walked casually towards Salonica. As soon as we were out of sight, we took to the fields at a run. When we drew near to Salonica, we went into a shop on a side-road and ate a meal; two Germans came in, and we greeted them with good day in Greek, to which they replied. We waited there until it was nearly dark; then we re-entered Salonica, fed again, and returned to our house of the previous night.

We were told by our host that the lorry had never started at all. I was anxious to leave on the next day, as I distrusted the ability of so many Greeks who knew about us to keep their mouths shut. Our runner decided that we should go by bus. He obtained tickets for us, handing in our identity-cards, while Yanni and I sat in a large coffee-shop. After a long delay the bus arrived, and we took seats, but not together. I dozed off in the heat.

I was awakened by a voice shouting, 'What's your name?'

I replied without thinking and in a loud voice, 'Bakas!'

It was fortunately the right one of the many pseudonyms I had used; otherwise the Greek policeman checking our names against the identity cards and the German military policeman with him would have arrested me.

At last we started. We passed quickly through the checkpost and were out of Salonica. It so happened that I had taken a seat on the left-hand end of a long plank which stretched across the bus. The plank, however, was a bit short. As we bumped along on the right-hand side of the cambered road, my end of the plank worked out of its slot and we all fell to the floor. This happened every ten minutes or so throughout the journey. There were many jokes and some altercations between me and the man at the other end of the plank, so that I became the most conspicuous person on the bus.

Then the bus broke down, plumb in the middle of the Vardar bridge, which had German guards on it. At least this gave me a good view of the girdering and construction of the bridge. We were soon ordered to get out and push the bus off the bridge. After some delay we set off again. We were stopped again at the checkpoint before entering Verria. The German guards checked our identity cards, moving along the bus. The driver gave them some cigarettes, and they then waved us on. The harvest was being threshed in the fields and our hearts were light as we drove up to Verria, where the bus completed its run. We sat in small cafés and wandered about the town, until our runner returned with the good news that he had found a lorry. We sat in the back with some peasants, and we bowled along at a good speed to the outskirts of Kozani. There we got off and took to the fields.

It was now evening, and we slept the night in a field, where we were plagued with mosquitoes. Getting up in the dark we circled Kozani before daybreak and reached the village where we had stayed previously. After a meal we took cover in the fields until dark and then walked towards the borderland. We were almost shot by an anxious ELAS sentry, and then we were safely back in 'Free Greece' again. Despite my ill-fitting shoes we made good speed to Rodhokhori.

When Yanni and I walked in, in the middle of lunch, we were given a hilarious welcome for our safe return. The usual accumulation of signals from Cairo awaited my attention. Among them was the news of the 'National Bands' agreement which had just been signed, in July.* At the prompting of Eddie and Chris the three current resistance movements', — ELAS, EDES and EKKA — had agreed to set up a Joint GHQ and to have all approved groups of guerrillas called 'National Bands'. As a result of hard bargaining ELAS had three representatives on the Joint GHQ and the others had one each. The three organisations promised to co-operate with and respect one another, and granted to one another the right of forming bands within territory hitherto claimed as the preserve of one particular organisation. Thus EKKA, which was centred in Phocis and Locris, and EDES, which was centred in Epirus, could start bands under their own aegis in an area such as Macedonia; and similarly ELAS could form bands within Phocis, Locris, or Epirus.

The difficulty of working this scheme was that none of the three organisations welcomed the idea of competition on its own home ground, and it was very difficult to find leaders on the away ground who had sufficient initiative or strength to form bands which would inevitably be regarded as rivals by the existing organisations. Thus in practice, new bands were usually not formed *ab initio* by local leaders. They found it was a better plan to send a few tough bands into a neighbour's territory, say that they were new bands, and disrupt the existing organisation. At this game, ELAS was more unscrupulous and more skilful than the others.

Under the agreement the British Military Mission was attached to the Joint GHQ of the guerrillas, and one of its officers sat on

---

* See C.M. Woodhouse, *Apple of Discord* (London, 1948) 138, 144 f. and 299 f.; and E.C.W. Myers, *Greek Entanglement* (London, 1955) 130 f.

the Joint GHQ as a representative of the Middle East Command. The role of the British officers vis-à-vis the guerrillas was that of liaison between the resistance movements and GHQ Middle East. It was envisaged that subordinate Joint HQs would be formed for individual large areas, such as Thessaly and Macedonia, and that the senior British officer there would act as liaison between it and the Middle East. It was a sensible and orderly arrangement.

A clause in the agreement which was regarded as very important made provision for any new organisation of guerrilla forces to gain recognition from GHQ Middle East and from the Joint GHQ in Greece. Once recognition was granted, the new organisation would be represented on the Joint GHQ and have the same rights as EDES, EKKA and ELAS. By a coincidence, this clause had been under discussion at the time that I was in Salonica negotiating a provisional agreement between EDES, ELAS and YBE on the same principle. When therefore I reported the Salonica agreement, GHQ Middle East and the Joint GHQ in Greece recognised YBE in principle and acknowledged its right to enter the field subject to certain provisos. At the same time EDES was entitled to bring its own bands out of Salonica.

The next step was to inform the leaders of YBE and EDES of the new situation, and to ascertain from them where they intended to establish their first bands. There could be no formal recognition until this was known and personal contacts were made. We had only two channels of communication, ELAS and ISLD. When I asked Karatsas and his colleagues, they promised to send the messages which I prepared to the leaders of YBE and EDES, but no acknowledgement was ever received from Salonica. It was stated later by the YBE and EDES leaders that no messages had ever reached them. I sent the same messages to Cairo for transmission through ISLD agents in Salonica to the leaders, but these did not reach their target either. I was of course unaware that both channels were being unsuccessful. As I learnt later, messages from Joint GHQ, sent through ELAS runners, never reached the leaders of YBE.

The full report on conditions in Salonica which I now sent to Cairo owed much to the help of Yanni, who had obtained a lot of valuable information with commendable objectivity. For example, we described the nature and resources of EDES and YBE in Salonica; the proceedings at the two conferences; and the general attitudes towards EAM and ELAS, one of admiration in the great majority of people who were ill-informed (e.g. Vasilios) and of detestation among those who had had experience of EAM's methods. We gave figures for the strength of the Greek police in Salonica. We tried to judge how the police would act in certain circumstances: if Allied help was at hand, how they would act towards the German forces; and if Allied aid was not forthcoming, whether they would resist any attempt by ELAS to take control in Salonica. We supplied notes on the leading men in the police force. There was also a good deal of detail about the positions of German units, aerodrome construction, railway development, and targets suitable for bombing. The siding with the mines at our crossroads was one of them.

ELAS HQ in Macedonia was now of the opinion that it was important to move their troops into forward positions, i.e. onto Mounts Kaïmatsala, Paiko and Vermion and towards the coast of Pieria. At this stage a German attack on Siatista took place. In the course of it the excellent ELAS officer Yanni Lamiotis was killed. Although Kite and another ELAS leader, Ipsilantis, destroyed a number of German trucks with landmines, the Germans captured Siatista without difficulty. They then advanced to Tsotili and the outskirts of Krimini. We therefore moved our headquarters to a higher village, Pendalofos.

Meanwhile, Johnson with Bill Daniels, his wireless operator, and an ELAS force had set off on their journey to Mount Paiko. When they were crossing a shoulder of Mount Vitsi, they were ambushed by Germans in wooded country, and Johnson was shot through the shoulder. The ELAS men all disappeared. Johnson and Daniels made their way back through the scrub, moving only at night. When they reached us, Johnson's wound was full of maggots, which meant at least that it was not gangrenous.

Some weeks later, when his shoulder was better, he set off again and got through to Paiko, where he established his HQ. He was able there to make contact with Tito's man Tempo in Yugoslavia, whom I had met in May. When Cairo decided to send a British Mission to Tempo, it was dropped on Mount Paiko and was passed on by Johnson into Yugoslav Macedonia. At this time, I was in touch through ELAS with a British Mission led by Smiley in Albania. I passed some stores and a wireless operator to him. It was, of course, made possible only through the willing co-operation of ELAS.

The ELAS command was somewhat disgruntled at my actions in Salonica. However, personal relations were still cordial; for the ELAS forces were still being built up. There were numerous drops of supplies, which included a few two-inch and three-inch mortars. The Elasites had been patted on the back for their part in the operations late in June. They appreciated the value of the training we gave their squads in demolition and commando work, and they had fought quite well during the German attack on Siatista. They began to acquire pretensions. ELAS proclaimed itself an army and numbered its divisions on the model of the regular Greek Army. Thus ELAS HQ in Macedonia became the HQ of the 9th Division. The change of name was farcical, but the aim was political. ELAS laid claim now to being the regular army of 'Free Greece', in contradistinction to the armed forces of the King and his Government in exile and to the exclusion of the other guerrilla movements which were recognised by the Joint GHQ.

ELAS was fortunate in Macedonia in having a reputable military commander. Hitherto the best they had been able to manage was a rather doddery veteran of the Greco-Turkish War of 1922, one Jojo, who had been dug out of some village. When the old man had a heart-attack and retired, his place was taken by Colonel Demaratos, who had commanded the real 9th Division in Albania in 1940–41. He had been one of the four leaders of YBE when I was in Salonica. But on hearing what I had to say there he had felt that it was his duty to support the Allies by joining an organisation of which they approved, even if it was ELAS. So he came out of Salonica and brought some good staff officers with him. This was one very welcome effect of my visit to Salonica. It was just what ELAS had wanted, and it was also to prove of value to me, because two of the staff officers provided me later with inside information about ELAS.

At Pendalofos our HQ was very close to the headquarters of ELAS. Hitherto I had preferred to live in a neighbouring village, but pressure of business now made it desirable to be in the same place as ELAS. One result was that we came to know much more about each other's activities. For example, ELAS took complete control of the dissemination of news in Pendalofos and outside it. All radio sets had to be surrendered on penalty of death, and an ELAS loudspeaker in the market square gave its own garbled version of events. No one could produce leaflets or news-sheets except ELAS, which set up a printing-press in Pendalofos and printed a local newspaper. Naturally, EAM-ELAS figured as the hero; all other organisations were denounced as traitorous. All arms had to be surrendered on penalty of death. ELAS was the dispenser of justice under martial law and the controller of all civilian movement.

We had managed hitherto to keep the relief of civilians in our hands, but the flood of refugees which resulted from the German capture of Siatista left me no alternative but to commission ELAS to set up soup-kitchens; for nobody else could produce the food at short notice. I contributed money under the usual conditions of non-discrimination.

As ELAS tightened its control, it met with more opposition. In one respect it modified its propaganda. In my early days in Macedonia the EAM line had been that the Albanians, the Yugo-slavs and the Bulgarians were brothers of the Greeks, and that they, like themselves in the past, had been led astray by Fascist or Royalist regimes. Once they threw off these shackles, the argument ran, and accepted the leadership of the resistance movements, they would prove to be real brothers and form a Balkan entente.

This naive propaganda sprang from the hope that with the establishment of closely related regimes a Balkan entente would come about, and that the basis of the entente would be the Communist International. Hence the bitter opposition by the leaders of YBE ('the Defenders of Northern Greece') who believed that EAM-ELAS wanted to betray North Greece to the Russians. At that time YBE had been correct. The Russian plan for the Balkans was to set up a Soviet Republic of Macedonia at the expense of the national territories of Greece and Yugoslavia and to a lesser extent of Albania and Bulgaria; and EAM-ELAS had supported it.

Some indications of this Russian plan had appeared in May. At that time a group of Yugoslav guerrillas had taken refuge near Florina wearing the red star on their cap and a flag on their sleeves. When I sent Cairo a description of the flag and asked what it was, the answer came back that it was the flag of IMRO, a movement for an autonomous Macedonian state.* ELAS, however, sported a national symbol on its cap, namely the Greek letters ELAS, which stood for the *National* Popular Army of Liberation. A compromise was then arrived at, whereby the flag and the letters were both removed, and the two groups of guerrillas appeared as brothers under the five-pointed red star of Russia.

---

*   'Vatrashna Makedonska Revolutsionna Organizatsia' or 'Internal Macedonian Revolutionary Organisation', founded at Salonica in 1893.

Again the ELAS policy towards the Komitaji and the recruiting of men from the Bulgarian-speaking villages had been aimed at holding the brotherhood together. But by July ELAS realised that their open declaration of this policy was alienating a great many people in Greek Macedonia and particularly in Salonica, which was full of refugees from Greek Thrace in fear of the occupying power, Bulgaria. We heard no more of the Balkan brotherhood for some months.

A more sinister form of opposition to ELAS than that organised by YBE came from a Colonel of the Greek Army called Poulos, who recruited an anti-Communist force in Salonica and its environs. He and his men had collaborated with the German troops in capturing Siatista and advancing to Tsotili. There and elsewhere they inflicted considerable losses on ELAS, which was not surprising as the Germans fed them with ammunition and supplies. ELAS naturally described them as jailbirds; but it is probable that most of them were the survivors of movements which ELAS had suppressed.

However, Poulos and his men were only one example of the growing opposition in Macedonia to ELAS. Already in June, when Johnson was operating near Servia and Kozani, he found that the ELAS troops who were supporting him were unable to enter certain villages. When he made enquiries, he learnt that these particular villages were occupied by 'Pontii', that is by refugees from Pontus in Turkey who had come to Macedonia under the scheme for an exchange of populations in 1923. This group of Pontii had organised an independent band to fight the Germans, but the leaders of the band had been killed by ELAS.

In the latter part of July all the area commanders in the British Military Mission were summoned to Pertouli in western Thessaly for a conference. I went by car with an ELAS party, which included the Bishop of Kozani. The car, a degutted butcher's van, had no seats except the front one on which the Bishop and the driver sat. The rest of us bumped up and down on the floor, as we rumbled over the pot-holes and the rubble from Tsotili to Grevena; then we forded the river of Grevena, trundled on through the low and forested parts of Mourgana to Kalabaka, and followed the road from there to Porta on the edge of the Thessalian plain.

The radiator boiled over frequently, and we had to push the car up the river-banks. On one such occasion, we all got out except the driver and the Bishop of Kozani. In the struggle up the river bank, the car finally went head-over-heels, and the Bishop emerged with his purple robes covered with sump-oil. His appearance and language were uncanonical. From Porta another car took us up to Pertouli. This journey illustrated the successes which ELAS had won against the Italians; for it was no small thing to control a road from near Kastoria to the rim of south-western Thessaly, a matter of well over a hundred miles.

The conference was valuable for a variety of reasons.* We had all made attacks in June on the enemy's lines of communication, and we were now able to compare notes on the assistance we had received from the resistance movements. There were plenty of strong, indeed caustic views. The members of the original mission had a marked preference for EDES and its commander, Napoleon Zervas. This was natural enough, in view of their experience (p 15 above). For it was Zervas who had alone supported the mission throughout that difficult and depressing winter. At that time the members of the original mission had formed a strong dislike of ELAS, and most of them had seen no reason to change it. Rufus still battled on in the cause of ELAS, and poured scorn on the EDES movement.

It was good to meet Chris for the first time since our work together at Haifa (see p 14 above). His experiences in Crete and in Greece had made him a much more forceful person than he had been at Haifa. He was an admirable second-in-command, and had a much deeper understanding of Greek character and Greek politics than the other members of the original mission, Eddie included. My favourite among the company at the conference was Tom Barnes, a delightfully bluff and direct New Zealander, who was the senior liaison officer with EDES and had a high opinion of Zervas.

The conference was attended by David Wallace, a representative of the Foreign Office, whom Eden had sent out to investigate and report on the situation.† Like most of the British officers, he was in his twenties, and he had a quick mind and ready understanding. He was concerned solely with the political aspects of the resistance movements, and he had read my reports on EAM-ELAS in Macedonia. We talked at length about the political background and contacts of EAM-ELAS, and the possibilities of trouble later.

* See E.C.W. Myers, *Greek Entanglement* 224 f.
† Information from the Mission went usually through the filter of SOE in the Middle East and in London or through GHQ Middle East and the War Office.

I was able to add two points to my reports. One was that the EAM-ELAS movement in Macedonia did not emerge at all until Russia's entry into the war; then it attacked several targets north of Salonica. The other was that some Yugoslavs had been introduced to me at ELAS Headquarters at Omale. Their leader, Tempo, wanted me to arrange supplies for his guerrillas in southern Yugoslavia, and there was no doubt that he was finding it difficult to establish the Tito movement which was in conflict with the Chetniks of Mihailovitz, the Serb leader, who had been active since 1941. Chris also talked to me about the political aspects of EAM-ELAS. He was the only member of the Mission who had met the inner caucus of EAM, the so-called Central Committee, when he had gone into Athens early in 1943. He knew that the Central Committee was predominantly Communist in origin and in policy, and he had seen through the propaganda of the ELAS movement.

The conference was a great success. It enabled men to meet who were known to one another only by pseudonyms in Middle East telegrams; to discuss our views of the different movements; and to feel that we were a united force, however far from the centre our areas might be. As the wireless messages from all stations went to Cairo, we did not have immediate and direct communication with one another. It was arranged that in the future we should try to keep in touch by runner with our HQ at Pertouli, as far as it was possible.

I walked the eighty or so miles to our HQ in Macedonia in the company of Booth, whom I had taken with me to Pertouli. The two of us struck across the high country and went via Kastania (where Rufus had his station), Koutsouphliani, Krania and Philippaei. It was a glorious walk in perfect weather. We felt exhilarated and almost carefree as we descended to Pendalofos.

CHAPTER FIVE

An Abortive Operation

This and the following chapter cover the period August to Novem-
ber 1943. The Russians defeated the German armies and advanced
beyond the Dnieper. Anglo-American forces landed in Italy on
3 September, and the Italian Government surrendered on 8
September. British forces seized Leros, Cos and Castellorizo, but
lost them on 17 November. Australian and American forces
advanced in New Guinea.

When we were being forced back to Pendalofos in July, we had
lost our dropping-ground at Omale. The reserve one at Philippaei
which we still held was not suitable for bodies. The next lot of
British officers was therefore dropped in Thessaly, and three of
them came on to Macedonia. Arthur Wickstead and Bill Winlaw
had read classics at St John's College, Cambridge, where I had
known them slightly, and Ronald Prentice had been in the Cairo
Office, where I had met him late in 1942. I sent Winlaw to Pieria
to work with Kikitsas and Lazanis, who were in command of the
ELAS forces there. Wickstead and Prentice came to Pendalofos.
The HQ of the Mission informed me that some other officers
were coming to join me for a specific operation.

A decision had been taken after the attacks in June that in
future only an occasional operation should be mounted against
a major target. I was ordered to undertake the first such action.
For this purpose I was told to take Jim Power under my command. He was stationed on Lower (southern) Olympus. I had
already studied the Peneus bridge in the Tempe Pass as a possible target during my stay on Kissavo, but I decided now that
there was more chance of success if we went for the Haliakmon
bridge, north-east of Pieria. Either target could be attacked only
if ELAS would co-operate. Indeed it was intended that we should
use such operations as this to test the value of ELAS. I imagine
that the choice fell on me largely because ELAS had been more
co-operative hitherto in Macedonia than elsewhere.

For the operation I was sent three officers: Scott, known as
Scottie, an RE officer; Inder, an Anglo-Indian, who was a demoli-

tion officer; and Jock Hamilton, a Scots Commando officer, who had served only with EDES and had yet to form an opinion of ELAS. Together with them came a sergeant, a Palestinian Arab called Khouri, who had evaded capture when his unit was left behind during the retreat in the Greek campaign, and had joined the ELAS movement at its inception in Central Greece. A bold cut-throat himself and a keen fighter, Khouri had been with the notorious 'Ares' (Velouchiotis) until the first officers of the Mission arrived in Greece, when he had joined them and taken part in the demolition of the Gorgopotamos Bridge.

Scottie and Khouri had been members of the party which had destroyed the Asopos Bridge on 20 June. As far as I remember it, their story was as follows.* The railway bridge, spanning the deep and precipitous gorge of the Asopos River, had been selected as a target in advance of the June operations, and Eddie had asked ELAS to join the British in the task. ELAS GHQ said eventually that they would not do so. Nettled by the attitude of ELAS GHQ, Eddie said scornfully that the British would do the job themselves, at which ELAS GHQ laughed.

As the only approach to the bridge was through the railway tunnels at either end, and as these tunnels were guarded at the entries and the exits by German troops, the British party had to find a way down the gorge, which was said to be impassable. They did so in several stages by felling trees and using ropes. At the last stage Don Stott (a New Zealander whom I had tried in vain to teach Greek in Cairo), Khouri and one other succeeded in reaching the last bend of the gorge beyond which lay the bridge. They then retraced their steps, leaving fixed ropes at the worst points, and collected three more men (Creed, Scottie and Inder), and explosives in water-proof bags.

The six men then descended the gorge, left the last bend just after dark, and approached the foot of the main pier, which was known to be defended with mines. When they came to the barbed-wire apron, they found it open. Going through the gap, they made their way to the pier. A German party had been working on the pier, and had lifted the mines and left the barbed-wire apron open. When two of the British party were already among the iron girders of the pier, a searchlight came on, and shed a beam directly on to the pier. It came from the guardpost above on the bridge-end. The two men pressed themselves tight against the girders, sure

---

* See E.C.W. Myers, *Greek Entanglement* 180 f., for a fuller account.

that they had been seen. Then the beam moved along the arches for the whole length of the bridge, back again onto them, and then went out. It was evidently a routine inspection.

Shortly after this, Creed who was standing on the path between the pier and the guardpost saw a light coming down towards him. He soon realised that it was a lighted cigarette. Moving behind a bush beside the path, he waited until the man — there was only one — passed alongside him, and he then hit him with his full strength, knocking him over into the precipitous depths of the gorge. He fell without much noise. When the charges were laid and a time-delay was set, the party of six withdrew as they had come. They were round the bend of the gorge before the roar of the explosion cheered them on their way. It took them some twelve hours to climb up the gorge. If the Germans had succeeded in guessing how the demolition party had come, they would be waiting for them at the head of the gorge. But when they emerged, no one was there.

They then sent a Greek to photograph the bridge, in order to see the extent of the damage. The Greek came back with a photograph of the bridge intact. He had bought an old photo of the bridge in a village nearby. In fact the bridge was smashed and the main line was cut for some four months.

So far as our operation was concerned, we had a first-class team on the British side. Karatsas and his colleagues on ELAS HQ at Pendalofos raised many objections and difficulties, but I had Kikitsas on my side. The job was very much to his taste; for he was a fine officer and he had an unrivalled knowledge of Pieria. In the end ELAS detached him with 250 men to co-operate with me. Our plan was to move by night, as unobtrusively as possible, to the forested area south of Verria, which lies above the great Haliakmon gorge. There we should have explosives and ammunition dropped to us. The next step would be a reconnaissance of the Haliakmon railway bridge near the coast. The rest of our party and Kikitsas' force started off ahead of me. Before leaving Pendalofos, I briefed Prentice in handling ELAS HQ and running the station in my absence. It was a difficult job for a man who had had no experience of ELAS on the ground, but he had the right ideas from the start and the strength of character to be firm.

At this time 'Mick the Miller' (Guy Micklethwait), who had been with me in Cairo just before I left, was sent over from Epirus. He wanted to go to Thrace, and Cairo had put him under

Preparing to feast on requisitioned sheep

Offloading on the way to action

An ELAS unit with Major Prentice and Sergeant Kite in berets

Group at Pendalofos with Kikitsas (centre), Zotos (far left) and Wickstead (far right)

my command, with orders for me to pass him across the River Strymon. As my relations with ELAS were still good, I persuaded them that Mick was the man to help their movement in Thrace. They produced a couple of men who were said to have come recently from Mount Pangaeum, east of the Strymon. These men said that they would take Mick to Northern Pieria, then over Mount Vermion, Mount Paiko, Krusha Balkan, Bezik Dag, and so eventually to the Strymon river. I said the direct route through Salonica was preferable, but ELAS said they had no runners for Salonica, which I did not believe. So Mick set off, bound for Northern Pieria.

A day later, I met two EAM runners at Grevena who were going to Salonica, and I persuaded them to take Mick, if I could produce him in time. I caught him up by fast walking. We sat under a tree about noon, while I explained my plan, which was entirely new to him. It was that he should go through Salonica with a forged identity card as a Greek priest. His black moustache and beard, and his wild, shining black eyes made him look the part to the life, and I reckoned his chances of success were good, although he had little Greek.

Mick was at once willing and indeed delighted to impersonate the clergy. While I went on towards Pieria, he returned to Grevena, where I had left the EAM runners. They took him in safety to Salonica. There they got cold feet, but a Greek girl who was a member of EAM took him through by bus to the Strymon bridge. There his forged identity-card passed muster, and he was admitted into the Bulgarian zone of occupation. A few miles further on, the girl and he got off the bus with their suitcases, and walked up the slopes of Mount Pangaeum.

There he began his career as a guerrilla with ELAS. But after this splendid start Mick had a stormy passage. He soon reported that ELAS was not to his taste. Subsequently I asked Cairo that he should not remain under me but have a separate command. This saved me a good deal of trouble, because Mick later transferred his services to a rival band. With their support he was soon fighting against both the Bulgarian troops and ELAS on Boz Dagh.

After more fast walking by day and sleeping at night in bracken, which struck very cold as I had only a thin American blanket with me, I caught up the main party, which included Palaeologus with his wireless-set, Yanni and Alekko. We were now near the main road between Servia and Elassona, on which the German

convoy had been destroyed in June. All the villages on our side
of the road had been burnt to the ground. The crops were already
harvested, as the weather was hot and it was now early August.

Before we crossed the main road that night, I sat with Yanni,
Alekko, and Palaeologus under a tree. We were on the edge of a
village, in the dusk; it was the day of the month, the 20th, on
which we had dropped into Greece, and Alekko said it always
brought us excitement and good luck. We were happy to be together again after so many weeks apart, and the same affection
rose amongst us at once, although we were so different one from
another in every respect. I amused them by asking them the
name of a night bird which had a monotonous call. When they
told me it was a *bouffas*, I immediately greeted Palaeologus with
that name as a nickname, because the bird was so stupid and its
note was like his transmitting note on the wireless. 'Bouffas'
remained an affectionate nickname for Palaeologus, the youngest
of us.

Just before dark the convoy of mules and men moved slowly
down towards the main road. We crossed it after darkness had
fallen. The aim of Kikitsas now was to cross a large triangular
area of ground which lay between the main road and a side road
leading to Katerini, and then to cross the side road, all before
dawn, as the Germans used both roads. Shortly after midnight,
I realized that our guides had lost the way. This was not surprising, as there were deep ravines, and the guides appeared to
be going round in circles to avoid the ravines. There was a fair
chance that dawn would find us in the open between the roads,
where we should certainly be seen. At the worst a German force
might attack us and at the best they would know that a large
ELAS force was moving into Pieria. After consulting with Kikitsas,
I took over from the guides. I was relying upon the starry sky and
my sense of direction. Luck or judgement were on my side, and
the company of some three hundred men and a hundred or so
mules crossed the Katerini road while it was still dark.

As dawn was breaking, Jock Hamilton and I walked on ahead
of the others up a hill to the village of Kallithea which I had
visited in June. As the first houses appeared against the grey sky
of dawn, they looked ghostly and eyeless. We found that every
house in the village had been burnt in reprisal for the operations
carried out in June. As we walked on, Jock and I found we had
both been head of 'K' house and in the Rugger XV at Fettes,
he being some ten years my junior. We lay hid most of the day,

and then, moving mainly by night through high beech and pine forests, we came two or three days later to a camp high up near some open ground, which had been chosen as a dropping ground. During these days the ELAS forces split up into several detachments, each having its own camp. Yanni went with a different detachment to another dropping ground, which was to be under his control.

After arranging with Cairo for a drop of the explosives we needed, Scottie, Alekko and I with three ELAS men set off to reconnoitre the Haliakmon bridge. It was reckoned to be some seven hours distant. We put on civilian clothes, passed through the villages near the plain in the dark, and reached a bluff overhanging the bridge some time before dawn. Here we lay behind small bushes, from which we could direct our binoculars on the bridge. While it was still dark, a train approached from the north carrying a strong headlight. It stopped some distance short of the bridge, and then passed slowly through to the south side, presumably after a check had been made.

At dawn the air was hazy. A low mist rose from the river-bed, and the smoke from the German garrison's fire mingled with it. Shortly after dawn a train came up from the south. It passed through the surround of wire which was now visible, and stopped short of the bridge for a check. We could see that the checkpoint was opposite the main barracks of the German garrison. After the check the train moved slowly across the bridge, passed the second main barracks, and then ran out of the surround of wire. After this the guards and the gun-crews were changed. Their movements gave us a good idea of the layout of the defences; there were several posts with machine-guns or anti-aircraft guns and a very powerful blockpost inside the wire, which commanded the entry from the south.

As the sun was now up, we crawled back until we were out of sight of the garrison. We then set off on our long trip back, all uphill and by daylight this time. At first we made detours to keep clear of the villages we had passed through during the night. The heat and the dust became very exhausting. We decided we should go through the next village, which was one of the last near the plain, rather than make a detour. Two of the ELAS men were local to Pieria and might be recognised, but the third came from upper Macedonia. So he and Alekko went first; Scottie and I followed, each with one of the recognisable ELAS men. We all carried loaded revolvers in our pockets or in peasant satchels.

In the centre of the village Alekko and his companion were stopped by a Greek captain of gendarmerie who the ELAS man with me said was a dangerous man. Alekko began to abuse him, and a general shouting-match ensued. During it we all passed through. As I went through, Alekko was asking what the stars on the captain's shoulders were for, and then pretending awe and amazement that the gendarme was really so high and mighty as a captain. This buffoonery delighted the gathering crowd. Laughter put the captain to shame, and he let Alekko and his companion go without even asking to see an identity card. Just as well, as neither had one.

Safely out of that village, we took a ride in an ox-cart, built for carting wood, but it was so dusty, bumpy and painful that we were soon walking again. By the evening we were in ELAS country and we had a decent meal of eggs. We had been on our feet for some twenty-four hours with little break. As we toiled up the last slope towards our camp in the dark, we heard the planes overhead and knew they were dropping the explosives for the job.

While the drop was being collected, Scottie made a large model of the bridge out of fir trees, some of which we felled for the purpose; he instructed his demolition team of British personnel where to place the charges, carried out a dummy operation, and calculated the time he would need on the job. Meanwhile Kikitsas and I discussed how we should attack the bridge. We judged the garrison force to be some 200 or more Germans, perhaps 300 at most. Our 250 ELAS men were ill-trained and ill-equipped when it came to making a regular attack in force, but they could be effectively armed for close fighting with the Sten-guns which we had asked Cairo to include in the drop.

Kikitsas eventually accepted my plan. This was to enter the station south of the bridge shortly before dawn and, when the regular train from the south stopped, to seize the locomotive and the leading coaches. Two hundred of us would board the train and Alekko would drive the locomotive straight on into the compound and up to the checkpoint, where he would stop. The majority of our men would jump out, break into the main barracks, and shoot the Germans sleeping there. Meanwhile Alekko would drive over the bridge to the second barracks where a smaller party would jump out and attack. Alekko would then back the train on to the bridge, where the demolition squad would be at work.

If we carried the two main barracks, it was hoped we should

be able to capture the gunposts, which, as far as we had been able to see, all faced outwards. Of the rest of our force, some would mine the railway-line north and south of the compound, and others would hold two points on the main road, which would also be mined. If we succeeded in seizing the bridge, we would have to allow another hour for the further operations. The withdrawal would be over exposed country. It was a hazardous scheme, but the best we could devise.

The agreement of Kikitsas was reassuring to some extent. All the members of the British party accepted the scheme warmly, except for Jock Hamilton, who was to command the party holding the main road and would have preferred to be more in the centre of the action. The rest of us were to be on the train. My job was, together with Kikitsas, to command the first attack inside the compound. Scottie was to lead the demolition team.

All was happily arranged and agreed by the time that the canisters came in from the dropping-ground. It was then found that the canister containing cordtex had gone astray. This was fatal. The bridge was a steel girder suspension bridge, and the simultaneous detonation which could be achieved only with cordtex was essential to the demolition. Further, if the canister had fallen or were to fall into German hands, the enemy would probably reinforce the garrison on the bridge and be on the alert for any attack. When we asked Cairo to drop another, they replied that we must wait ten days, as their aerodromes were being changed. Kikitsas was dismayed. The chances of concealing the presence of so large a force would diminish day by day. Nevertheless, he agreed to adhere to the original plan, if a supply of cordtex was dropped, and if the Germans did not reinforce the garrison of the bridge.

A few days later, Inder, Alekko and two ELAS men went down to reconnoitre. They found the situation at the bridge unchanged, as far as they could see. But this time, on their way back, they were stopped by some guerrillas who were not ELAS men. When Inder said that he was an English officer, they refused to believe him. Alekko and he gave them the slip, were fired upon and were lucky to escape.

Kikitsas was furious. He said the guerrillas were members of PAO, formerly known as YBE. He and others gave instances of attacks by PAO-YBE on ELAS, and he wanted to dispose of this lot straightaway. I pointed out that to attack them would inform the Germans of our presence and prevent us from attacking the

Haliakmon Bridge. After a lot of argument, he agreed to send a message from me, through a neutral party, to their leaders. In the message I proposed a conference at a village called Elafina in a fine house, which had been built by a Swiss engineer before the war. At first the PAO leaders refused to come, suspecting treachery. As I had met them in Salonica in July, I was soon able to establish my identity with them by letter. In the end three officers came to confer with us at Elafina.

They were headed by Colonel Mousterakis and Colonel Aryiropoulos, both of whom had been with me at the conferences in Salonica. They assured me that none of the messages sent from Joint GHQ via ELAS runners had ever reached them, and they did not even know whether GHQ Middle East was prepared to recognise their movement. As they had not heard a thing from me or from any GHQ, the PAO leaders had decided to take the field once again. On previous occasions their small groups had been squashed by ELAS. This time they had tried with a large force to get a foothold in the hills. They had begun north of Verria, but had been driven off Mount Vermion by ELAS. It was a sheer coincidence that they were establishing themselves now on the foothills of Pieria. All they wanted was a space in which to get started, and freedom from interference by ELAS. There was ample space, they said, in the Greek mountains for all groups of guerrillas, and there were sufficient German posts for all to attack.

These points were put by the two PAO colonels to me and to Kikitsas and his colleagues, who included Lazanis, an influential man of a tough and brutal type, and a new arrival, Markos (Vaphiades). It soon became clear that Markos was the political power behind ELAS in Macedonia. He turned out to be the political commissar for the whole of Macedonia. At the moment he appeared to be a cordial and sensible man. The ELAS argument was that the organisers of the PAO-YBE movement had frequently collaborated with the enemy and had betrayed EAM members in Salonica; if they established themselves in the hills, they would give away the movements of ELAS units. They went on to say that anyone who wanted to fight the enemy should join ELAS. It was an established force, it had won many victories, and it welcomed all Greeks to its ranks.

The first conference was mainly spent in mud-slinging on both sides. They were all bogged down in past incidents and recriminations. My efforts to make them discuss the future had little

effect. But it was arranged that we would hold another conference, and in the interval I put pressure on ELAS. As YBE had
been recognised in July by GHQ Middle East and by the Joint
GHQ of ELAS, EKKA and EDES, the decision had already been
made in principle that YBE, or PAO as it now styled itself, was
free to take the field and free to co-operate with ELAS. Further,
ELAS in Macedonia had undertaken to carry out the orders of
GHQ Middle East, to attack the Haliakmon Bridge. It had accepted
supplies for the purpose. The essential thing was to accept PAO,
transfer them to some other pitch and clear the approach to our
target. I made it clear to ELAS that if they attacked PAO I should
recommend GHQ Middle East to stop all supplies to ELAS on the
grounds that they were using our supplies to attack Greeks and
not Germans.

This tirade forced ELAS to make some suggestions. Kikitsas
and Markos offered to let PAO move into the valley of the Haliakmon, which is precipitous and wooded. Once there PAO would be
pinched between the Germans at Verria and ELAS at Elafina. I
could not screw more out of them than this. Moreover, Markos
said that he had no authority to allow PAO to come into the hills
at all. He would have to refer the matter to the EAM Central
Committee in Athens, which was his boss. For the sake of the
attack on the Haliakmon Bridge, he would take a chance, and
let PAO move into the valley as an interim solution.

The second conference began some days later. On the first
day I got ELAS to agree to guide Aryiropoulos and Mousterakis
to Joint GHQ at Pertouli, in order that they might put the case
for the recognition of PAO. (They set off straightaway and did
reach Joint GHQ where they expressed willingness to sign the
'National Bands' agreement.) Apart from this both sides continued
to abuse each other. On the second day I started by talking to
the PAO officers alone, and explained to them that we were about
to attack the Haliakmon Bridge. They offered to do the job for
me themselves, showing all the conceit and obstinacy of a certain
type of regular Greek officer. They obviously thought that in a
joint operation ELAS would shoot me in the back. Indeed, they
could not understand how I had survived so long with ELAS. I
then explained that ELAS had already received the supplies for
the job from GHQ Middle East and that we were about to execute
the task. In order that we could go ahead with the operation,
PAO must move their force off our line of approach. The PAO
officers agreed to move their force if they could get a proper

area, and if a British Liaison Officer would accompany them.

The ELAS trio — Markos, Kikitsas and Lazanis — then joined us. The usual insults flew, but I guided the negotiations towards forcing ELAS to offer a locality to PAO. In due course the offer of the Haliakmon valley was made. The PAO leaders were horrified at the thought of entering such a trap, and flew into a tantrum. I offered to send a British Liaison Officer into the Haliakmon Valley with PAO (Jock Hamilton would have got this distasteful job). As lunch-time approached, the PAO officers looked like agreeing, provided ELAS made no further demands.

We broke up for lunch, and I got hold of Markos to put pressure on him. He finally confessed that he had heard from the EAM Central Committee that PAO was not to be admitted to the hills. For this he apologised and said he was sorry, etc. but his hands were tied, and so forth. It was clear that ELAS was hardening against my pressure. When we resumed after lunch, the meeting became very formal and polite. Neither side was willing to come to any final decision about PAO placing itself in the Haliakmon valley, and it was clear that the deadlock was unresolved. Finally they stood up, saluted one another, shook hands with me and departed. It was pretty clear that neither side was going to be capable of compromise. Mud-slinging had contained more hope than this new formality. All the same I stayed that night at the Swiss house in case anyone wanted to consult me.

At dawn I was awakened by the sound of machine-gun fire. An ELAS guard told me that PAO had attacked the ELAS outposts. I was on my own, except for an ELAS section which had been left with me, and only one man of this section was at his post. I set off towards the machine-gun fire, and I eventually came to a rocky and scrub-covered bluff where some ELAS men were lying under good cover. Desultory fire was being exchanged with another group — PAO — who held a similar bluff more than a mile away. At that range most of the shot was falling short or spent. I found that Kikitsas was in charge and had him fetched. Kikitsas told me the tale that PAO had attacked an ELAS outpost, and that ELAS had taken up the challenge. They would drive PAO out of the hills. It was less difficult than it sounded, for PAO were indeed on the last hill, and the plain below the hill was held by the Germans.

I made it clear to Kikitsas that I did not believe his tale. I spoke sharply about the folly of starting a civil war, and the effect it would have on relations with GHQ Middle East, and on their giving of aid to ELAS. After some altercation between us, I ordered Kikitsas to cease fire, so that I could cross over to PAO, persuade them to cease fire, and convene a conference to stop this folly. He agreed to cease fire from 2.30 to 3 pm, provided that I did not myself go as it was dangerous in this scrubby ground, but that a monk from a monastery which was situated in the valley between the two parties should take a message from me to PAO.

I therefore wrote an order to PAO to cease fire between 2.30 and 3.00, saying that ELAS had undertaken to do so, and I said that I would come at 3 pm to the monastery, where we should confer. The monk was willing to go. We saw him depart with my message. He rode on a grey pony, carrying a white sheet overhead on a long stick. He made his way through the valley, and disappeared into the shrubs beyond. He did not return. When 2.30 came, ELAS ceased fire. PAO continued to fire. At 3 pm Kikitsas ordered ELAS to resume firing, and I walked back to Elafina.

During the cease-fire on the ELAS side, while we sat looking out over the plain, we had seen some army trucks coming from the direction of Verria and driving across the plain to the foot of the hill upon which the PAO guerrillas were ensconced. Kikitsas had pointed the trucks out to me. He had maintained that they were German trucks bringing help to PAO — a clear case, he claimed, of collusion.*

Next morning Kikitsas was back at Elafina, well pleased with himself and with ELAS. He came himself to tell me what had happened. His men had attacked at dusk and driven PAO off the hill. In the confusion of the retreat, and in the darkness of this thickly wooded country, two groups of PAO had opened fire on one another. Many had been killed, and ELAS had had no casualties. Kikitsas' account was confirmed when I interviewed two prisoners who had been taken by ELAS. Both had fought in Albania, and their motives in joining PAO were patriotic. They were surprised to find the ELAS rank and file much like themselves and not the monstrous Communists whom they had been told to expect. Both agreed to join ELAS, now that PAO had disappeared.

---

* The Germans would of course be happy to stoke the fires of civil war between any rival Greek guerrilla bands. It does not follow that PAO had any understanding with the Germans.

It was now late in August 1943. During the next few days Kikitsas reported that the Haliakmon Bridge had been heavily reinforced. This was confirmed by independent evidence; for I sent Jock Hamilton down into the plain where he obtained information from villagers. We had a report also from one of four Cypriots, who at this time came out of hiding and joined us. There was no hope now of a surprise attack in force on the bridge.

At this critical period great difficulty was caused by a cipher jam in Cairo. As each station transmitted to Cairo only, it took three weeks for a top priority message from me to obtain an answer from Joint GHQ at Pertouli, both of us going through Cairo with all its attendant delays. I had of course reported the whole affair between ELAS and PAO stage by stage as it developed, and I asked for a ban on supplies to ELAS in Macedonia except for immediate operations against the Germans.

Replies to my messages came from Chris at Pertouli long after the event. Some caused me considerable annoyance, as he suggested that one should not give orders to an ELAS officer, that one should have recourse to mediation, and so forth. But I was glad that my recommendation to stop supplies to ELAS in Macedonia was approved. It was finally agreed that I should bring Kikitsas and Markos to Joint GHQ to discuss the whole episode. By the time this conclusion was reached some four weeks had passed since the episode itself.

In the meantime we had got some cordtex and some supplies for ourselves from a drop by a single plane. As the others in my party were much annoyed that we had had to put off the attack on the Haliakmon Bridge, we decided to move away from the ELAS contingent and make a separate camp on a ridge from which we looked east towards the sea. Our stay in the hills above Elafina had done us all good. We had even had some wheat bread instead of the eternal *boubota* (maize bread), and we had eaten a sort of thick paste, which was slightly sweet, made from the lees of grapes which were left in making wine. This stuff was called *threpsina* and was a great treat for us.

When we were about to move off to our new camp, I went up to the dropping ground to check that we had not left anything. I was walking alone through some bracken, when I came across two rotting corpses, the legs off at the knee and the trunks chewed by jackals. The smell of rotting flesh was nauseating. This confirmed a suspicion which I had that the ELAS squad on the dropping ground was an execution squad. Their commander was a queer chap with a bizarre expression. He had reminded me of Clearchus, the crazed executioner on Mount Kissavo. He got on well with us, but he was none the less a man of the same type. The two unburied corpses with the amputated legs were certainly his victims.

At this time I sent Jock Hamilton off in his kilt to act as Liaison Officer to ELAS on Mount Vermion, and I was not to see him again until after the war. Phillips, a newcomer who had dropped near Omale, was brought over to Pieria. I passed him on via Vermion to Paiko, where Johnson was already installed. At our new camp we lived in tents made from parachutes, pitched under a huge walnut tree. Every evening we had a camp fire. We were joined by Winlaw, who was with ELAS in Pieria, and later by Wickstead, whom I fetched from his station at Omale. I had sent Alekko down to the coast to look for some means of crossing the Gulf to Chalcidice, and he had found a friendly caique-skipper. I then proposed to Kikitsas that Winlaw should go as Liaison Officer to ELAS in Chalcidice. Kikitsas agreed to this and made the necessary arrangements. When Winlaw arrived he found similar trouble between ELAS and PAO in Chalcidice.

I was anxious not only about him but also about one of my Greek officers, Heracles, who had been away for some time reconnoitring the branch-line of the railway which runs from Edessa to Florina. His political sympathies were with PAO, and I was afraid that ELAS might kill him. Scottie and Inder reconnoitred all the bridges between the mouths of the rivers Haliakmon and Peneus. They found a number of good targets of a minor type, and we sent a plan of operations to Cairo. This plan was approved. It was successfully carried out with the help of ELAS but only when I had already set out for Joint GHQ.

My relations with ELAS had changed radically as a result of the PAO episode. I had penalised ELAS in Macedonia by stopping all supplies to them from GHQ Middle East, and Kikitsas and Markos knew why. Soon after the episode I was invited to attend an EAM rally at Elafina, and contrary to my usual practice I did attend. Several thousand villagers were assembled in a large clearing with high trees behind them. The speakers, Markos and others, slated PAO as a movement which was collaborating with the Germans. I then spoke in Greek in defence of PAO and against ELAS. My remarks were greeted with cries of 'Traitor', 'Fascist', and 'Death' from the back-row thugs, but I went on to the end with my speech, which was strongly rhetorical and evoked an emotional response.

One of our interpreters at this time was a Greek from this part of Pieria, and I had a particular friend in an ELAS captain called Katsantonis, a local man, whom I had known for some time. He had sheltered an Australian soldier who had been with me in Thessaly. Through these two men we got a clear view of feeling in Pieria. Sympathies were fairly strongly divided between ELAS and PAO and EDES was a weak third. My speech damaged the cause of ELAS considerably, because the people in the area had hitherto had the story only from the ELAS side.

Reports reached me that ELAS had attacked several villages near the plain which were opposed to ELAS and in particular a village called Koukkes. When I challenged Kikitsas about this, he maintained that Koukkes had accepted arms from the Germans, and that some PAO men had been helped by the villagers to make field fortifications against ELAS; in view of this, he said, ELAS had captured the village. I said I would visit the village and hear their version. Thereupon Kikitsas declared he would not allow me to do so and, when I asked on what ground, he said that it was not safe. I then wrote out a note in Greek and in English, saying that Kikitsas was not responsible for my safety, and that I was visiting Koukkes against his advice.

I set off with Alekko towards the village, which was in the borderland between the ELAS area and the German-occupied area. We were quite near it when Kikitsas appeared with a strongly-armed section and said he hoped we did not object to his company, as he also was going to Koukkes! This move stumped me. When we entered Koukkes the few villagers who had not fled were unwilling to speak out in the hearing of the Elasites.

This incident illustrated the difficulty of getting direct information in an area in which ELAS was attacking Greek opponents. There were several more villages which were said by ELAS to have taken arms from the Germans, and we were able indirectly by various means to confirm that this was indeed so. It was one of the consequences of the PAO episode; for the civil war which had broken out between PAO and ELAS was now being reflected by a split in the civilian population in the villages.

ELAS was of course eager to find out how much we knew and what we thought about them. At our camp under the walnut tree we had only one section of ELAS with us. They were supposed to guard us and get supplies, but they were also there to spy on us. After dark one night a young ELAS soldier, 'Byron', crawled into my tent and told me his history. He had become a

Communist at school at the age of fifteen during the German occupation, and had then joined ELAS and been trained in their political school. He had been put into the Intelligence branch which dealt with suspects, and Kikitsas had instructed him to watch and report on me and the other British officers. Now that he was seventeen, he told me, he had seen the light and become a convinced Royalist or at least a Conservative. Finally he suggested that I should tell him what he was to tell Kikitsas in order to deceive ELAS. I think his story was a true one, but it made no difference to me. I told him that I had no objection to Kikitsas hearing any views I might express. Byron was disappointed in me. He visited me another night, but I advised him to lay off in case ELAS got wind of him.

At this time the case of a Greek Air Force sergeant who was an agent of ISLD (an information service run by Cairo) came to a head. This man had been dropped into Macedonia with money and a mission to obtain information on certain points. ISLD worked separately from us, but in this instance the man had been instructed to report to me. When he came to my HQ, ELAS showed their dislike of him, and he reciprocated the feeling; this really finished his chances of success, because ELAS could keep track of him almost everywhere he might go. I advised Cairo to withdraw him and to drop another agent who could proceed on his business unknown to ELAS. Cairo did not agree. Eventually I persuaded Kikitsas to help him on his way into the German-occupied area, where he gave ELAS the slip for a time, apparently. Later I heard indirectly that ELAS had caught him. When I challenged him, Kikitsas denied it. Later however, he was seen by one of my Greeks (I think Alekko), and subsequently we heard that ELAS had killed him. I got some depositions later from witnesses.

This incident was typical of the situation which faced us. Any Greek sent in from Cairo was regarded by ELAS as a spy and was disposed of, unless he stayed under the wing of a British officer. For the ELAS police system had a monopoly of power throughout the hill country of Macedonia and controlled all movements of persons. In the towns, too, ELAS had gangs of cut-throats, known as assault squads, and they were often able to track down anyone who fled from the hill country into populated centres which were only nominally under German control.

What had happened in Pieria had very serious aspects. ELAS had shown itself determined to wipe out a resistance movement which its own representatives at Joint GHQ had agreed to recognise in principle. The action of Markos and Kikitsas near Elafina had made a mockery of ELAS's participation in the Joint GHQ and of the promised collaboration with other resistance movements against the common enemy. Nor did the damage stop there. The bloodshed of the engagement near Elafina spread out in the villages of Pieria, where reprisal and counter-reprisal was carried out against the unarmed villagers. That way lay demoralisation and disaster. It was vital to bring Markos and Kikitsas before the Joint GHQ.

CHAPTER SIX

Civil War

There was some truth in Churchill's comment on the situation in Greece after July, 1943: 'This [the actions which formed a cover for the landing in Sicily] was the last direct military contribution which the Greek guerrillas made to the war, and henceforward the scene was dominated by the struggle to gain political power at the end of hostilities' (The Second World War, V, 472–3). As far as the grand strategy of Churchill was concerned, Greece was now on the side lines and his own mind turned to helping the partisans not in Greece but in Yugoslavia (SWW, V, 121). Yet the very presence of Greek guerrillas was damaging to enemy morale and kept large enemy forces active in the southern Balkans. 'The struggle to gain political power' had been dominant from the start of the resistance movements, a start which had preceded the arrival of the first British parachutists. After July 1943 the struggle became more intense and more open because the movements were stronger and the day of liberation was thought — erroneously in fact — to be close at hand.

At that time the position of King George and his Greek Government was particularly difficult. He and the members of his Government were generally disliked in Greece as supporters of the Metaxas regime, and their armed forces outside Greece were inactive and disaffected. On 3 July the King promised in a broadcast to the Greek people that his government would resign and a general election would be held immediately after the liberation of the country. The tacit assumption that he and his Government would be in control during the liberation did not go unchallenged. EAM-ELAS demanded that their voice should be heard outside Greece, and the Greek forces in Egypt mutinied. The gulf between the Greek Government, which was recognised by the Western Powers, and the strongest of the resistance movements was now seen to be wide and deep.

When I set off with Markos and Kikitsas on our journey to the Joint GHQ, I left Wickstead in charge of Pieria. He had had a slow start, as he had skinned a big toe on his first cross-country walk with me, and this later turned septic and crippled him for a time. But he had sized up the situation with ELAS, and I was happy to leave him in charge. Winlaw had now set off for Chalcidice, Hamilton was on Mount Vermion, and Phillips and Johnson were on Mount Paiko. Scottie and Inder were in charge of the attacks on the railway targets which had been approved, and Kikitsas had named a capable ELAS officer who was to support them with some ELAS troops.

For Markos, Kikitsas and myself the journey to the Joint GHQ at Pertouli was something of a holiday. I organised donkey and mule races on the way, and we had amusing arguments about many things. Our personal relationships were entirely friendly and easy, but none of us concealed the difference in political outlook which divided us.

One day my donkey came in last, being a slow and obstinate animal; when I came up with the other two, I said I should make my donkey the 'Responsible' (*ypefthenos*), that is, the EAM agent in his village. When they asked why, I replied because he was the slowest and most obstinate of them all. This delighted them. Their jokes were on the themes of gigantic lice, from which all Elasites suffered, as well as some of us; of 'sending so-and-so to GHQ', which was a euphemism for bumping him off en route; and of 'the monkey-man', which was a nickname I had invented amongst ourselves for the PAO commander Aryiropoulos, and which Kikitsas had found out from one of our party.

We had about five days together, ending with a drive in a guerrilla car along the fringe of the Thessalian plain from Kalabaka to Porta Pazari. We travelled up from there to Pertouli by lorry. On the way I met and talked with Kissavos, the first ELAS commander I had known. It was several months since Karayeoryis had said he would demote him at my suggestion. Kissavos must have known this but he bore me no ill-will. He had evidently been promoted.

At the Joint GHQ Chris was in charge of the Mission, as Eddie had gone by plane to Egypt with delegates of ELAS, EAM, EKKA and EDES and had not returned. In fact he never did return. The ELAS and EAM representatives had caused great difficulty in Egypt and the Lebanon by their intransigent attitude and excessive demands. They refused to recognise the Greek King and the Government outside Greece, and they promoted mutinies in the Greek forces in the Middle East. Eddie fell a victim to this trouble. He was blamed for the results of a policy which he did not initiate

Author between Sarafis and Despotopoulos in an ELAS HQ group, April 1944. A photograph given by Sarafis.

British Liaison Officers at Pendalofos 1944 with Jock Hamilton on the right.

Parade of ELAS Andartisses at Pendalofos, March 1944

Chris waiting to salute the dead. Pendalofos, March 1944.

and against which he had warned the Higher Command at Cairo.

When we arrived at Pertouli, all the delegates had returned, and it was one of them, Tzimas (known as Samariniotis), who represented EAM in the discussions about PAO. Ares represented ELAS. The representatives of EDES and EKKA held less high positions in their own resistance groups, and they were less forceful characters.

The Joint GHQ had already interviewed Aryiropoulos and Mousterakis, and Aryiropoulos had returned to Salonica. It had been agreed that Mousterakis was to represent PAO at the Joint GHQ, if Middle East and the members of the Joint GHQ should come to recognise PAO. A decision on recognition had been deferred for our evidence. Markos, Kikitsas and I therefore appeared to give evidence. The real difficulty in the way of recognising PAO was the presence in the organisation of men who had contacts with the Greek police-force and with the security troops in Salonica, both of which were of course acting under the Quisling Government.*

After much argument the Joint GHQ agreed to recognise PAO, provided that certain persons were discharged and certain contacts were abandoned. When GHQ Middle East was informed, it approved the decision. Mousterakis was sent off to convey to Salonica the decision, which bore the signatures of the members of the Joint GHQ, including those of the ELAS representatives. In fact, Mousterakis never got to Salonica. He was put into an ELAS prison at Dheskati, as I learnt in December.

The other aspect of this problem was the suspension of supplies to ELAS in Macedonia for wiping out the PAO group in Pieria. Here the case was a more difficult one to argue. I held to my position that any movement which attacked Greeks was to be given supplies only for an immediate operation against the Germans. Chris supported me. He was as fully aware as I was that ELAS aimed to acquire a monopoly of power, and that we could only hope to hold it back from attacking the other resistance movements by using sanctions in supplies. In fact ELAS in Macedonia continued to be penalised: no supplies were sent from the Middle East except for immediate operations against the Germans.

At Pertouli there was great excitement over the Italians. When

---

* The Government set up in Greece and supported by the Germans; such governments were named colloquially after Quisling who headed the first such government, in Norway.

Italy collapsed on 8 September 1943, General Wilson gave the
Mission orders to contact all Italian headquarters in Greece and
obtain their surrender or, better still, their collaboration against
the Germans. In Macedonia there were Italians only at Kastoria.
Prentice established contact with them, but negotiations broke
down when the Germans moved in.

At Lidoriki to the south of Thessaly, Creed had an amusing
experence. He and a sergeant went into Lidoriki, armed but with
a white flag. While they were interviewing the Italian commander
with a view to his surrender, a truck stopped outside, and two
German officers came into the room. The Italian Commander then
said that there was no question of his not continuing to fight
alongside his German allies. To Creed's surprise, the Germans
appeared to accept the immunity of himself and his sergeant under
the white flag, and he therefore took his leave. Formal salutes
were exchanged. As soon as he and the sergeant were out of sight,
they took to their heels. It was only later that they learnt that the
two Germans had not been accompanied by any troops.

In Thessaly the Italians came over in large numbers. The Pinerolo Division of 15,000 men, complete with arms, ammunitions
motor transport and field guns, marched to Kalabaka and offered
to fight under the command of GHQ Middle East, of which
Chris was the representative, against the Germans. The first
official contact was made by an Italian cavalry colonel in a smart
uniform at the head of a column. He was met by a British Liaison
Officer called Harker, a cheerful soul who had no Italian. The
Italian colonel made a flowery speech in Italian, and a Sicilian
corporal, who had been in the USA and was later known to us as
Joe, came forward to interpret. When the Colonel had finished,
Harker turned to hear the translation, and Joe said simply, 'You
not listen to that bastard, he say nothing.' Needless to say, the
offer of the Pinerolo Division was accepted.

The Commander of the Pinerolo Division was General Infante,
a distinguished officer who had been Military Attaché in London
for many years. He spoke good English and played a good game of
bridge. During the negotiations he made it clear that he would
never co-operate with ELAS or any other resistance movement
alone, and that he had come over only because the British Mission represented GHQ Middle East. When the division joined us,
the representatives of ELAS and EDES and EKKA signed an
agreement recognising the Italians of the division as co-belligerents
and promising them equality in supplies, etc; in particular they

guaranteed that any Italian who chose to give up his arms and not fight would have the same standard of rations as a guerrilla had. Any surplus supplies, arms and ammunition not allocated to Italians in fighting units were to be distributed fairly among the three resistance movements, in proportion to their numbers, as was more or less the case with supplies from the Middle East.

The immediate problem was to feed 15,000 Italians. Because no one area had the resources, it was decided to divide the Italians into three main forces and place one in Roumeli, one in Thessaly and one in Macedonia. The field-guns and their gunners stayed in Thessaly; they were to hold Kalabaka, which they did successfully at the outset.

When my business was finished, I set off for Krimini, where one of the Mission stations in Macedonia was situated. I was accompanied by an Italian major, a regular little Mussolini, who grumbled at every discomfort. We took Italian cavalry chargers and rode via Kalabaka and Mourgani, where we stayed the night with an Italian battery post. They were a good unit. They did not hide from me their suspicions of the Greeks, by whom they meant ELAS, and their suspicions were only too well founded. As we got into Macedonia, rumours reached us that the 4,000 Italians who had gone to Macedonia had surrendered all their arms to ELAS. While I was at Pertouli the rains had started, and the 4,000 had marched in heavy rain. With Greek guides their route had been circuitous and arduous; they had slept in the open, and the villagers had stolen anything loose from them, such as boots and equipment. When they were nearing Grevena, they were addressed by General Kalabalikis, a new ELAS commander whom I had not yet met. He painted the rigours of guerrilla warfare in gloomy colours, and he explained that the Greeks knew the country better and were more inured to the harsh conditions. Why not hand over their weapons to the Greek guerrillas? Why not live in the villages on the same rations as the guerrillas had in the open? His oratory carried the day. To a man the 4,000 laid down their arms. Kalabalikis astutely drew up a formal agreement which was signed by the Italian Commanders of all the units.

On hearing the news my little Musso major was furious. I took him to see General Demaratos, the ELAS military commander, who had commanded the 9th Division so successfully against the Italians in Albania. After listening to a long and bombastic speech by the major, Demaratos said nothing but handed him the formal agreement. The major read it for the first time; it punctured the poor little windbag. I arranged for him to go back to General Infante. Meanwhile ELAS had acquired the arms of the other Italian groups by less subtle methods. Force was used in Roumeli. Then the Germans made a sudden drive into the hills. They caught many disarmed Italians, and shot them as traitors. There was nothing I could do to help the Italians in Macedonia, except try to keep ELAS to the agreement that the Italians should receive the same rations.

We were now passing into early October 1943. The British Military Mission had changed its name to the Allied Military Mission with the arrival of some American officers. It was a change without a difference as far as Macedonia was concerned, because no American officers were attached to our HQ, and no change of policy was initiated. When I came back to Pendalofos, Prentice had been running the West Macedonia HQ for over two months and had done it admirably. He was slow, calm and deliberate in manner, and he would not be pushed by the ELAS command into the decisions which they wanted. He was being strongly pressed by Karatsas for 20,000 gold sovereigns, then the equivalent of about £100,000 in paper money. The harvest was now in and Karatsas wanted to buy grain for the troops in Macedonia for the winter months.

Before Eddie had disappeared into Egypt he had approved the provision of gold sovereigns for this purpose, but I had been opposed to it on the grounds that ELAS would get the supplies by requisitioning anyhow and would keep the gold sovereigns for other purposes. The 4,000 Italians were a further complication. Karatsas included them among the troops in Macedonia, as they had come over to our side, and this accession pretty well doubled the total demand, so that he reached his grand total of 20,000 gold sovereigns. I advised Cairo against, and I told Karatsas that, as ELAS had made the agreement with the 4,000 Italians and had not consulted us, ELAS alone was under a specific obligation to feed them. As Cairo adopted my policy, Karatsas did not get the £100,000 and he had to feed 4,000 Italians at the expense of ELAS.

One morning after ELAS HQ had been informed of this, Karatsas sent up a message in the usual way and asked if I could call on business. I found him rude and abusive about the sovereigns, and when I firmly repeated the ruling on the Italians, he lost his temper completely. He shook with rage and cursed me for always 'smiling and laughing' at him (one word in Greek has both meanings).

Acting very much the British officer, I then told him that I would leave him until he had recovered his temper, and I marched out in a formal manner.

When I got back, another message had just come in for me to decode. It partly explained the attitude of Karatsas. Having acquired almost the whole armament of an Italian Division, ELAS had attacked EDES.* A civil war had begun, which in fact was to last for more than four months. EKKA remained neutral. The Joint GHQ ceased to function. An enquiry by the Mission pinned the blame on ELAS as the aggressor. A new phase in our relations with ELAS had begun. Karatsas had inaugurated this phase with particular venom, because, but for me, as he must have thought, he would have got £100,000 into his coffers just in time.

As soon as this civil war started, GHQ Middle East turned off the tap of supplies to ELAS as the aggressor. It made no difference to ELAS in Macedonia, because I had already done so with Chris's approval for ELAS's attack on PAO. In addition I asked GHQ Middle East to cease sending gold sovereigns for the relief of the devastated villages of Macedonia, because I believed that ELAS would extort them from the villagers. I also held Karatsas to the obligation of feeding the Italians. It was no wonder Karatsas was hostile to me. He was no doubt blamed by his own GHQ for his failure to extract more golden eggs from the British goose.

The war had begun in Thessaly and Agrapha, where the forces of Zervas were driven back rapidly by the now superior fire-power of ELAS. The Macedonian troops of ELAS were not involved at the outset. ELAS and EAM put abroad the usual tales, that EDES was collaborating with the Germans and that Zervas was receiving German subsidies and ammunition. When the Germans took advantage of the civil war to attack EDES in Epirus, Zervas found himself ground between the forces of ELAS and those of the Germans. According to ELAS, German forces which raided villages in the hills were led by Edesites. Now the Germans were very well informed about the Greek resistance movements. They did all they could to inflame feeling between EDES and ELAS, even dropping pamphlets which pronounced sentence of execution on all Elasites and promised a free pardon to all Edesites. It is then likely enough that German raiding forces were led by Greeks dressed up as Edesites in ELAS areas and as Elasites in EDES

---

* For the circumstances see C.M. Woodhouse, *Apple of Discord* 167 f. and *The Second World War*, V, 475 f.

areas. As I have mentioned earlier, the Germans had raised 'security forces' of Greeks, commanded by a Colonel Poulos, which served against the guerrillas. ELAS put it out that Colonel Poulos was a member of EDES. As ELAS had a complete monopoly of all newspapers and radios in the hill country of Macedonia, their propaganda had an extraordinarily powerful effect. A counterblast could be given only by the Allied Mission, and one problem was how we were to get through to the public.

The first step I took was to see Colonel Demaratos, the commander of the 9th Division in West Macedonia, who had come to join ELAS after my visit to Salonica. I complained formally about the rudeness of his subordinate officer, Karatsas, and said I should not deal with Karatsas again unless he made an apology to me. Demaratos knew that I knew that Karatsas was in fact the boss, but I enjoyed exploiting the pretences of the ELAS system of command. Subsequently Karatsas made a full apology, formally on the instructions of Demaratos.

My main point, however, was to discuss with Demaratos his own position in regard to the civil war. I explained the attitude of the Mission, and told him that GHQ Middle East had cut off all supplies to ELAS everywhere pending an enquiry. I left him to think the matter over. Soon afterwards he consulted me about his duty. He saw his command might involve him in a conflict with the British; he disapproved of the civil war as a Greek, and he disapproved of the Communist control of ELAS. He therefore decided to resign his command, and I expressed my support of his decision.

His resignation made a great impression on the ELAS rank and file, and on the peasants in Macedonia, for he was a well-known figure. It was a brave action. He withdrew to his native village, Aetopetra, and survived the war. Another friend of mine, who had been influential as a journalist and a Venizelist politician in Kozani and had joined EAM, told me that he could no longer participate in a movement which aimed to achieve a monopoly of power at the price of a civil war. He withdrew from EAM and left the hills. His fate is not known to me, but I doubt if he survived; for EAM and ELAS were particularly anxious to liquidate anyone who left their ranks and might exert political influence against them. Members of ELAS were particularly vulnerable because they had taken the oath on pain of death to stay in ELAS until after the liberation of Greece. Anyone absconding was likely to be killed without question, if caught.

Shortly after the resignation of Demaratos, London broadcast a condemnation of EAM-ELAS as the aggressor in the civil war against EDES, and named Ares in particular as the promoter of the attack; but, because ELAS possessed all the wireless sets in their areas, this condemnation did not reach the ELAS troops, far less the peasants in the hill country. Its only effect in the mountains was to enrage the ELAS command still more against the British Mission.

The counter-measure which Karatsas took was to restrict our movement. He told me that in order to protect the British Mission from attack by 'those collaborators with the Germans, the Edesites and their agents', he must ask me to keep all members of the Mission within whatever village or place they were stationed. We both knew that this was absurd, as there was no EDES unit anywhere in Macedonia. But he knew that I knew that he was issuing a thinly-veiled threat that any member of the Mission leaving any village would be shot, and no questions asked. It was clear from later signals that this instruction came from ELAS GHQ, because it was announced to all stations of the Mission. Karatsas took special precautions with me; he placed a guard on my house, in order to 'protect' me.

These steps by Karatsas suited my book well enough. When the payment of gold sovereigns for the relief of villages was stopped, Karatsas had stimulated the burnt villages to send deputations and to dun me with their complaints. The deputations came in droves during some six weeks, beginning from the time when London denounced ELAS for beginning the civil war. Each deputation consisted of some twenty villagers, and the leaders of each were members of EAM. They presented a complaint which had been duplicated quite obviously in the ELAS Headquarters at Pendalofos.

As each deputation arrived, I heard the complaint and then replied, insisting that the ELAS guard on my house should come forward and witness the show. I gave the facts about the civil war, London's condemnation of ELAS as the aggressor, and the withdrawal of the support of GHQ Middle East from ELAS as the promoter of civil war between Greek and Greek. I referred to reports for which I did not vouch, that money given for relief had been extorted from the villagers and used for party purposes, and I made it clear that the Allies could hardly be expected to pour gold into an area which EAM-ELAS was able to control for its present purposes. I then asked for questions from the dele-

gation. Some of the questions usually enabled me to counter the
ELAS propaganda and spread doubt about the truth of their
statements. At the end of the session I always commented on the
peculiar fact that, although each village claimed to have acted
spontaneously in sending a deputation to me, all deputations
presented the same formal petition on identical paper.

The great advantage of this method was that it touched the
villagers' sense of humour as well as their intelligence, and it
made them question the motives of ELAS in the war against
EDES. When Karatsas complained, I asked him to attend and reply
himself to any charges. He came only once because I cornered him
on his promise to feed the Italians; for he was feeding them from
food-supplies which had been reserved to help the villages that had
suffered from reprisals. Karatsas decided to stop any further
deputations, but it took a week or two to re-direct them. By that
time in any case, the damage to his cause was widespread.

We settled down to our confinement in the large village of
Pendalofos. I had Prentice, who was my adjutant, and Evans, a
young journalist by profession who had recently arrived; two
Greek officers, Heracles, who had returned safely from a successful
reconnaissance of the Edessa-Florina railway, and Zotos, who had
distinguished himself at Himarë during the war in Albania; Sergeant
Kite, an excellent Commando NCO; Leo Voller, an RAF sergeant,
who was my wireless operator; and several other NCOs who were
recent arrivals. Time being heavy on our hands and our minds, we
organised various competitions in card-games and especially in
tavli, the Greek form of backgammon. We made friends with the
village children, for whom the NCOs improvised a number of toys,
and the children showed us their games and toys. The most
ingenious was the *psevdhaetos* or 'false eagle' (what we call a kite).
One made a huge dunce's hat of paper, put a thin frame across the
open end, and set it on the ground with the point upwards. Then
one put a lit splinter of pinewood or a candle on the frame, and on
a calm day the hot air would lift the 'false eagle' into the empyrean.

Shortly after the first rupture with Karatsas, one of three
wireless operators, who had recently arrived, fell very ill. I asked
Cairo for advice, but before the reply came, he was dead. The
cause of his death was blackwater fever. At the time I too was ill
with malaria but mine was of the benign tertian variety, with
which the mosquitoes of Kozani had infected me. I got out of
bed to conduct the funeral. I had a high temperature, which may
account for the vivid impression I retain.

The corpse had been laid out on a low bed in his military uniform with his hair brushed and with sweet-smelling herbs beside him, and the women of the house, clad in black, sat wailing on the floor of the room. Another officer (Prentice) and I had difficulty in lifting the corpse from the bed into a crudely-made wooden coffin. As we did so, the women came up wailing, and threw walnuts and almonds into the coffin. It was raised up by the bearers, who were the men of the house, and as it was carried down a flight of stone steps into the paved court-yard, the nuts fell through the gaps between the planks of the coffin, and bounced down the steps on to the paving.

I marched slowly behind the coffin with Demaratos and Karatsas. The British contingent and an ELAS contingent marched behind us. A pall of dank mist lay over the village as we walked through mud and over wet cobbles to a derelict cemetery at the other end of the village. I read the service in English and Demaratos read it in Greek. Both nationalities saluted the dead man. The emotion of the Greeks, including the ELAS troops, who knew that we had stopped their supplies, touched me deeply. They were sincere in their grief, that this Englishman, who had come to help in the liberation of their country, had lost his life on Greek soil.

When the civil war got under way, we soon began to see some of its effects in Pendalofos, where ELAS still had its headquarters for West Macedonia. Every morning, shortly after dawn, an ELAS firing squad executed Greek civilians, whose crime, presumably, was to be hostile to ELAS. From the house in which I stayed, the figures could be seen against the skyline, small figures which fell, not always at the first volley, of which the sound came echoing down to us. These public executions were intended to terrorise the villagers. They certainly did so, and few adults dared speak to us. Inside the village several houses were used as prisons for political prisoners. These houses were soon known to us from the horrible groans and shrieks which issued from them.

At this time EAM-ELAS instituted 'People's Courts', in which martial law was administered. I knew these courts to be a travesty of justice. For example, a respected and relatively well-to-do villager, who was known to me and to a local interpreter, Bill Daniels (the son of an American Greek), was imprisoned and beaten, and was then put on trial. As it happened, I was seeing Karatsas that evening and he mentioned that he had been delayed by a case in the People's Court. I asked him to tell me about it, and he gave me the following account.

This villager had been overheard by an Elasite, who was in his house, when he expressed the opinion that the English might bring the King back to Greece after the war. For this he was put on trial. The prosecution had argued that the Russians would not wish to bring the King back to Greece; therefore, when the villager said that the English might bring the King back, he was trying to split the Grand Alliance of England and Russia; and that he was therefore sabotaging the war effort. On these grounds he had just been condemned to death as a traitor.

I remarked that the sentence seemed unduly severe for a mere expression of opinion. Karatsas appeared to be surprised that I did not applaud his argument. I asked Cairo to let me attend the People's Court as an observer, but Cairo was not willing to let me do so.

Before the outbreak of the civil war Prentice had been trying to protect an agent of Zervas, who had tried to start an EDES band in West Macedonia in accordance with the Joint GHQ agreement. This agent had had little success, and had finally disappeared from our knowledge with the outbreak of the civil war. Many peasants were being brought in from the countryside to Pendalofos and to neighbouring villages, where they were interned as civilian hostages and made responsible for the good conduct of their villages, which had been won by ELAS from EDES. The intention was to shoot them if their villages did not remain loyal to ELAS.

We heard of these hostages from the old widow, Aphrodite Ioannou, whose house was our headquarters. She came from a village in Epirus, where her relations had supported Zervas. Some of them were among the hostages. They suffered terribly from cold and hunger, and Aphrodite used to smuggle food to them. We also saw strings of men, women and children handcuffed or chained to one another, being driven like sheep into Pendalofos by ELAS troops.

In July 1944 I was to visit some of the villages from which such hostages had been taken. I was told then that many died on the march or were clubbed by ELAS men on the way over the mountains in the snow, and that many who reached Macedonia did not survive their imprisonment. The full horrors of the civil war quickly became known to the villagers and to the rank and file of ELAS. Undoubtedly the bulk of ELAS in Western Macedonia was opposed to the civil war. Only a small proportion believed the propaganda to which they were subjected. Yet revolts from

Communist control did not occur. This was largely because the Communists took the initiative in individual cases. Those who were known to be leading moderates in ELAS were posted elsewhere, or 'sent to GHQ' and so liquidated.

On the ground that GHQ Middle East had betrayed ELAS by cutting off supplies, it was stated by the ELAS high command that the movement could not maintain its full strength for the winter months. Therefore anyone who wished to be released for the winter should volunteer. This gambit was tried first in the case of a so-called battalion of 200 men; those who volunteered for release were about 165! A new tactic was then adopted. All ELAS troops were subjected to a medical examination. This was of a perfunctory nature. Many were discharged as 'unfit'. The truth was that they were not medically but politically unfit in the opinion of ELAS; for they were mainly the men who had fought in Albania.

The places which they vacated were taken by youths of fifteen or sixteen, who were conscripted under martial law; for EAM-ELAS was now openly proclaiming itself to be the one and only government of 'Free Greece'. These youths were subjected to a course of political indoctrination. They were then blooded, being detailed to act as executioners. Thereafter there was no turning back; for not only was their outlook warped, but they were known to the families of their victims. The seeds of future vendettas were sown in the soil of civil war. Girls too were recruited into ELAS and trained as soldiers; they staged a parade in Pendalofos.

As the winter hardened, ELAS had difficulty in finding food for the 4,000 Italians. We heard about their plight from the Italian officers who came to ELAS HQ in Pendalofos and talked to us, if chance offered. ELAS had tried by propaganda and by favouritism to convert some of them to Communism, but they had had little success. On one occasion, I protested strongly to Karatsas on this head.

Another device for reducing the number of Italian mouths to be fed was to tell the Italians that they were free to go home, either by walking round the head of the Adriatic or by taking a boat from the coast of Albania, and that in either case, if they kept to the high country on the way, they would be passing through safe areas liberated by the guerrillas. When the offer was made, many Italians set out on this forlorn journey. A few came back suffering from frost-bite and malnutrition; some returned to die in Pendalofos. I doubt whether any saw Italy again.

One evening the ELAS guard on our house was eluded by two ragged men. They proved to be Serbs, supporters of Mihailovitz; they had been captured by the Germans and put into forced labour at Salonica. From there they had escaped. The Greeks who had helped them escape had passed them out to the hills, where ELAS picked them up. Seeing that ELAS was Communist in its organisation and outlook, the Serbs had concealed their membership of Mihailovitz's movement. They were then brought to Pendalofos, where they were questioned closely. They realised that ELAS suspected them. In any case they were told by ELAS that they would be passed on to Tempo, whom they knew to be Tito's lieutenant in the south of Yugoslavia. They believed that, if they fell into his hands, they would not survive. Hence their escape to me, in the hope that I would protect them from ELAS and send them out to join the Royal Yugoslav forces in Egypt. One of them had been a pilot in the Yugoslav Airforce.

I sent an urgent signal to Cairo, and kept the men while I waited for a reply. Meanwhile Karatsas bombarded me with indignant demands that they should be handed over. From discussions with him it emerged that ELAS had an agreement with Tito, whereby any national of the other country would be handed over to ELAS or Tito as the case might be. This was an interesting example of international Communism at work. The reply of GHQ Middle East was simply an order to hand the Serbs over to ELAS. When I explained this order to them, they went without protest or complaint to what they believed would be an unpleasant death.

Another sign of international Communism was manifest in the fact that Tito attacked Mihailovitz in Yugoslavia and Hoxha attacked Kupi in Albania at the same time as ELAS attacked EDES. There was no room for doubt that these attacks were concerted by the Balkan Communist Parties. They may have been timed to start in October partly because there was a chance that the Germans would have to withdraw from the Balkans that winter or next spring. Shortly after the ELAS order confining us to the village, Tzimas, who ranked next to Siantos and had been the EAM representative at the former Joint GHQ, appeared in Pendalofos. Using the pseudonym Samariniotis, because he was of Vlach blood and Samarina was a famous Vlach village, Tzimas was the most able in a conventional sense of the EAM leaders; for he was a well-educated lawyer, and he had charm of manner and a sense of humour. At this time he had with him an American airman who had been shot down over Greece. Tzimas was giving him a royal time, priming him against the wicked English and making him speak about America or whatever at banquets and meetings, where his speeches were completely misrepresented by EAM interpreters. Any intelligent child could have seen through it, but not so this simple-minded airman. I spoke strongly to him and even ordered him to stay under my command, until his HQ in Cairo could instruct him what to do.

Tzimas, we learned, was going to Tito's HQ to be EAM's liaison officer with the Yugoslav movement. The sending of this top-ranking Eamite on this mission showed how much value EAM placed on collaboration with the adjacent Communist movements in the event no doubt of actions after the German withdrawal. Karatsas, who ranked much lower, was terrified of Tzimas; on one occasion when the three of us were together and Tzimas criticised Karatsas, he could not control his trembling. When Tzimas left, the American airman went with him. In January he came back a sadder and a wiser man with a deep hatred of ELAS and EAM.

At this time we had developed a good source of information from within ELAS Headquarters at Pendalofos. Some staff officers who had been brought from Salonica by Demaratos were indispensable to ELAS. At the same time they supplied me and Prentice with the ELAS secrets to which they had access. One of them was Manolessos, the champion fencer of Greece. He had been arrested and deported by the Germans, but he had jumped out of a train south of Salonica. The local ELAS unit caught him and at first maltreated him, but eventually he was given a post in ELAS Headquarters as a staff officer.

He was particularly daring in sending notes to me at night with urgent news. From them we learnt that ELAS were finding it difficult to crack Zervas, whose men were fighting well, and that many ELAS units were being moved from Macedonia to Epirus, in order to attack Zervas from the north. We also learnt that ELAS was now finding it almost impossible to feed the Italians; that the Germans were moving troops out of the Kozani area; and that this probably meant an attack on Pendalofos. It was clear that ELAS was beginning to feel the pinch. Our stone-walling tactics were telling gradually.

At the start of the civil war in October, the area commanders (as I and my counterparts were styled) had been asked by GHQ Middle East whether we advised evacuation of the Allied Mission on the grounds that the Mission personnel was in danger and that we were unable to control ELAS. I advised against evacuation, arguing that the danger of ELAS liquidating us was small and that our very presence had a restraining influence. The same question was to be asked twice in 1944. Each time my answer was the same.

There were, of course, other reasons and considerations. One did not want to leave a job half done and abandon hope of military operations inside Greece under the direction of GHQ Middle East. For without our presence there would be no means of supplying anyone. If resistance declined dramatically, as it was likely to do without us, the Germans would be able to divert troops to other areas. As far as the internal affairs of Greece were concerned, our withdrawal would result soon in the liquidation of EKKA and then of EDES, both organisations which GHQ Middle East had supported throughout their existence. For us to abandon fellow-fighters and personal allies in this way seemed to us almost a betrayal. More important than that, however, was the future of Greece, our first and only ally in the year after the fall of France. The only hope that we could see of enabling the Greeks to hold free elections after the liberation lay in the continuation of the Military Mission as a means of holding the ring while this group or that fought one another.

CHAPTER SEVEN

Operations Resumed in Macedonia

This and the following chapter cover the period December 1943 to April 1944. British and American forces were fighting south of Rome and won successes in New Guinea. British and Chinese forces advanced in Northern Burma.

The capitulation of ELAS began when they asked me to take over the feeding of the Italians and to resume the relief of the villages on any terms I wanted. In Thessaly and in Roumeli the Mission had been paying for both operations throughout the civil war. I arranged for Karatsas to attend a meeting between me and the Italian Commanding Officer, at which Karatsas formally expressed his inability to support the Italians and I undertook on behalf of GHQ Middle East to give such help as I could.

Some of the Italian officers were known to me through the QMS in ELAS, a long-eared Macedonian called Diplas, who was rather a friend of mine. I was therefore able to appoint a Captain Castiglione to organise working parties. His job was to fetch supplies from Grevena and other markets. The purchase of these supplies was done by Diplas at prices agreed between him and me, and Captain Castiglione had access to me at any time. At the same time I undertook the relief of the villages which had been burnt by the enemy. My conditions were the same as before (see p 48). British officers should go in person to meet the village committees, which were to comprise the priest, the schoolmaster, and the pre-occupation president, and two men elected by the villagers.

These conditions put an end to Karatsas' blockade of the Mission, and it ensured that EAM members of the committees were usually in a minority. Like boys out of school, we all raced round the villages, checking lists and giving out the money to the recipients in person. Snow had fallen, and the drifts were deep in many places. We often slept twenty or thirty in some hovel which the enemy had left standing. These villagers had lost everything. They had suffered from exposure to the bitter wind, which froze streams solid in icicle cascades. Yet they did not complain

that the Allies had provoked the reprisals, and they wished us well.
Their only shame was that Greeks were locked with Greeks in
civil war.

At the end of one of these trips I inspected the Italians, now
nearer 3,000 than 4,000. They were encamped in three hill villages
between Smixi and Philippaei. As I had given them warning of
my intended visit, I found them assembled on parade in the
village square of Dhoutsiko, high up on the Pindus range. I was
hardly worthy of the occasion. My battledress tunic, very dirty
in itself, was almost covered by a leather jerkin. I had no cap,
and I was wearing blue riding-breeches and puttees.

When I walked onto the parade-ground, the Italians in their
nondescript clothing stood strictly to attention. I roared, 'Stand
at ease!' in English but nothing happened. I repeated the order
in Greek. Still nothing happened. I then mimed the motion of
standing at ease several times, but with no result. Finally I asked
for an Italian who knew Greek, and explained my desire to him.

At last he shouted the necessary order in Italian, and the
men stood at ease, not putting one leg sideways as we do, and
as I had done in mime, but putting one leg in advance of the
other. The sight of 3,000 men unexpectedly making this move
nearly made me laugh. I then spoke through the interpreter,
urging them to maintain their self-respect and their discipline as
a military unit, and expressing the hope that they would return
as a unit to Italy next year. I ended, '*Viva l'Italia*' and 3,000
voices shouted, '*Viva l'Italia*'.

When I left Macedonia, Wickstead took charge of the Italians.
They stuck together longer than any other Italian unit, but eventually the men scattered. Most of them found billets in the houses
of villagers, and worked on their land. There were some other
Italians who had been taken prisoner by ELAS near Grevena
in March 1943. They were outside my control, but I gave ELAS
money and medicines for them. Later that autumn an attack by
German troops cut the line of ELAS supplies. At the time this
group of Italians was moved back to Samarina and had no food.
Many of them ate grass. The grass proved poisonous, so that
many died and others suffered from severe dysentery. In general,
whenever individual Greeks had the means, they were very generous
to the Italians; but there was not always enough food to go
round.

The Germans had promptly taken advantage of the civil war.
They began by attacking Zervas' flank in Epirus. They followed

this up in October by a large-scale drive delivered by two mountain divisions against the guerrillas. They operated simultaneously from Thessaly, Macedonia, Albania (via Ersekë), and Epirus. ELAS, bent on other things, put up little or no fight. Their units withdrew into the depths of the thick forest, while the Germans passed through the mountains, burning every village in their path. At Pendalofos we took our dump of explosives and ammunition to a secret hiding-place. Most of the Mission stores and personnel withdrew to a remote village called Heptakhori. ELAS units fell back towards Pindus. They held Pendalofos with the help of our demolition groups and machine-guns, but the other villages where we had stayed — Rodhokhori, Krimini, Omale, etc — were burnt to the ground.

A copy of the German plan of attack was captured by a Macedonian unit of ELAS and an Italian mortar section, which together cut off the tail-end of a German raiding column. This plan showed many more Mission stations than really existed. With their usual thoroughness the Germans had marked a station at every village at which we had ever stayed. The capture of the plan was divulged to us by Manolessos, and he smuggled most of the information to us for GHQ Middle East. In particular we learnt the strength and the component units of the two German divisions which were engaged in the drive. Subsequently, in the spring of 1944, Chris saw the actual documents. Later, in December, the Germans launched an attack against us in West Macedonia, when we managed to hold Pendalofos but lost Grevena temporarily. Much of the town was burnt. On this occasion Kite, Zotos and Heracles destroyed German vehicles by laying land-mines.

Christmas came with more snow. The second German drive had ended, and we were still billeted in Pendalofos. We had broken Karatsas' blockade, and in the ten days before Christmas Prentice, Evans and I were away from Pendalofos giving out relief in many of the newly burnt villages. It was hard frosty weather, and the snow lay deep. At Omale every single house had been destroyed. I spent the night with some thirty villagers in a lean-to against one of the few surviving walls, and we sang songs and talked deep into the night. They had no bitter feelings towards us for attacking the Germans or Italians and bringing these disasters on their village. They were ready to suffer any hardship for liberation, but they did not conceal their hatred and fear of EAM and ELAS, which did little to protect the villagers. In some villages, where an EAM member was ex officio on the committee (often the schoolmaster was an Eamite), they could not voice these feelings but we were always warmly welcomed.

At Grevena, from which the Germans had withdrawn, EAM staged a hostile demonstration. A crowd of people upbraided us for giving so small a sum, and for distributing it ourselves and not through ELAS. I gave them the obvious answer that the Allies did not have unlimited funds for relief, and that ELAS was engaged in a civil war which distracted their soldiers from protecting the villages. This displeased the extremists.

One man was arrested by ELAS troops as he was pursuing me with two Mills hand-grenades, in the hope of doing me in. Later, at my request, ELAS let him go, but sooner than I had suggested, and he was caught at the same game in a village outside Grevena, where I was dispensing relief. During this time other officers were visiting the villages north of Pendalofos. Our range extended to the district round Heptakhori where I had posted a British officer called Backhouse, who had recently arrived.

We all returned to Pendalofos on Christmas Eve. We agreed that relief was worthwhile and indeed important, both on humanitarian grounds and in its value for the good name of the Allies. In all South-West Macedonia 250 villages had been burnt in part or wholly. As I had laid it down that relief would be given only in person by a British officer, some of these villages were beyond our reach, being either in the enemy-occupied area, or too remote. The sovereigns which we gave for relief were used to buy corn, mainly from the German-occupied centres, such as Ptolemaïda, Kozani, Amyntaion, etc, and the corn was transported at night into the liberated area. Thus the gold was employed to stimulate the circulation of foodstuff within the country; no other means could have achieved this circulation in these hard times.

The merit of the direct method in giving relief was that EAM-ELAS could not embezzle the gold immediately or, when it was distributed, claim the credit. At the same time we could check to some extent on the correctness of the claims made by each village, and we could narrow the circle of recipients to villages in our immediate sphere of operations. This experiment was reported to Cairo. My recommendation that it should be used elsewhere in Greece was adopted, and it became general later. I also provided some money for the purchase of saws, in order to equip mills and make timber available for building houses in areas where we could oversee its use.

Our own Christmas was all the happier for a resumption of

contact with the outside world. Nobby Clarke, a stout-hearted Yorkshireman, had crossed the Pindus range in deep snow with despatches from Chris and with some personal mail for us, the first for months. On Christmas Day we had a Christmas party in Aphrodite's house for the children of Pendalofos. There was a Christmas tree, and we gave out balloons and toys, of which some had come in a recent drop and others had been made by the NCOs of the Mission. Aphrodite cooked us an enormous *Kastanopeta*, or sweet-chestnut pie. She was distressed that I was not there to eat a slice, because I had been called out to deal with the distribution of relief in Pendalofos and in the neighbouring village of Vithos.

It was a busy time too in our signal traffic with Cairo. After the collapse of Italy British forces had been landed on Leros and Cos, but were overwhelmed by the Germans in the course of November.* Some of the prisoners of war had then been moved from the islands to Athens, and during early December they were being taken north by rail. We were asked to derail or hold up the trains and liberate the prisoners. A suitable plan was not easy. The prisoners-of-war would be in poor shape, and if they escaped onto the snow-bound slopes of Mount Olympus they would not be likely to survive. I made arrangements with Scottie, whom I had left in charge in Pieria, that ELAS would provide military help on a large scale, and that consignments of rations would be dropped to him so that he could make dumps at suitable places. The plan was to move any escapees away from Pieria into the Dheskati and Grevena area.

However, the Germans had taken full precautions. The first train was successfully derailed. But it was a decoy train, and the trains carrying the prisoners passed through to Salonica. Only four sergeants and four privates escaped. They managed to break out of a truck when the train was on the move. They had fallen head-first onto the snow, one of the sergeants being injured, and had taken to the hills. Scottie's party found them later. An attack on the line north of Salonica was made by Bill Johnson from his base on Mount Paiko, but again the trainloads of prisoners passed through on the way to Germany.

The Germans retaliated by attempts to wipe out the British stations in Pieria and on Mount Paiko. They advanced from several points in considerable numbers. They were well equipped

* See *The Second World War* by Winston Churchill V, 185 f.

and well supplied, and our people had to move out at short notice in very severe weather. They were on the run over Christmas. Johnson's party escaped from Mount Paiko to Mount Kaïmaxitsala, but it was impossible to conceal their tracks in the snow, and the Germans were so close behind that they could not have a fire at night. During one such night, Phillips, a big powerful chap, died of exposure. The others buried him in the snow, and escaped north-westwards into an ELAS area. Scottie's party was chased from mountain to mountain. They made their escape from Pieria by getting across the Elassona-Servia road. While he was on the run, he managed to keep his wireless working, and we knew that he was in a dangerous situation.

One day I was decoding a message about Scottie's party when an EAM demonstration started outside. I sent Evans out to explain that I was too busy to see them and to send them away. As the uproar continued, I left the decoding and went outside. There I found about 300 people, including some ELAS troops and some well-known agitators. They were demanding arms and ammunition and gold for ELAS and making all the usual requests, in the usual insulting language. I told Prentice and Evans that I would give this crowd some of their own medicine. I obtained silence and spoke my mind in unmitigated terms.

I told them what the Allies and the Allied Mission had done for the Greek people in the past and were doing at this time, and what they were giving in return, abuse and insults and ingratitude; how the Greeks in Albania had fought with the bayonet against the Italians, and how the ELAS troops either fought at long-range against fellow-Greeks in a civil war, or joined this rabble under EAM agitators; how they could not leave us in peace even on Boxing Day to transact business with Cairo for their protection, and so on.

At this unexpected outburst most of the demonstrators withdrew, but their leaders broke into the house with shouts. They were soon ejected by Prentice, Evans and myself. I sent at once for Karatsas and reported the incident and the participation of ELAS troops. He said that he would punish the offenders, and I said that if he could not stop such nonsense I would report him to the General Headquarters of ELAS. We had no more such demonstrations. The Bishop of Kozani came to complain on behalf of the civilians in the demonstration. He went away with a straight answer, and I later heard from Chris that he had asked for me to be withdrawn from Macedonia.

Next day, 27 December, I set off to meet Scottie's party coming out of Pieria. Although I did not know it, it was my last day at Pendalofos. Prentice was left in charge there. I set off before dawn with Kite and two ELAS men, and we saw the sun's red light appear on the snowy peaks of Olympus. The ground was as hard as iron, and the river below Pendalofos lay solid in its bed. We walked in a battledress top plus two sweaters, a leather jerkin, despatch-rider breeches, puttees, army boots and two pairs of socks. We had small packs, and carried a revolver and a tommy-gun or rifle. This kit had proved far superior to the Arctic gear which Cairo had dropped: rubber thigh-length boots, thick woollen garments, and huge wind-proof wool-lined coats, which weighed a ton. Our kit was perfect for walking, and it was warm enough if you were not benighted.

We made fast going to reach Dheskati in two days, arriving some hours after dark, very much exhausted. Scottie and his party were there. They had escaped intact from Pieria, after a difficult move high up in the snow. Wickstead, whose big toe had been suppurating since October, had arrived in advance on a mule with the wireless party, and Palaeologus and Alekko had come with Scottie. It was very nice to be with Palaeologus and Alekko again, for the last time as it proved.

Scottie's party had buried most of their kit in Pieria, but a supply of rations had been dropped for them near Dheskati. They laid on a Christmas party for 30 December, the day after our arrival. The pièce-de-résistance was an egg on which two large moustaches were drawn. It was set facing me in the place of honour, and it represented Colonel 'Eggs', famous for his moustaches. The egg was toasted in the whisky which had been dropped to us in metal water-bottles (to its detriment, I was told, since I did not sample it, preferring ouzo). I visited Wickstead, who had had a rotten time of it with his foot. He lay under a pile of rugs trying to keep warm, and he had as his companion the injured sergeant who had escaped from the p-o-w train.

I interviewed the eight escapees. The four sergeants were regulars. They were fed-up, because they had served their time and when already on the way home had been intercepted in Egypt and sent on the Leros expedition. They wanted to get out of Greece. The four privates, from the Royal West Kents, were keen to stay with us, and they could help with the wireless sets. I arranged for the four sergeants to be taken to Bill Ford's station on Mount Pelion, from which they would go by sea to

Turkey. Heracles, who had grown more and more angry with
ELAS, and was in some danger from ELAS, was to go with them.
He lost his life in December 1944, a victim of the ELAS attack
on Athens. The four privates stayed with us and were most useful
as qualified signallers.

While I was at Dheskati, a signal came from Chris, summoning
me to a conference at Neraidha, and outlining a new set-up for
the Allied Mission. Eddie was not returning to Greece, and Chris
was taking command. He wanted me to act as chief liaison officer
with ELAS, and to be in charge of all the Mission stations in ELAS
territory. This entailed moving from Macedonia to Thessaly. I
should have a larger command than I had in Macedonia, and a
more important job politically, but I preferred the more active
life in Macedonia. I told Scottie of the message, and I said that I
would try to come back, but in the meantime he was to take
command of the Mission in Macedonia.

I briefed him fully of the dispositions. Mick the Miller was in
the Bulgarian sector on Boz Dagh, operating now with independent
bands, and at odds with the ELAS bands. Winlaw was in Chalcidice,
whither I had got ELAS to pass him by caique; he was operating
with ELAS, but he was also in touch with Intelligence officers
from the Middle East, who were under ISLD. Johnson was now on
Kaïmatsala, but he was due to return to Paiko as soon as the
German drive was over. Jock Hamilton was on Vermion, where
Backhouse was to join him. Evans was on the move to Mount Vitsi
where he would set up a new station. Prentice was in charge at the
Pendalofos HQ, where Scottie and his party were to join him.

I managed to speak to Prentice over an ELAS telephone, a
crazy line with several conversations going on simultaneously
and at cross-purposes. I told him the plans for the new set-up,
and he asked at once that I should take him with me. I also
told Palaeologus and Alekko that I was probably going to the
headquarters of ELAS and that I could not take them with me.
Palaeologus said he would hang on, in case I could move him
later to join me. Alekko decided that, if he was not to be with
me, he would rather go to Egypt. It was difficult, they said, to feel
for any Englishman as they did for me, after all our experiences
together. I arranged for Alekko to go out with Heracles and the
others.

Later he got involved in the mutinies of the Greek forces in
Libya and Derna. He escaped and rode to Egypt on a bicycle
with both tyres flat. He wrote to me saying that he had gone

further than Graziani, but more slowly. It was not possible for Palaeologus to join me. He returned to Egypt, where he was demobilised. He married a Greek girl in Cairo and I received a photo of the happy pair.

Prentice and Scottie had both seen me negotiating with ELAS. They knew the importance of taking a strong line and sticking to it. If I did not return, they would be of much help to my successor. While I was still at Dheskati, a boy came to my house at night with a letter written in a quavering hand which I had difficulty in reading. It was from Mousterakis, the PAO representative on the Joint GHQ who had been sent on the journey to Salonica, and it said that he was starving in prison at Dheskati. I sent for Kikitsas who had come out of Pieria with Scottie and was now the senior ELAS officer at Dheskati. He agreed to treat Mousterakis better, pending orders from ELAS HQ for his release. Kikitsas was very pleased that we had started giving relief again to the villagers, and I authorised him to tell the villagers near the pass above Servia that British officers would be giving relief there soon.

Kikitsas and I were on more friendly terms than any other British officer and ELAS officer in Macedonia. We respected each other and ever since my early days in Macedonia we had been through a good deal in close company, both militarily and politically. His last remark to me was a typical one. 'You're a good officer but a bloody awful politician', words that equally expressed my idea of him. I never saw him again. He was leader of most of the military operations which ELAS carried out in Macedonia, right up to the liberation.

After the war I saw a photograph of a triumphal procession of ELAS troops entering Salonica with Kikitsas in the lead, wreathed in garlands, smiling quizzically as he often did, with his head tilted on one side in a bird-like manner. He was a very neat figure of a man, typical of the traditional Andarte of the Greek War of Independence; and he was a born guerrilla fighter, with a love of battle in his blood. He fought on under Markos in the years after 1944. He was eventually executed by EAM because he opposed the policy that the Communist party advocated for Macedonia.

The local boss at Dheskati was Lazanis, a nasty and cruel ruffian. He was chasing me with a demand for arms, ammunition and sovereigns, in order to re-establish ELAS after its withdrawal from Pieria. He said that the German drive was coming next to Dheskati. He also organised some deputations of EAM followers from villages nearby, who came to demand arms for ELAS and relief for themselves. This was the same old story. I knew perfectly well that ELAS had stocks of arms and ammunition in reserve for later use. My knowledge was based on my own figures. I had kept records of all stores dropped by air since May and of the Italian arms and ammunition acquired by ELAS from the Pinerolo Division, and I had the original returns which had been made to me during May for all the ELAS units in Macedonia. Indeed I knew where most of the dumps were, and I had informed Cairo of their position.

In any case, even if ELAS were given arms to fight the Germans, they could not save Dheskati. I knew they would simply withdraw again and probably divert most of any arms we might give them to their dumps. Anyhow, I told Lazanis that the ban on supplies to ELAS had been imposed because ELAS had started the civil war against EDES; and that, if he and his fellows had directed their efforts only against the Germans, then ELAS in Macedonia would not be short of ammunition at all.

Lazanis saw that he could get no further with me, and asked me to see General Kalabalikis, who had succeeded Demaratos as Commander of the 9th Division. I did not see Lazanis again. He too fought on under Markos after 1944 and was killed in a guerrilla action, a hard and unattractive Communist of the criminal type. He was like Ares, except that he had no charm of manner at all.

I met Kalabalikis in a village outside Dheskati, a small, alert, vigorous man in his late fifties, a good Venizelist officer who had been cashiered by Metaxas. His primary interest was in military matters. He admired Kikitsas and the conduct of ELAS, as far as he had seen it. He also had his eyes open to political matters, but he knew ELAS only from the upper end of the command. He appealed to me for arms to resist a German drive on Dheskati in the name of the Allies and in the interest of the defenceless villagers, against whom we had excited reprisals.

He was clearly an honest man with a mind uninfluenced by Communist ideas, and I therefore explained my position to him fully. He was quite unaware of the ELAS background in Macedonia, the attacks on the independent bands, the frustration of PAO and EDES in Salonica, the reasons for Demaratos' resignation from the command, the extent of Communist control in ELAS, and the existence of ELAS dumps for later use. I told him all this over lunch, when he and I were alone with a bottle of wine, which he had got in my honour. As I trusted him fully, I told him he was right to keep his command of the ELAS 9th Division, and to use his opportunities to help the Allied cause.

I also told him what I had not told Lazanis, that we expected a drop at Dheskati to re-equip Scottie's party and to provide ammunition for use by ELAS against the Germans — but Germans only, if an attack developed. We parted good friends after this one meeting. He behaved consistently well, and his influence played some part in preventing action by ELAS in Salonica in December 1944, when the British forces in Athens were being attacked by ELAS. Thereafter he tried to preserve the better elements of the 'Resistance' in a non-political organisation called rather pathetically 'the organisation for the (politically) unorganised Andartai', and he corresponded with me until his death.

On this occasion, the drop did come. The Germans attacked, and ELAS used some of our ammunition. But they put up a feeble defence and Dheskati was added to the list of burnt villages. By then I had said goodbye to Macedonia, and was travelling fast to Neraidha.

CHAPTER EIGHT

ELAS Proves Recalcitrant

I took the familiar route by Mourgani to Kalabaka, which had been burnt by the Germans in late October when the Pinerolo Division had been disarmed. I ended my journey with a very long day's walk, and reached Neraidha after dark. Chris and some of the others were at the house of Worrall who was stationed there; I was too exhausted at first to talk, and they gave me ouzo and tea as I sat silent. When we had settled down, Chris said he had some good news for me, that I had been awarded the DSO. I remember saying that there must be some mistake, but I recovered from my exhaustion sufficiently to thank Chris and the others for their congratulations. Chris outlined the new set-up. The problem was to end the war between ELAS and EDES, and to keep ELAS on a tight rein until the time was ripe for Noah's Ark, the code-name for the guerrilla attack on German forces withdrawing from Greece. All Mission stations were to be ready for Noah's Ark by April. It was important to settle the civil war before then, and to have all targets detailed and ready for assault. Chris himself would visit the headquarters of the Mission in the individual areas. I was to be in command of all Mission stations in the areas controlled by ELAS, and to liaise with the GHQ of ELAS. Arthur Edmonds was to succeed me in Macedonia, and John Mulgan was to replace Arthur in Roumeli. Chris made it clear that despite my preference for Macedonia he needed me to deputise for him at ELAS GHQ, and that GHQ Middle East had approved the new arrangements.

Neraidha was a dark and depressing place. There was sleet and slush everywhere, and the house in which we met was dirty and over-crowded. When I had finished handing over to Arthur Edmonds, I set off with Gordon Creed, who was Liaison Officer with EKKA, and with Doc Felton, yet another graduate of St John's College, Cambridge, who had recently come in and was to move to Macedonia later. We walked south, while Arthur rode off north on a fine horse he had acquired to join Prentice at Pendalofos. We stopped a night on the way with a BLO, Ross Bower, who had combined adventure and romance. He had recently married the daughter of a Greek colonel, and she was having a hard time of it under the drab conditions of life in a hill village. Next day we reached my new abode, Viniani.

I stayed in the house of Uncle Joe, the American Greek, who was proud of possessing a bath, although there was no running water for it. It was a historic house in the sense that Chris and Zervas had shared a double-bed in it before setting off to join Ares for the attack on the Gorgopotamos bridge. It had no other merit. It was so dirty that I developed a strong dislike for it. The double-bed stank; I had it washed and scrubbed but with little effect. The bedbugs were so active that they bit one's wrists as one sat writing at the table during the daytime. When spring came, the flies were appalling. The food too was worse than in Macedonia, partly through inadequate catering but mainly through bad cooking. Chris seemed quite content with it all.

I found that the same dirty conditions prevailed at many of the other stations in Roumeli (Central Greece). A few had gone to the other extreme, and had all the luxuries that money and parachute silk could buy. But I was now stuck at Viniani, and because I had to be adjacent to ELAS GHQ I could do little about it.

The immediate problem was to force ELAS to come to terms with EDES and to terminate the civil war. While Chris and Jerry Wines, the American major in charge of the American side of the Allied Mission, went to a conference at Plaka near Merofilo on the Arachthus river, my job was to press ELAS GHQ to come to terms. Here the all-important man was Siantos, the acting secretary of the Greek Communist Party and the political boss of ELAS and EAM. He presided at ELAS GHQ and his political deputy was Despotopoulos, an Athenian barrister. On the military side Ares was the most powerful personality, but he was usually off on some business with his *Tagma Thanatou*, 'The Death Squad'. The military commander was General Sarafis, who had been captured by ELAS and under duress had accepted command in April 1943 (see p 34 above), and the Chief-of-Staff was for a time Mandakas and later Papastamatiades. The ELAS GHQ was also the centre of comings and goings by ELAS commanders and political leaders, such as Roussos, Zevgoyannis, Partsalidis, and other Communist leaders.

I saw most of Siantos, Despotopoulos, and Sarafis. Of the three, Siantos had a humble origin. His home village was near Neraidha, and he sometimes talked in peasant Greek, with a peasant's directness and simple humour; but he had been trained in Moscow and was a shrewd and far-sighted tactician in the field of diplomacy. The official secretary of KKE (the Greek Communist Party) was Zachariades, but he was interned in Germany during the war; Siantos, as acting secretary, had organised EAM and ELAS, and his power over his colleagues at GHQ was complete. They were clearly frightened of him. I regarded Siantos as a genuine Communist, aware of the undoubted faults of capitalism and of an Athens-controlled democracy in Greece, and completely regardless of the bloodshed which a change to Communism must entail; ambitious for personal power and ruthless in his treatment of others; a fanatic, but true to his convictions.

Despotopoulos was an educated man, and as a barrister he knew and used all the tricks of contentious argument. He was prepared to argue until his opponent flaked out with exhaustion, and he had added to his battery of linguistic cross-fire all the duplicity of Communistic dialectic. It was in part because of his skill in debate that we called him among ourselves 'the slimy Despot'. In our official dealings we had many friendly moments and bore each other no grudge. But we were fundamentally antipathetic. His opinion of me was no doubt vitriolic.

Sarafis, a regular staff officer of the Greek army with a fine reputation in prewar days, had a combination of acidity and conceit, found more often in French than Greek regular officers. He was singularly unco-operative in every way. He treated ELAS as though it was a regular army and he treated himself as if he was a regular Commander-in-Chief, equal to Alexander or Montgomery or de Gaulle. As we made little effort to bolster his view of himself, he usually treated us with hauteur and coldness. He was, of course, a powerless figurehead and a mere puppet, whose earlier reputation was meant to give a touch of respectability to ELAS in circles not familiar with the actuality. His past was known to us, and we did not blame him for having accepted a position of command under the circumstances of April 1943. Sarafis, too, knew that we knew his past history and understood his present position. He was pitiful but in no way likable.

Other figures flitted to and fro across the stage of ELAS GHQ. Mandakas was a Cretan, a regular officer, large, bluff and ponderous in conversation. Originally head of the unsuccessful branch of ELAS which was started in Crete, he had come over to join ELAS GHQ. He probably possessed some administrative ability, as he was later put in command of the attack on Athens in Decem-

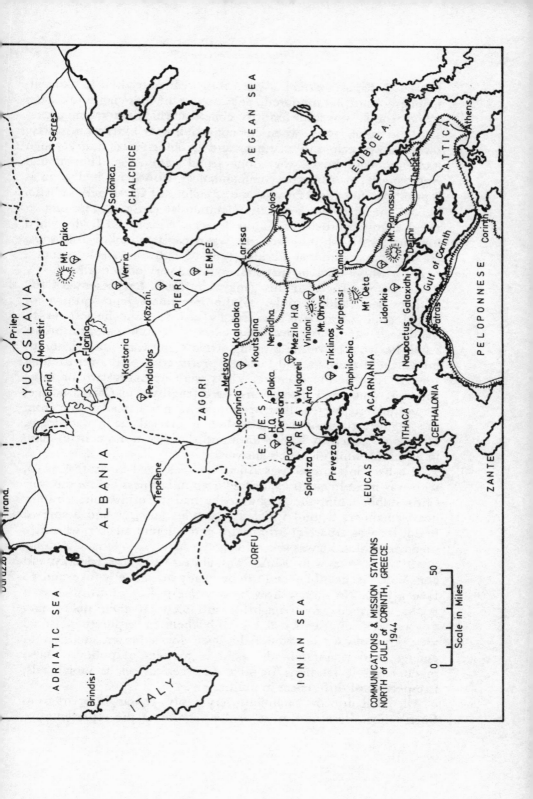

COMMUNICATIONS & MISSION STATIONS
NORTH of GULF of CORINTH,
1944.

Scale in Miles

0   50

ber 1944. Papastamatiades was a rough character like Lazanis, ill-mannered and ill-humoured, but capable of enjoying a joke. His worst trouble was an inferiority complex which made him aggressive and rude. Ares, when he appeared, was bluff and hearty, direct in speech and manner, and he blossomed under rough handling. One knew where one stood with Ares. The original *Kapetanios*, or Andarte commander in ELAS, he had a great reputation for his bravado and toughness. Cruel and sadistic, he did the dirty work for the Communist cause, and he perpetrated many murders of fellow Greeks. Finally KKE disowned him in 1945; he shot himself and was decapitated by his followers. He was the traditional Turkish type of bully in Greek legend, a man for whom I had an instantaneous and very deep dislike.

As liaison officer to this gang of ruffians, I represented GHQ Middle East, and I spoke as the immediate representative of Allied policy; for Chris was usually on tour, and he left me to handle all the ELAS problems except on some specific points when he would give me a ruling. Their GHQ was in a neighbouring village, Kerasovo, and I usually preferred to walk over to them for the sake of the exercise. Visits were normally two or three times a week, and discussions were lengthy. On Chris's advice, I used an interpreter, though neither he nor I needed one from the linguistic point of view, and I had never used one in Macedonia. What one gained by having an interpreter was a moment of time in which to think out one's answer.

The best interpreter was Allen, a Greek aged thirty-five or so, who was most loyal to us; he had been in business before the war. Chris dubbed him the 'Pasha' as he had a Turkish air, a rather heavy manner, behind which lay a quiet humour and a shrewd brain. He was a perfect interpreter and a sound adviser, who gave no advice unless he was asked for it.

My technique with ELAS was always to be as friendly and courteous as possible, and to be ready to make a joke and to take a joke. No matter how bloody the policy of ELAS was, I could tell them my straightforward view of their policy and yet remain on friendly terms with them in a purely personal way. This always left the field open for a better situation to emerge, and it undoubtedly paid in matters of policy. It also made ease of relations possible between us all as individuals, irrespective of differences in politics etc.

Allen fell into the technique very easily. It was different from Chris's line. He stood more on his dignity as the representative of GHQ Middle East, and he made it clear that he demanded good manners from the ELAS chiefs. He was less cordial in his approach and more concerned with intellectual debate than I was. On occasion his line sometimes ended in a deadlock. To give an absurd instance, Chris heard that Papastamatiades had declared he would spit in Chris's face for some reason or other, and when Papastamatiades became Chief-of-Staff at ELAS GHQ, Chris said he would not negotiate with ELAS when Papastamatiades was present unless he made a formal apology. As far as I know, Papastamatiades never did apologise, and the situation was something of an impasse.

We had several other interpreters. 'Uncle Bill' was a man of fifty or so, who held a British commission from the First World War, a first-rate person but not as intelligent as Allen. He was interpreter to Jerry Wines at this time. Others were George, a young engineer, who was loyal but temperamental and tired by much travelling; and another, bald-headed George, an older married man, whom I sent off to serve with Mulgan at one stage. There were two excellent Cypriot runners, who ran messages to neighbouring stations and were fine walkers; they had both survived in Greece from the days of the Greek campaign in 1941. In our own HQ at Viniani we had Allen as quartermaster and accountant, Sicilian Joe as batman, and his Italian underlings. The staff of wireless operators was headed by Joe Sherrard, an RAF flight-sergeant; they usually numbered three or four. At first I had as my adjutant Hamish Torrance, a major in the Parachute Regiment. Hamish was a tough Scot who had been landed in Narvik before the raid there; speaking no Scandinavian language at all, he had passed himself off in German company as a silent Norwegian. He was great fun in every way, but he was far too active a man to be doing the sedentary job of Adjutant at Viniani. So I asked Cairo for someone else, and sent Hamish to be an aide to Tom Barnes in Epirus.

Another interest at Viniani was the handling of some Russians who had been disowned by ELAS. These Russians were of two types, the 'Asitini' from the Caucasus who had joined the Germans, and the Russians proper who had been captured by the Germans. When ELAS had captured or liberated these Russians as the case might be, they had served at first in the ELAS units. There had been a few of them in Macedonia. But when ELAS attacked EDES, the Russians in ELAS refused to fight against Greeks. Their only wish was to kill Germans. In consequence

ELAS disowned them. They approached Chris, who arranged that they should be fed and maintained by the Allied Mission. When I came to Viniani, there were ten Russian officers there who took meals with us, while the others, some fifty or so, lived and fed in the village. They were a considerable expense and they tended to create trouble with the villagers.

Chris had arranged for one party of Russians to escape to Italy together with a Liaison Officer called Bunny Warren. They had volunteered to go. They sailed from near Naupactus in the Gulf of Corinth, and during the night they got into the open sea beyond the German naval posts on Ithaca and Leucas. When they came in sight of the heel of Italy, now in Allied hands, the engine of their caique failed. They had run out of fuel. The Greek skipper had kept some of the money which he had been given to buy fuel, and he had cut it too fine. A north wind rose and drove them before it all night; as they had no sails on board, they just drifted. At dawn they saw land and put in. It proved to be Zante, the island south of Ithaca. They obtained fuel and started off again. The sea was rough when they were spotted off Ithaca by the Germans, who fired across their bows. Bunny Warren asked for a volunteer to swim to the shore and report the fate of their party. One Russian, a big powerful man, dived overboard and managed to swim to land. Eventually he reached me and told me the story. The others were captured by the Germans and executed. We tried for several months to trace Warren, but in vain. This attempt had been made with Cairo's approval. We now had to try and find another route.

Meanwhile the number of Russians increased gradually until it reached 250 in all. Because the Russians and the 'Asitini' kept quarrelling with one another, I put them in separate camps. They were under the charge of a Greek interpreter, whose name was Phokion; he had been born in Russia and spoke excellent Russian and English. The Russian officers had also been rather a nuisance. Young chaps who stood on their rights, they were under the influence of a more educated man, who was probably a Commissar. Phokion suspected that one of the officers was in fact a Greek and not a Russian. I asked the Commissar, who said he was not a Greek but a Russian who had learned Greek; but when I questioned the suspect, he broke down and burst into tears, confessing that he was a Greek of Russian extraction and wanted to go back to Russia. I made the Commissar witness his confession, and then handed the boy over to ELAS who could make use of

The author at breakfast in the Mezilo marquee, 2 August 1944.

Group outside the Mezilo marquee at a reception given by the Mission for the Russians, ELAS HQ and PEEA. Allen (far left), Mrs Svolos, Papastamatiades, Popov, Svolos, author, and last three on the right, West, Siantos and Despotopoulos.

West, Popov, author and Rough-neck outside the Mezilo marquee

Desborough, West and Popov

his knowledge of Russian. It was after this episode that I formed the two camps and placed them under the general supervision of Phokion.

One reason for forming the two camps was that the Russians in Viniani were always hatching up excuses for a party; it was Stalin's birthday or Red Army Day, or the battle of Stalingrad, and so on. A dinner would be held with unstinted ouzo. I would be guest of honour, and blood-thirsty speeches would be made, in which each speaker recounted his deeds of valour in killing Germans, etc. When everyone had spoken of the number of Germans he had killed with his own rifle and his own hands, the party would get violent, and dancing and fighting would begin. These affairs were in my view better conducted in a camp than in the village. So off they went, as soon as I could get it organised, to camps in a remote area in the hills.

One camp which the Russians took over had been occupied by Poles, who had themselves deserted or been released by ELAS from the German forces. In Macedonia I had had a group of Poles who had fought well, and I now persuaded ELAS GHQ that we should use the Poles in Central Greece as assault troops under our command. The Russians we intended to send to Russia. They were escorted in convoys of thirty or so to Epirus and were taken off from the coast by light naval craft. I insisted that each man should sign a paper, saying that he went of his own free choice and at his own risk. There were no further disasters. One or two refused to go; they stayed with the Allied Mission as muleteers or batmen.

Before the last lot was due to go, I received an angry signal from Cairo asking on whose authority I had sent all these Russians out of Greece. I replied 'Cairo's authority', and quoted the signal authorising the plan. I was told to stop the business. After the war I met a friend who had been in the Foreign Office. He told me that he had seen a signal from Eden answering a complaint by Molotov and saying that Colonel Hammond was a trustworthy officer, and that all Russians sent out by him had signed a paper volunteering for repatriation. The Russians were in fact repatriated via Italy, Egypt and Persia. As the Russian Government did nothing at all for Russian soldiers in German hands, one wonders whether our Russians survived their repatriation.

Our impression of these Russians was that they were simple and rather brutish people. They lived for killing Germans and for drinking bouts, and in their camps they fought with one another,

using stones to re-inforce their blows. Several received bad injuries.
The worst offenders were sent to me by Phokion. Regarding me
as their 'little Father', or commanding officer, they reported
themselves for punishment, and they accepted my orders without
question. Usually I sent them to a camp we had for 'bad' Italians,
where they were poorly fed and roughly treated. On receiving my
orders, they went off unescorted and duly reported themselves
at the camp for internment. If I had ordered them to parade for
execution, I think they would have done so. These Russians were
young men who had grown up since the Revolution, except for
one man who could remember the First World War. He was one
of those who hesitated to sign for repatriation; he did so finally
because he had a family in Russia.

None of them could understand at all the possibility of there
being two political parties in Greece. To them the war meant
killing Germans and carrying out orders. Tough, unimaginative
and unintelligent peasants, they were suspicious of each other,
and would accuse each other of having curried favour with the
Germans before they came into the hands of ELAS.

To return, however, to ELAS GHQ and the need to end the
war between ELAS and EDES in time for Noah's Ark. Since GHQ
Middle East had condemned ELAS for starting the civil war by
attacking EDES, we had stopped supplies to ELAS and continued
supplies to EDES, which was being attacked simultaneously by
the Germans in Epirus. Zervas fought well on his home ground,
but he was gradually driven back into Western Epirus; for ELAS
had not only more troops but far more ammunition, much of it
seized from the Pinerolo Division. In fact, although ELAS was
unaware of it, GHQ Middle East did decide to stop sending supplies to Zervas, and it was only by sheer chance that ELAS was
willing then to treat for a settlement, because their ammunition
was running low and they found themselves unable after some
months of warfare to demolish EDES.

A meeting was held at Plaka in January 1944 during an armistice. It was attended by Chris and Wines; by Sarafis and Roussos
for ELAS; by Psarros and Kartalis for EKKA which had remained
neutral; and by Zervas and Komnenos for EDES. Negotiations
lasted for three weeks of wet weather, poor food and general
discomfort. As usual, the ELAS representatives were not pleni-
potentiaries. They referred everything back to Siantos at GHQ
and my job was to bring pressure to bear on Siantos. He wanted

to gain by other means the objective which he had failed to win by force: not only a peace, but a united guerrilla army, acting under the command of GHQ Middle East, and independent of the Greek Government and of the Greek Army outside Greece. In such an army ELAS would have an outright majority over EDES and EKKA, but ELAS generously offered senior commands in the proposed joint army to the leaders of EDES and EKKA. This was on the face of it most plausible, and Siantos had a battery of good dialectical arguments to support his claim. But it was the same game, to swallow the other resistance movements, just as EAM had swallowed many political parties but remained under KKE control.

When I first met Siantos, his line was that whoever had started the civil war (he never admitted that he had) it was a great mistake. The sensible thing, he said, was to bury the hatchet and unite against the Germans. Greeks were always apt to split on political issues, but now they must unite even as the great Allies had united. He himself had the highest regard for Great Britain, although his political sympathies were more to the left, and he knew that the future of his country lay with the destinies of Britain and the USA; for Greece was a mercantile sea-going country and the prosperity of Greece depended on obtaining markets through our favour.

This was all sound argument, but it remained mere words; for to Siantos 'unity' spelled only one thing — the monopoly of power by KKE and by Siantos at its head. However, we had to leave the Greeks to fight the ELAS proposal out of court; it took them a week or two of wrangling, but the issue was never really in doubt, since they could never agree on mutually acceptable persons to act as commanders; and in any case, Zervas was too wily a bird to enter the trap.

Meanwhile I pressed Siantos from several angles. The Allied offensive was imminent, and the Mission had to be ready for the Noah's Ark operations in the spring. It was not difficult to make Siantos believe that Allied troops would soon be landing in Greece, and that they would necessarily be British or American at this stage of the war. If ELAS had not come to terms by then, I suggested that they would be regarded by GHQ Middle East as little short of mutinous; in fact, time was short if ELAS wished to be reinstated in the favour of the Allies. I also discussed arrangements for resuming supplies to ELAS, for preparing Noah's Ark operations, for resuming relief to burnt villages and so on, in order to dangle the carrot of Allied support before ELAS.

When the Siantos plan for a united guerrilla army failed, he began to negotiate for a hard settlement with Zervas; the aim was to tie him down in as small and as vulnerable an area as possible. This went on for days. Siantos claimed ELAS salients in the area between Arta and Kamarina, between Pramanda and Gotista, and the whole of Zagori. As Siantos was intransigent, and as Zervas in the end could be pushed by Chris, a treaty was finally concluded on 29 February much to the disgruntlement of Zervas. The three resistance movements agreed to respect one another, and, in a secret clause, to obey the instructions of GHQ Middle East and to aid one another in the Noah's Ark operations. When I finally got Siantos' consent at ELAS GHQ, a consent which I had been able to forecast as likely, the civil war was over at last. There was great relief on all sides. No one had lost face, and no further blame had been pinned on ELAS. Bygones were bygones, in the best tradition, but Chris and I knew there was no change of heart. Psarros and Kartalis left Plaka ahead of the others, and had tea with me at Viniani on their way south. Psarros was a regular officer of moderate political views; he possessed great charm of personality, but less toughness of fibre and less intellectual acumen than George Kartalis. Both were glad the civil war was over, but they distrusted the future policy of ELAS.

Even before the Plaka agreement was signed on leap-day 1944, rumours had reached me that ELAS were preparing a political manifesto, in which they would claim to be the sole representative of the guerrilla movement in Greece. Siantos had failed to achieve his military objective, the formation of a single guerrilla army, but he was continuing with the civil side of his plan. A number of politicians began to arrive at Viniani. On 25 March, the anniversary of Greek Independence, ELAS GHQ broadcast the news of the formation of PEEA, a 'Political Committee of Greek Resistance', which claimed to be the Government of the liberated Greek people in the mountains. As such, PEEA was to have full power over the liberated areas, until the final day of liberation of all Greece in which the Allies would co-operate. The authority of PEEA was accepted by ELAS, which put itself under its orders and became its armed forces. At the same time PEEA declared itself willing to accept any other genuine resistance movement which was willing to fight for the liberation of Greece.

The first office-holders of PEEA were announced. The President was Bakertzis, a regular colonel, known as the 'Red Colonel', who had hitherto been second-in-command of EKKA. (He had been brought back to Greece at the request of the Allied Mission in June/July 1943, in an attempt to bridge the gap between the Greek regular army in Egypt and the guerrilla movement; Chris wanted him to serve in Macedonia at a Joint HQ either as a member of ELAS or as an independent, but to my relief he had finally joined his old friend Psarros in EKKA.) The Minister of War was Mandakas. The Minister of the Interior was Siantos. Other ministries were filled in similar style, not always by known members of EAM. One minister was Tsirimokos, a leader of ELD, a small democratic party, and other ministers represented parties that had existed in the early 1930s before the dictatorship of Metaxas but were now mere names.

The formation of PEEA was an extremely clever move by Siantos. ELAS could always be treated by the Middle East as a mutinous force (as the Greek armed forces in Libya were later), but PEEA was something more difficult to deal with. It represented itself as a provisional government, loyal to the Allied Cause, but independent of any émigré Greek set-up. It cashed in on a reality, the spirit of resistance within Greece. Moreover, if liberation should come about through the withdrawal of the German forces from Greece, this provisional government, PEEA, might claim to represent the new spirit of Greece and might be able to seize control of the cities and use its armed forces — ELAS — to carry out its orders, and, above all, keep the King and his Government out of Greece. In fact, of course, PEEA was only the old EAM, an amalgmation of amorphous and spurious political parties, controlled by KKE; but Siantos had created a strong bargaining-counter in the political game.

It was also shrewdly timed. It concealed the discomfiture of ELAS in the war with EDES. It announced the claims of ELAS to be the greatest of the resistance movements; for EKKA and EDES, though invited to join under the aegis of PEEA, had refused to do so. If, as Siantos probably thought, the Allies expected the Germans to withdraw in April, the plan he made in February for the formation of PEEA was calculated to produce its maximum effect just before the moment of liberation.

By the time of liberation it might be expected that many politicians would have left Athens and joined PEEA, and the strong element of bluff with which PEEA had started would not be called. Siantos had certainly not lost the initiative, even if he had failed to win the military game against EDES.*

As far as the Mission was concerned, the answer to this new move by Siantos was simple enough. We were a military Mission, and we liaised only with military formations. As the Allied GHQ in the Middle East recognised only one Greek Government, that of the King in exile, the Mission did not recognise the existence of PEEA at all. The GHQ of ELAS began at once to say that they could not execute the orders of GHQ Middle East as transmitted through me, unless the Minister of War in PEEA approved them. Of course we could reply that no army can serve two masters, but this was a double-edged argument. If GHQ Middle East was the effective master at the moment because it could grant or withhold supplies, no one could deny that after liberation PEEA might well be the master. My job was to report on PEEA as well as on ELAS; the fact that it sat at Viniani made the task easier.

Rumours reached me that ELAS was massing troops in the south near EKKA territory. Here, our Liaison Officer, had become rather scornful of the EKKA rank and file, who were more and more preoccupied by their fears of ELAS and were concerned more with means of resisting Communism than of resisting the Germans. As he was evidently becoming rather impatient and tactless, he was summoned to Viniani. After some probing, Chris asked him whether he would be prepared to act on orders which would necessarily involve him in close co-operation with EKKA. When he said in all honesty that he did have reservations, he was told he had better leave for Cairo. He was ready for a change since he had had a longish spell in Greece. He collected his kit and passed through Viniani to our landing-ground at Neraidha, whence he went out by air. This was an example of the strain

*   The impact on the situation outside Greece, of which we were unaware inside Greece, was described by Churchill, *The Second World War* V, 477. 'On April 5 ... the office of the Greek Provost-Marshal in Cairo was occupied by a hundred mutineers, who had to be surrounded by British troops and Egyptian police and were removed without trouble in lorries to an isolation camp. At Alexandria a leader of the Greek seamen's union had barricaded himself in his house with thirty supporters, and was defying the police. Five ships of the Royal Hellenic Navy declared themselves in favour of a republic and demanded the resignation of every member of the existing government. All the members of the Greek Government tendered their resignation to the King, but agreed to remain in office pending acceptance.'

on one's patience and tolerance which was imposed by the role of Liaison Officer, and at the same time of the need to carry out the policy of the Mission, however irritating the situation might be. And nothing could have been more exacting than the nursing of EKKA's faint hopes. His successor was Ponder, an Australian schoolmaster, rather dour and obstinate, but patient and shrewd. He had been in command at one of the Missions in Roumeli, and he had subsequently been in charge of a camp for Poles. On his arrival at Lidoriki as Liaison Officer with EKKA, Ponder reported that there was friction between EKKA and some ELAS units. Similar friction was of course a commonplace between EDES and ELAS, but EDES was capable of defending itself. On the other hand EKKA was only some 800 men strong. I feared the worst and warned Ponder to keep out of any fighting between ELAS and EKKA.

I made strong representations to ELAS GHQ, warning them of the consequences if EKKA was attacked; for no one would believe that EKKA was the aggressor, if a clash on a large scale should develop between the two parties. I then asked Bakertzis to tea, not as President of PEEA, which I ignored, but as a personal friend of Psarros, to whom he had acted as second-in-command of EKKA before joining PEEA. I had already met Bakertzis at Pertouli and elsewhere. On this occasion he was amiable enough, and, when pressed by me, he swore that he was a devoted friend of Psarros, and that no trouble was brewing between EKKA and ELAS.

On the following day, Ponder reported a large-scale attack by ELAS on EKKA, an attack which was led by Ares at the head of his 'Death Squad'. A few days later I was woken before dawn by an Andarte who climbed into my room. He was a founder-member of the Death Squad, and he had just been engaged in the battle with EKKA. He told me that some 400 of EKKA's force, including Psarros, had been captured, disarmed and marched off in a column. Then on the orders of Ares they were machine-gunned and massacred to a man. This was his story. He had come to tell me because it had sickened him. He climbed out of my window in the half-light and set off for the German-occupied area, hoping to escape before he was caught as a deserter from ELAS. His story was certainly true. EKKA had ceased to exist on 17 April, 1944.

The destruction of EKKA had several effects. It cleared the route of ELAS to Athens, for EKKA had held the foothills of

Parnassos and Oeta. It enabled ELAS, if the occasion should arise, to occupy the main cities of Greece without the possibility of being anticipated by any other resistance movement. And it isolated EDES more than ever; for EDES was now confined to the remote hill country of Epirus. These points might seem to be of great value to ELAS and PEEA. But they were offset by much more serious disadvantages. The annihilation of EKKA horrified general Greek opinion much more than the civil war between ELAS and EDES had done. The reasons for this were that Zervas, the leader of EDES, was not regarded in many quarters as a reputable politician, and that the scene of conflict was very remote from Athens. But the EKKA area was close to Athens, and Psarros was regarded as a most honourable man who held moderate political opinions. Thus thoughtful people in Athens came to realise more clearly what ELAS was becoming.

The destruction of EKKA gave GHQ Middle East yet another foretaste of what ELAS might do, if it was ever able to occupy the cities of Greece for even a few days. As far as I was concerned, the policy I had to advocate was clear, the suspension of all supplies to ELAS in all areas, while an enquiry was being held, unless particular supplies were needed for Noah's Ark operations. With this policy GHQ Middle East and Chris agreed. It was put into effect at once. I never forgave Bakertzis for his treachery. As President of PEEA he had, I believed, signed the death-warrant of his friend Psarros. Fortunately one very important member of EKKA survived; for George Kartalis had been in Athens when EKKA's forces were being liquidated.

I had had a few brushes with ELAS GHQ before the elimination of EKKA. The first clash concerned the relief of the victims in the villages that had been burned by the Italians and the Germans. Whereas I had re-started relief in Macedonia in December 1943, it had not been resumed elsewhere, because relief had hitherto been given mainly through EA, the 'self-help' run by EAM in the villages. No one now doubted that EA had used the money to support and strengthen the Communist elements. ELAS was of course unwilling that relief should not continue to be handled by EA, but I made it clear that relief would be given on my terms or not at all. ELAS GHQ eventually gave way with a bad grace, but only after I had told a deputation of villagers why relief was being withheld.

When relief was resumed in all areas on the system which I had used in Macedonia, I insisted that ELAS GHQ should print me a sheet which explained the object of the relief and asked the villagers not to believe the 'German propaganda' which was being spread abroad, to the effect that the English were trying to bribe the villagers and to corrupt them with the 'yellow leprosy', i.e. gold sovereigns. In fact I knew, and ELAS GHQ knew, that this propaganda had been the propaganda not of the Germans but of EAM itself. This sheet was issued with the relief money in the villages. It caused much amusement among the villagers, to the annoyance of the EAM-ELAS bosses.

Another clash concerned our interpreters. Although they were employed by the Allied Military Mission, they had in fact no military status, and GHQ Middle East was unwilling to grant them any status, because it would involve pension rights and raise other problems. ELAS often tried to impound and grill them. I had resisted all such attempts in Macedonia, by saying that they enjoyed the immunity of British troops. When PEEA was formed, a message reached me that an old and loyal interpreter called Papacostas, who had helped to build the landing-ground at Neraidha, had been arrested at ELAS GHQ. Papacostas was, we knew, hostile to EAM; his family had been in danger from EAM, and one of his sons had fled to Athens. I immediately rang up Despotopoulos, who maintained that as a Greek subject in liberated Greece Papacostas was liable to the Greek laws of PEEA, and that the Allied Mission had no right to obstruct PEEA in its dealings with a Greek civilian. If I had engaged in legalistic argument I might have been on awkward ground.

I therefore stated that Papacostas was under the protection of the Mission and of GHQ Middle East, and I ordered Despotopoulos to release him at once on the authority of GHQ Middle East. I gave this order in the presence of a witness at my end of the phone, and I ordered Despotopoulos to repeat the order verbatim to me. After some stammering he did so, and Papacostas returned from Kerasovo within a couple of hours.

This settled the matter. I instructed all Liaison Officers in ELAS areas to take the same line, and to quote this case as a precedent. It was also clarified with ELAS GHQ that, if a civil charge was preferred against a Greek interpreter, the commander of the Allied Mission could either hold a court-martial, or at his discretion permit him to be tried in a civil court of PEEA with a representative from the Mission speaking in his defence, and that, if found guilty, he could either be punished by the commander of the Allied Mission or be handed over to ELAS. I never had any more difficulty, but Arthur Edmonds in Macedonia got into a very difficult situation when ELAS arrested an interpreter on a charge of assaulting a village woman, and he failed to insist that they should follow the arranged procedure. I got him to take a stronger line and then interceded with ELAS GHQ, who sent the man to be dealt with by the Mission.

I also heard of two Greeks who were said to be 'British agents', and were imprisoned by ELAS in Acarnania. We sent details about them to Cairo, from whom we received their names. I was then able to persuade ELAS GHQ to send them to us. They proved to be ISLD agents, who had been picked up by ELAS and maltreated. As their cover was blown, I sent them out from Neraidha later.

There was a continual stream of messages from the Mission commanders in the ELAS areas with complaints against ELAS or with demands to be exempted from the general ban on supplies to ELAS. I remember a very harassed appeal from Jock Hamilton on Mount Vermion in Macedonia, an area close to the enemy; he had faith in the co-operative spirit of the local ELAS commander and he wanted the ban on supplies to be lifted. There were similar complaints and appeals from ELAS commanders, which were transmitted to me by ELAS GHQ. The Mission's wireless system was so planned that every station transmitted every message direct to Cairo, partly in the interests of security and mainly in order that Cairo should have complete knowledge and keep control of the general situation. In consequence, a great deal of wireless traffic came from Cairo to my HQ at Viniani. Cairo forwarded to me not only any message addressed to me, but all messages concerning ELAS areas, on which my advice was wanted or of which I should be informed.

At the same time Barnes in Epirus transmitted copies of all complaints made by Zervas to and against ELAS. There was an unending series of border incidents, both before and after the peace, and many of these were serious and dangerous. As ELAS had no wireless link with Cairo, they sent messages to Cairo through my station and were given a separate code for the purpose. When PEEA was formed, I received many messages also from the Foreign Office and from the Greek Government to deliver to PEEA. These made it clear that Siantos' stroke of genius in forming PEEA had caused consternation in political circles. At this time, too, Chris was on tour. When the conference at Plaka was over, he and Wines visited Barnes in Epirus, Edmonds in Macedonia, and Sheppard and Power in Thessaly. He sent long reports and signals to me at Viniani.

The pressure of wireless traffic and the amount of business with ELAS GHQ made it very difficult for me to get away from Viniani for more than a night or two. However, I managed to visit Worrall at Neraidha. He was handling the problem of the 12,000 Italians of the Pinerolo Division, who had been disarmed by ELAS and discarded to starve. Although Chris never allowed ELAS GHQ to deny their responsibility for the Italians, he had taken over their maintenance. It was not possible in Thessaly to keep them in central camps. Instead, they were placed in villages as labourers, and the villagers who housed and fed them received a certain amount in gold (I think a third of a gold sovereign a month).

Worrall's job was to run this system. He also had two camps, one for 'bad' Italians, which was guarded by an ELAS unit under a tough called Thoma, who caused much trouble, and another in which sick Italians were housed and nursed by the Italian doctor, to whom we supplied drugs. Worrall handled this task well and was worshipped by the Italians. Although he had plenty of Italian batmen, his own house was very dirty and he himself fell ill later. He also ran the landing-ground on the Neraidha plateau, to which a road led from the Thessalian plain. When the ground was not being used, it was usually camouflaged with cut bushes. In the spring the plateau was covered with fine grass and wild jonquils, which had a strong scent. We paid a rent to the owners of the land which was required for landing aircraft.

A Major Harris was with me at this time. He had come in as an aerodrome engineer to report on the Neraidha ground and then to go north and build landing-grounds for the Noah's Ark operations. He was a rough and temperamental character, and needed much encouragement to stick to his job. He had an interesting story. At the end of the Greek campaign, when the British force at Kalamata surrendered and officers not on the normal establishments of the units were allowed to try a get-away, Harris as an aerodrome engineer took a chance with some of the others. They got a caique south of Kalamata and put off, but while they were still close inshore, German troops reached the coast and German planes attacked them. Harris swam ashore and took to the hills. Later, he was about to escape in another caique when he heard that Crete had been lost. He then walked to Athens, dressed as a peasant and carrying a satchel with a revolver in it. On the

road a German motor-cyclist with a tommy-gun on his handle-
bars passed him, came back to re-pass him, and turned and stopped
to hold him up. Harris fired first from his satchel and killed him.
He hid the German and the cycle behind some bushes; he then
followed the foothills parallel to the road.

He reached Athens early one morning and walked into a large
square, where a vegetable market was being held. He walked
around for some time, and then telephoned the American Embassy,
where he had an acquaintance. His friend said he would pick him
up within an hour. Several hours passed and the friend did not
come; Harris rang again and was told it was not after all possible
to collect him. Later he tried the Swedish Embassy, where he also
had an acquaintance. The Swede collected him and placed him
with some Greeks, who looked after him. They equipped a small
sailing boat for him, and he sailed in August for Turkey. There
was enough food on board, but with unthinking generosity the
Greeks had put in a large barrel of retsina wine and no water. In
consequence, he was usually either thirsty or intoxicated. When
he reached the Turkish coast three weeks later, he was almost
off his head. No one believed that he was English. In the end he
was passed to a British Consul and sent on to Syria, where his
identity was established. Later he volunteered for service in
Greece and came to Viniani. His experiences had made him
erratic in his attitude to others, and I had to change his interpreter more than once. He was later killed in a plane which crashed
in mist on a mountain near Neraidha.

Another visit was to Mulgan, the area commander of Roumeli,
who had his headquarters in South-East Thessaly. A New Zealander who was on the staff of the Oxford University Press,
Mulgan impressed me as the best officer in the ELAS area; quiet,
intelligent and resolute, he took a firm line with ELAS, and he
was a bold commander in his operations. I later recommended
him for the Military Cross, and Chris supported the recommendation, but it was not accepted. He had wrecked a number of
trains. On each occasion the Germans stepped up the reprisals,
which took the form of shooting civilian hostages. ELAS never
minded about these reprisals, dismissing them with the catch-
phrase 'all for the struggle', because the Germans were shooting
well-to-do and well-educated Greeks who were anti-Communist.
When the derailment of a train led to the execution of fifty
hostages, we stopped operating in the area for a time.

John Mulgan got on well with the ELAS commander, a regular

officer who was a native of Katarraktes in Epirus. As I knew his home village, we became friendly. At this time, ELAS GHQ always pointed to Mulgan's area as the one in which ELAS co-operation was freely given, because Mulgan treated ELAS properly. It was a regular gambit of ELAS to have one such model area, but Mulgan deserved his luck. On this trip I saw Phokion at one of his Russian camps. These occasional escapes from Viniani did me good, because I grew weary of my rather static head-quarters job.

When I sent Hamish Torrance to work with Barnes, there was an interval before Cairo sent John Clows in May to be my adjutant. He was very good-hearted, rather slow to learn and not very discerning, but he got on well with my staff at Viniani and stuck to his orders. His arrival made it easier for me to get away for a few days at a time. Together with him came Walter Parkes, a member of 'A' force, which organised the escape of prisoners-of-war. Cairo sent strict instructions that Parkes was not to be exposed to any risk of capture, as he had been twice a prisoner and had twice escaped. At the time one asked no more, and I only learned his story later.

His real name was Frank Macaskie. He escaped first from a prisoner-of-war camp in Greece, and then volunteered to return and organise escape for others. When he did return, he was betrayed and caught. He was put in the Averof prison, where his identity was discovered, and he would have been executed but for an escape with the help of Greek friends. This time the Archbishop of Athens, Damaskinos, concealed him, and he got away safely. He had returned again with a double task, to organise an escape route for escaping prisoners-of-war and to be available for entering Athens on its liberation. Months later, when the Germans did withdraw, Macaskie was in Athens and watched them go from the balcony of the Bishop's palace. When he came to me, I knew nothing of his history.

Three Polish officers arrived with Clows and Parkes. Their job was to contact the Greek end of an underground route which led from Poland across Europe to Athens. When they made the contact, they were able to pass messages by runner from Greece to the Polish resistance movement within a fortnight or so.

During this time, a variety of people came to see me at Viniani. Jack Botha, a South African, related to the famous Botha of the Boer War, was one. He was distributing relief in Southern Thessaly in accordance with my instructions, and he came to Viniani to discuss some problems. He was a difficult customer with a dislike of the English, but a sound man when one got to know him. We saw eye to eye on the methods of giving relief, and he was fearless in dealing with ELAS. Three or four Greeks presented themselves with ELAS support as Trade Union Leaders from Athens; they wished to be flown out from Neraidha in order to attend an international Congress of Trade Unions. When I pressed them for their credentials, they claimed to have been elected in 1935 before the establishment of the Metaxas regime. They were, I was sure, crypto-Communists, and Cairo did not agree to fly them out.

A delightful Greek called Seferiades, a lawyer who had helped to receive the first parachute party in 1942, came to stay with me. He had been acting as an impartial arbitrator investigating the death of Hubbard, a New Zealander who had been shot at Triklinos by ELAS troops at the beginning of the civil war. His finding was that an ELAS officer was guilty of negligence, but that the shooting was accidental and not deliberate. The finding was accepted by us and by ELAS.

Woman trouble arose very occasionally at a Mission Station. In one case it was not clear what was going on, and Chris sent a girl down to see me. He wrote saying he passed the problem to me as 'a fatherly old gentleman', being then thirty-six years old and married. The girl fell ill on the way at Neraidha, and when I was visiting Worrall there I interviewed her. She was clearly up to no good; the only way to get rid of her was to pass her south to Galaxidhi, our southernmost station, and thence through ELAS to Athens. This was successfully accomplished.

A more difficult case was that of a girl called Jane. She turned up at Viniani with her cousin, who had been a Mission interpreter. Jane wanted to join us. When I saw her, I remembered her as the daughter of one Metaxa, a Greek Naval Officer (retired), who had been very friendly with me in Athens in 1941. He was now in the Middle East Command. Jane had come up from Athens. She was seventeen or eighteen, had good English and good looks, and was full of adventurous spirit. I told her that the hills were no place for her, and arranged with Cairo that she should be taken out on the next plane. Until then she worked for Worrall at Neraidha, where she met a Sergeant Lee Oldfield. They were married after the war.

The American side of the Mission produced a great character in the person of Doctor Moyers. As far as we could gather, he was a qualified dentist and veterinary surgeon, who had also been a rodeo star in his youth. He was the complete Uncle Sam type; small, skinny, and with three bristles on his chin, lion-hearted and loud-voiced. When he arrived to be our doctor and set up a surgery in a village near Viniani, we sent him as his first patient Nobby Clarke, who had a raging toothache. The Doc had not yet received the equipment which was due to be sent in, but he succeeded in extracting the tooth. Nobby swore he would never go near him again, and no British 'other rank' ever did. But the Greeks loved him, as he amputated their limbs and cut them up to their heart's content. They admired a doctor who really did something.

I was one of Doc's patients too. Ever since the first attack at Pendalofos, I had had malaria once a month. Fortunately Kokkinos, a delightful doctor at Tsotili, had some quinine, of which he used to give me large doses to stop the fever. We had asked Cairo for supplies of quinine or of a better drug of which rumours had reached us, but none was sent. Doc had quinine only, and he treated me once a month in the same way that Kokkinos had done.

The Doc made his mark with ELAS GHQ in a forceful way. Botha, who was giving out American drugs as part of his relief work, told the Doc and me separately that the drugs were being confiscated by EAM and then sold for gold. Before I could see Doc, he had ridden to Kerasovo, marched into ELAS GHQ and told Sarafis what he thought of him and of ELAS. Physically slight, Doc used terrific language and told Sarafis he was the son of a bitch and much more to the same effect, which sounded even more abusive when translated literally into Greek.

ELAS GHQ rang me up in great indignation, and I waylaid the Doc on his way back. The trouble was that Botha had no evidence that would stand investigation, and therefore we could not charge ELAS formally with selling the drugs. The Doctor would not see this at all: but as we got on very well in other ways, he agreed to deal with ELAS GHQ in the future through me. Shortly after this he was in a village when Ares arrived and made a fiery speech. Doc's interpreter gave him the gist of it, and Doc immediately got up and gave Ares his view of Ares and ELAS in the most unmeasured terms. Ares, who was the terror of the villages and of the ELAS rank-and-file, was apparently stunned by Doc's invective.

A less pleasing American was an officer of Greek extraction, called Joe. He had attached himself to Doc as a fellow American, but after a few days Doc sent him back to Viniani. Neither Doc nor I could stand him. Wines posted him south to succeed Ponder in the area which ELAS had taken from EKKA. I had not wanted him there, but Wines was not prepared to accept my recommendation to send Joe out of Greece. His successor, West, did so, however.

PEEA reached its zenith in the latter part of April. A successor to Bakertzis as President of PEEA was announced with many fanfares from EAM-ELAS: Professor Svolos, a well-known and respected democrat of non-extremist views. When he had been installed, he called on me, and we had a long talk. He was a Macedonian born in Monastir (in southernmost Yugoslavia), and he aspired to a larger Greek Macedonia without subscribing to the Communist policy of an independent Macedonian state. He had had some experience of Greek politics. He told me that he admired EAM and ELAS for leading the Greek resistance. When I suggested that EAM and ELAS had their failings and might be dangerous under Communist leadership, he agreed that this might be so, but he thought that PEEA would act as an amalgamation of parties and have a moderating influence on EAM-ELAS. When I asked him which of the other party leaders in PEEA could counterbalance the Communists, he said he had come to convert the Communists to his own way of thinking, and that he himself as president would give a more moderate direction to PEEA. I told him frankly that he would not succeed in converting or even in modifying the Communist control of PEEA, EAM and ELAS, which was deeply entrenched and ideologically intractable. He would not be shaken.

Svolos was a prominent man in the University of Athens. He had a shrewd intellect, a charming personality and was sincere and honourable, but he sadly overestimated the power of the intellect, and in particular that of his own intellect in politics of this kind. I warned him of the dangerous influence which his adherence to PEEA would have, if he failed to change his colleagues' minds. In the long run, Svolos passed more and more under the influence of Siantos. I noticed that he began to use the arguments which Siantos had advanced on earlier occasions. He became in fact a fellow-traveller of the Communists without apparently realising it.

In his train, Svolos brought some reputable intellectuals of

Reception for the Russians at Mezilo. Author at the head of the table, Popov on his right and Allen (seated) looking towards the camera.

Brigadier Barker-Benfield and Uncle Bill talking to an ELAS officer, August 1944.

General Scobie between General Sarafis and General Napoleon Zervas

Reunion 1953 at Pendalofos. Author in centre, Aphrodite on his left and Vasilios in the white suit.

Athens University, notably Angelopoulos, a good economist; Kokkalis, a distinguished surgeon; and Hadzibeis and Askoutsis, both Venizelist Republicans of the old school. Quite a stream of minor politicians and generals appeared from Athens. Some were given office in PEEA or joined so-called ministries, while others who showed their suspicion or who aroused suspicion were interned in a neighbouring village, from which they were not allowed to move. Two eminent generals were Sarayannis, who was offered the Ministry of War but wisely refused it, and Gregoriadis, who paraded himself as the commander of the ELAS Youth Movement. He gave me a copy of a play on Pericles written by himself and protested his love of England in spite of our failure to recognise PEEA. The more I saw of him, the less fit he seemed for any command. A cross-cut of Athenian intelligentsia turned up, led by old Rogas, who had translated the plays of Shakespeare for the National Greek Theatre. A more sinister figure was Mrs Svolos, a small and acid woman, who was a keen Communist. She addressed meetings of the village women, dilating upon women's rights and on the need for female suffrage.

Siantos had very cleverly given to the Greeks who were living under the occupation just what they most wanted, and had most missed, a chance to play the game of politics. They had indeed been without it since Metaxas seized power in 1936. Many who came to join in the game did not know the stakes for which Siantos was playing. When they came to realise that the game was controlled by KKE and that Siantos meant to seize power, they were sometimes too far committed to withdraw. Moreover, the terrorism which Siantos exerted through ELAS could be switched on to his political colleagues; they then realised that the families they had left in Athens were in fact hostages, whom the assault squads of ELAS in Athens could liquidate. Up to a point, then, PEEA was a great success for Siantos.

But PEEA soon passed its zenith. The prominent men who joined were few, and they did not set a fashion. Most of the old party leaders had either got away already and entered the King's Government in Cairo (such as Kanellopoulos and Papandreou) or preferred to stay in Athens. It became more and more clear that PEEA was simply a camouflaged version of EAM. It was not recognised by any of the Allies, except Russia, which alluded to it on Moscow broadcasts; and it was even denounced as an impostor by the King's Government. Nevertheless it served the purpose of

Siantos. Its very existence increased his bargaining power, for it threatened trouble on the day of liberation, unless it could be converted or hoodwinked into accepting the orders of GHQ Middle East.

When the spring weather came, and Chris was in Thessaly on the last stage of his tour, the Germans launched a series of drives with the three mountain divisions which were kept in the Balkans to invade the guerrilla areas. They went straight through the main Pindus range from north to south. Almost all the Mission stations north of Viniani had to be abandoned. ELAS put up very little fight, and all the units disappeared into the forests. There was still snow on the mountains. Hamilton and Backhouse lived on beech-nuts for five days on Mount Vermion in Macedonia, and many others had similar experiences. Pendalofos was evacuated. Rufus Sheppard got away just in time from Kastania, losing a lot of gold sovereigns which were at the station. Chris went off the air, while his party was on the run through thick country. But the drive passed, leaving little in its trail except more burnt villages and more contempt for ELAS's passivity.

We were ready to move out of Viniani, but the Germans came no closer than Karpenisi. When Chris and Wines arrived, they were due for a rest, and I was anxious for a change of air. I had been suffering from dysentery as well as malaria, and I decided the best cure for dysentery was mountain spring water and exercise. I had used this drastic cure in Epirus before the war. So I set off to tour the area once held by EKKA, in order to report on the situation there, and then to visit American Joe near Galaxidhi. Parkes and the Poles were to go with me in order to be nearer Athens.

From Viniani we crossed the Agrafiotikos, and climbed several thousand feet up to Karpenisi. I went at full speed and reached the town before the others. I had to secure the release of an unfortunate woman, who had been interned and maltreated by ELAS on some trumped-up charge of collaboration with EKKA. One of the Mission HQs had been in her house, and ELAS were probably punishing her for being pro-English. Anyhow, I got ELAS to release her.

From Karpenisi we followed a high ridge with some beech-woods on it throughout a long day, and then came down and followed a long valley on the south flank of Mount Oeta. My dysentery was now better. We passed through Lidoriki where we stayed the night with a Greek family whose name we had been given by Gordon Creed. The father had been in America. One of his sons had joined ELAS, and another had lately joined EKKA, when Psarros came into the hills. The older son had been in one of the ELAS units which had eliminated EKKA. The younger had escaped in the final stages of the attack and crossed the Gulf of Corinth to the Peloponnese, where he joined the so-called Security Battalions of Rallis, the then head of the Quisling Government in Greece. This younger son had in fact little option, for if he had kept on the run ELAS would almost certainly have got him sooner or later. As a member of a Security Battalion he was armed and could fight against ELAS.

The father disowned both sons: one as a near-Communist who had murdered the EKKA survivors, and the other as a traitor, serving the Quisling Government. The mother and the sister seemed to share the father's views. They were delightful people, and could not have been kinder. This case and many others which I came across showed the tragic effects of a civil war in an enemy-occupied country.

At Lidoriki we met Beïs, 'the Bey', as he was affectionately called. He had welcomed and helped the original party which blew up the Gorgopotamos Bridge in 1942, and he had later joined ELAS because he could not join the Mission. There was no other organisation in his area at that time. Chris had invested him with the BEM, awarded for his services in 1942. When we met him, he had been boarded out of ELAS on medical grounds and was living in Lidoriki. He was a man of fifty or so. In December 1944, when ELAS was planning to seize Athens, the Bey was conscripted into ELAS again and joined in the attack. He then discovered who it was that ELAS was attacking — the English. He changed into civilian clothes, crossed over at night, and made contact with some members of the Mission who were in Athens. He ended up on our side. Later the Greek Government imprisoned him as an Elasite. Chris managed to have him liberated and sent home to Lidoriki. He was another example of the victims of a civil war, an honest villager, hearing nothing except what ELAS gave out in 'Liberated Hellas'.

My visit to the area, once controlled by EKKA, showed me that ELAS was hated by the people, but was none the less very powerful. ELAS had executed many civilians on charges of collaboration with the enemy when they had really done nothing except support Psarros and EKKA. I interviewed the ELAS commanders in the area. Like so many others in Roumeli, they were either embittered regular officers who had been retired as a result of a political coup d'état at one time or another, or else they were rough, bestial types, such as Ares himself.

We then went on south to Joe's station, north-west of Galaxidhi. Joe, an American officer, was the opposite number of an English officer, whose name I have forgotten. It was a dim station, and Joe and his colleague were doing little of value, except to act as a remote base of communications with Macintyre, who was operating in Attica. One problem I had to investigate was the loss of 200 gold sovereigns, which dated back to Gordon Creed's time. We suspected the Greek cook and his wife. I caught him out by a well-worn trick. Beginning in a friendly manner with another officer present, I told him of the loss and asked him to describe his activities and movements on the days in question. He rambled on happily, and I appeared to take all he said as gospel. An hour later I had him in again, and frightened him by taking a cold and suspicious attitude, and I then asked him to repeat his story in full. He thereupon contradicted himself hopelessly and under further pressure he broke down, wept, and admitted he had taken the money and disposed of it. He was dismissed and his name was recorded at Cairo, but I expect that nothing more was done.

We then spent two days at Galaxidhi on the Gulf of Corinth. It was an idyllic spot, and we bathed and sailed. It was the first carefree rest I had had since my entry into Greece. Parkes and I thoroughly enjoyed it. We were shot at one day in a craggy ravine by some ELAS troops, who could not be blamed, as I was wearing an old German forage-cap to keep off the hot sun. This ELAS squad was a tough one. The men were covered with lice, and all were bearded. They liaised with ELAN, the so-called ELAS navy, which operated in the Gulf against German-controlled caiques. We sailed in the Gulf one morning and passed boats which were being sailed by Germans on leave at Itea. On one of our days at Galaxidhi, two German gun-boats raided the port. Fortunately we were on land at the time, and we joined in the general rush for the hills.

When we left Galaxidhi, Parkes and I intended to go to Agoriani on Mount Parnassus, where we had a small station. As we would be crossing the main road between Amphissa and Itea, I planned to take Parkes to see Delphi by moonlight, because he had never been there. But at the last moment we were told that there were German patrols at Chryso on the road near Delphi. So we went straight through to Agoriani, where the station was commanded by an excellent sergeant, who had attacked German posts in several villages near Delphi. He confirmed reports which we had had from ELAS GHQ of atrocities committed in the villages near Delphi by German troops on punitive raids. Some of the troops came from French Morocco. When this visit was finished, Parkes and I made record time back to Viniani, taking less than three days and arriving very exhausted. But this sort of trek kept me hard physically, and it relieved the monotony of dealing with affairs at GHQ.

When I got back to join Chris, our relations with ELAS were approaching deadlock. Noah's Ark had been deferred from April until some unknown date. There was now no immediate prospect of a landing in Greece by the Western Allies, which might have restrained ELAS. Our forces were moving slowly in Italy, and the Russians were beginning their spring offensive. Indeed, I was amused to hear an EAM broadcast of news in a village square which reported the Russian advance in one day as thirty kilometres and the Anglo-American advance as thirty centimetres. ELAS may have begun to hope that the Russians would be the first to enter the Balkans. Anyhow, their GHQ was maintaining a difficult attitude. They were continually bickering with EDES over frontier incidents, which were sometimes serious and involved several units on both sides. Zervas himself had been hard-pressed by a German drive from Ioannina, and he was penned up in a comparatively small area. Chris decided to hold a further conference between ELAS and EDES, and he wanted me to go with him and Wines.

The conference was held in gloomy weather in April at Koutsaina, where I was astonished to find Mousterakis as the local ELAS commander. He had made the same choice as Sarafis. ELAS sent Despotopoulos and a very cantankerous officer who had fought on the Turkish side against us in the First World War; EDES sent Phrontzos and their Chief-of-Staff, Nikolopoulos. The fact that Siantos and Zervas did not attend suggested that the conference was unlikely to be constructive. Our object was to improve relations between ELAS and EDES and to gain their co-operation or at least their promise of non-intervention with one another during Noah's Ark, that is during attacks on the Germans, as they withdrew from Greece. Chris was also able to reveal that Allied troops in the form of RSR Groups (Raiding Support Regiments) would shortly be entering Greece.

The conference was conducted in a formal manner with Chris

presiding. The first day passed more smoothly than anyone had expected. The ELAS representatives were polite and accommodating and promised full co-operation over Noah's Ark, the infiltration of the RSR Groups with their supplies into Epirus, and their movement thence into ELAS territories. Chris was pleased on the first evening, and optimistic that the situation was improving. I remember saying that I mistrusted the tactics of ELAS and believed that they wanted as much information as we could give them, but that there was no change of heart at all.

On the second day they began to cavil. They made impossible demands of EDES, such as that ELAS should control the Arta area and operate there during Noah's Ark. Chris on the other hand wanted EDES to operate in the whole of Epirus — from Arta to the Albanian border — and also on the Metsovo-Ioannina road. The meeting became very stormy. Abuse and recriminations passed between ELAS and EDES. In the evening we saw Phrontzos and Nikolopoulos alone; they made it clear that they would not agree to the demands of ELAS which would expose both Arta and Ioannina (the two main towns of Epirus and the centres of civilian support for Zervas) to the possibility of occupation by ELAS when the Germans withdrew. For Phrontzos and Nikolopoulos were clear that ELAS were interested less in attacking the Germans than in seizing the centres of civil administration. Even if Chris had wanted to press Zervas to accept such demands, he could not have succeeded; for we now had little leverage to put on Zervas.

On the third day we had a separate talk with the ELAS representatives in the morning. The gloves were soon off on both sides. Chris's aim was to pound ELAS into taking a more reasonable attitude. His attack included the liquidation of EKKA, the bickering with EDES, the embezzling of relief money and medical supplies, the victimization of civilians, and so forth. It was made clear to the ELAS representatives that, unless they became more co-operative, they were in danger of receiving little help from GHQ Middle East.

Despotopoulos and the Turkish-Greek officer counter-attacked by accusing Chris of prejudice against EAM-ELAS and of misrepresenting their case to GHQ Middle East. They accused EKKA and EDES of collaboration with the Germans, and they accused Chris of failing to condemn the Security Battalions as traitorous. Despotopoulos excelled himself on the subject of money for relief by arguing that the British object was 'philanthropy' and that, once we had handed the money over, we had been 'philanthropic' and it did not matter to us who ultimately received the money.

Chris rubbed in the salt by explaining that the relief money was given solely because ELAS itself was incapable of organising the movement of supplies; men, he said, do not eat gold. The food which was needed to save the victims of enemy action was, he pointed out, already in the country, and any capable and patriotic group of Greeks could arrange for a proper distribution of the foodstuffs. However, ELAS had shown itself completely incapable of doing this, and that was the only reason why non-Greeks gave out relief-money at all.

When the abuse died down, the general upshot was clear; ELAS did not intend to soften their attitude, and the deadlock remained. When we all met again in the afternoon, there were acrimonious exchanges. The only point of agreement was that the RSR Groups were to be given free passage to help in the Noah's Ark operations.

CHAPTER NINE
Entente Achieved

Chapters IX and X cover May to August 1944. British and American forces captured Rome on 4 June and advanced into Northern Italy. The invasion of Western France was on 6 June, and American forces landed in Southern France on 14 August. Paris was liberated on 25 August. Churchill met Tito on 12 August. The Russians advanced to Finland, Poland, Rumania and Bulgaria, and the Warsaw rising took place on 1 August with disastrous results for the Poles. Further advances were made in Burma.

The failure of the Koutsaina conference was more disappointing to Chris and Wines than it was to me. My recent experience of ELAS GHQ and of PEEA had made me hope for less than they did. Military co-operation with GHQ Middle East in Noah's Ark was far less important to ELAS than jockeying for position when liberation came. Therefore they would not yield an inch of ground to Zervas; indeed they intended to drive him into as small a corner of Epirus as they could before the day of liberation. In the same way the existence of PEEA was designed not to step up resistance to the Germans, but to give the Communist Party a flying start in occupying the cities of Greece when liberation came. The ELAS leaders knew that the Germans would leave Greece in any case, whether ELAS attacked them or not. All they wanted from GHQ Middle East was some credit, or at least not an open breach or a denunciation. What mattered to them was to obtain as much credit as possible in the eyes of the outside world and of the Greek people in the cities; for they knew that the halo of romance still surrounded the resistance movements in some quarters.

My view was that time was on our side. ELAS and PEEA would come to feel more and more isolated, and if they were led to expect a large-scale offensive in Greece by troops of the Western Allies, they would have to toe the line politically by joining the

Greek Government and by co-operating with Allied troops. The uncertainties on our side were whether any Allied troops would in fact land in Greece, and when the Germans would pull out.

Chris had reported the progress of the conference on the local wireless set. Cairo was very upset by the failure to improve the situation and suggested that the Allied Mission should be withdrawn altogether. Chris and I were each asked independently to give an opinion on this suggestion. We both replied that it would be disastrous to evacuate the Mission, which formed the only restraint on the excesses of ELAS and provided the only hope of securing military action against the Germans.* Cairo agreed not to evacuate the Mission but issued new instructions. Chris and Wines were to go out at once and report at home. I was to take command of the Allied Mission, and Wines's successor, Colonel West, was to be sent into Epirus shortly.

This was a blow to me. I had told Chris before the conference that I wanted to go home on leave, having completed four years of service overseas and also having had a lot of malaria. He had agreed to recommend me for leave after the conference at Kout-saina. The new instructions ended my chances; for Chris was clear that I was best qualified to carry on the policy of the Allied Mission in his absence. So I entered on my last three months in Greece, from May to August 1944. Both the military situation and the political outlook were at their worst; but as I had told Chris, time was now on our side, provided that we did not weaken in our attitude to ELAS and PEEA.

When Chris and Jerry Wines left for the landing-ground near Almyros, to the south of Volos in Thessaly, it seemed to me probable, in the light of Eddie's experience, that they would not come back into occupied Greece. Chris maintained contact with me for some time by sending signals from London, but he soon ceased to have any directing hand. Events on the spot had so

---

* This proposal was made again in July and rejected by Churchill, *The Second World War*, VI, 96. 'The King of Greece asked us to denounce ELAS and withdraw the military missions which we had sent to help them fight against Hitler ... but after a long talk on 15 July with Colonel Woodhouse, a British officer who was serving with the missions in Greece, I consented to let them remain for the time being. He argued that they were a valuable restraint on EAM and that it might be difficult and dangerous to get them out, but I feared that one day they would be taken as hostages and I asked for them to be reduced.'

often to be settled without delay.*

My general policy was approved and I received every assistance from Cairo. It was, in brief, to stonewall ELAS; to maintain the position as guaranteed to Zervas under the Plaka agreement; not to recognise PEEA; to insist that PEEA must be liquidated before EAM could be represented in the Greek Government; to infiltrate the RSR Groups; and to select and train small ELAS groups which would join us in attacking Noah's Ark targets. The officer with whom I dealt mainly at Cairo was a Colonel Street, and we established a first-rate understanding, although we never met.

Relations with ELAS GHQ gradually improved. They knew that I should not yield from the Plaka position, but that if they played straight I would give them some credit. We continued to give relief to the villages, and ELAS kept their hands off the money, as far as we could tell. Worrall had developed appendicitis and been flown out, and in his place I sent John Clows and later John Cook to take charge at Neraidha, while ELAS removed Thoma at my request and put in a more co-operative commander. I persuaded ELAS GHQ to nominate an officer and special troops in each area, who were to work with us and the RSR Groups for the Noah's Ark operations on specific targets. I explained that these were special tasks, and not the general operations in which the main ELAS forces under the command of GHQ Middle East would be playing a part.

The old irritations continued. There were several frontier incidents, of which both ELAS and Zervas, aided by Barnes, gave fiery reports. I made it clear that I regarded those as unimportant. However, I said that, if general fighting broke out between ELAS and EDES, the past record of ELAS would be taken into account and ELAS would be denounced by GHQ Middle East as unworthy of Allied recognition. We all knew fairly well where we stood in relation to one another. There was also at this time a strong leader at the head of the Greek Government in Cairo, Papandreou, who had united the party leaders and formed a 'government of national unity'. He had denounced

---

* We were little affected by the important events which were taking place at the so-called Lebanon Conference of 17—20 May 1944 (see C.M. Woodhouse, *Apple of Discord* 191 f). They led to the formation of a Greek Government, headed by Papandreou, in which EDES and EKKA (in the form of George Kartalis) participated and EAM-ELAS refused to participate. The EAM delegates to the Conference did not return to Greece until July.

PEEA, and he had had pamphlets to that effect dropped by Allied planes in the mountains.

While my chief problem was with PEEA, EAM and ELAS, I also had to make arrangements for Noah's Ark and maintain the establishment of the Allied Mission. At this time we had some seventy officers; there were also a large number of other ranks, mainly wireless operators, interpreters and Commando sergeants, and detachments of Poles and some survivors from the Greek campaign of 1941.

The AMM in the Peloponnese was nominally under my command, but in effect it constituted an independent unit under John Stevens and later MacMullan. The stations of the AMM there had quarrelled decisively with ELAS, and because the AMM existed on sufferance from ELAS it was confined to a number of precarious positions between the ELAS strongholds and the German fringe. Its function mainly was the provision of intelligence reports. I remember indignant signals from John Stevens, when Ares, after liquidating EKKA, crossed into the Peloponnese and badgered the AMM. Stevens complained that we were off-loading our 'rubbish' into the Peloponnese. In any case, the AMM in the Peloponnese could not contribute much to Noah's Ark.

North of the Isthmus, we were well placed for action against the main railway and the main road which led from Athens to Salonica. MacIntyre and Sheppard were in Attica. MacIntyre had a special task, to save the Marathon dam from demolition by the Germans (the dam held the water-supply for Athens, which then had a population of between one and two millions). Our posts lay on the flank of the road and the railway, with Mulgan, Power and Scott holding the key positions near Lamia, Tempe, and Pieria, and with Johnson threatening the Gevgeli Gorge from Mount Paiko. All the target areas were controlled by ELAS. Our difficulty was to get the Raiding Support Regiments into these eastern areas; for, setting out as they did from the Allied base in Southern Italy, they had to land in Epirus in EDES territory and then cross into areas which were all controlled by ELAS. We relied entirely upon ELAS honouring the agreement they had made with us, that the RSR units would be conducted by ELAS to their targets.

The only other route northward out of Greece ran between the ELAS area and the EDES area. This was the main road through Epirus from Arta to Ioannina and thence to Albania, where there were further German garrison troops. Here we wanted EDES to operate alone; but ELAS claimed a right to act solo, and especially to the north of Ioannina, where they claimed they were able to join hands with the Albanian Communists, who had liquidated their rivals under the leadership of Abas Kupi. The rivalry between EDES and ELAS in Epirus might at any time endanger the movement of the supplies which were landed on the coast near Splantza and then transported through Epirus into Macedonia or Thessaly.

The route was hazardous enough in any case. Edmonds in Macedonia had already sent convoys with mules to collect supplies from Epirus. While escorting one of these, Jock Hamilton was lost to us. When German troops intervened at a road-crossing he fought a small rear-guard action and was wounded and captured. He was put into a Gestapo prison in Salonica, beaten and maltreated. One morning he was stripped of his clothing and taken from his cell, as he thought for execution, when a higher officer appeared and read out a personal pardon from Hitler. He was sent to an ordinary prisoner-of-war camp, and survived to complete his undergraduate career at Oxford.

When the weather grew hot at Viniani, I moved my HQ to Mezilo, while ELAS GHQ and PEEA moved to Vatinia nearby. I had a large marquee built with pine-wood and roofed with canvas parachutes outside an unused village school-house. The village was high up on the steep flank of a mountain, and a rapid watercourse flowed into a gorge, where a fine stream ran below us to the south. We constructed a shower-bath by the marquee and we suspended a lavatory pan over another water-course on the mountain-side. As we slept in the open or in the marquee, we had a good fresh-air existence, and we all felt much fitter than we had been at Viniani. The gorge was spectacular. Semerdzis, a Greek artist from Athens, who had attached himself to PEEA, made a fine painting of this gorge which he showed in an exhibition of Greek art after the war. He insisted on painting a portrait of me in the Andarte style of the 1820s, ferocious with giant moustaches and piercing eyes, but he wanted too many gold sovereigns for it; so I never owned it.

The villagers of Mezilo were typical of most mountain villagers. They hated and feared ELAS, but they would do anything for us. They even refused payment. The hatred of ELAS which was general in the mountains had spread now into the plain of Thessaly. Whereas in 1943 I had moved freely in the plain without fear of betrayal to the Germans, now Mulgan reported that ELAS units were having considerable difficulty because the villagers were opposed to them and this inevitably limited the activities of the AMM in Thessaly, of which Mulgan was head.

It had always seemed important to me that the outside world should obtain some picture of life inside Greece at this time. I had in the past asked Cairo to send in some accredited journalists, but without success. I now repeated my request, pointing out that lack of news would simply mean that the Allied press would have a misplaced prejudice in favour of ELAS. This time Cairo seemed to be willing in principle, but they wanted the agreement of ELAS in advance. When I asked ELAS GHQ, they claimed the right to vet a list of any names proposed and to reject anyone they judged unsuitable. I then urged Cairo not to grant ELAS the power of selection but to send accredited journalists from a wide range of newspapers, informing ELAS at the same time of their credentials. As the journalists would be entering a theatre of war, they would be war correspondents and would be attached as such to the Allied Military Mission. I pressed hard for this to be done from June onwards but without success. We were to pay the price for our failure after the liberation.

By early July PEEA, ELAS, and EAM found themselves in something of an impasse. PEEA had ceased to attract personalities from Athens, and the King's Government had hardened against them. ELAS was not getting any supplies from GHQ Middle East and was unlikely to do so, as long as it looked to PEEA as its civil government. The RSR groups were coming in, the Allied invasion of France had begun, and the Germans were beginning to make some troop movements which suggested that they were getting ready to withdraw from Greece.

My opinion was that if we held on firmly, PEEA would have to come to terms with the Greek Government. In that event EDES would have an important part to play, and I decided I ought to visit Barnes and Zervas in Epirus. Recently Clows had fallen ill and had been sent out by plane, and his successor, Dobson, was now sufficiently trained to hold the fort. There was one uncertainty still unresolved. We knew that ELAS had been preparing to receive a plane on our landing ground at Neraidha without asking our leave, and I judged from rumours which reached me that ELAS was expecting some Russian officers. I told Cairo of this, but they dismissed the suggestion as absurd.

While I was preparing to go to Epirus, the first RSR group passed through Mezilo on its way to John Mulgan. I addressed the man in the open air. The gist of what I said was that they had come to do a military job and should not concern themselves with Greek politics; and I assured them that the ELAS groups would co-operate with them against the Germans, as they had co-operated earlier with the AMM forces. It was a great thrill to see British troops again, and it made a fine impression on the Greeks to find their allies amongst them once more as fighting units.

I set off for Epirus with a Cypriot runner called Nikos, and we made good speed across the Achelous gorge and up to Vulgareli. This area had been the scene of the ELAS-EDES civil war, and there was very bitter feeling against the ELAS troops who now held it. Many villagers told me of the execution of members of their families and of beatings and imprisonments. It was particularly sad to me, because I had known these villages so well before the war. Next day we reached the main road on the south side of Ioannina. We crossed it that night, and we reached the headquarters of Zervas and Barnes at Dervisana in time for breakfast.

Tom Barnes was a straightforward New Zealander, a courageous man and a forceful personality, who reckoned that he had trained Zervas to behave like an Englishman. He had been with Zervas since late in 1942 and he detested ELAS. Barnes and I had met at Pertouli in July 1943, just a year before, and we had liked each other from the first. Hamish Torrance was his second-in-command. It was nice to see him again.

Tom's HQ hummed with activity and flies; it was the dirtiest HQ I had ever seen, and that was saying something. Tom was very suspicious that I would upset Zervas, and in fact I knew I probably would do so. Anyhow, I asked Tom to be with me while I saw Zervas, so that he would not feel I was working behind his back.

As acting commander of the Mission, I had to form my own opinion of Zervas and EDES. What I had seen so far was not very encouraging. The EDES troops had less discipline than those of ELAS, and the RSR group which passed through Mezilo had contrasted the pilfering in the territory of EDES with the efficiency and the discipline of ELAS units. I had met Zervas for a short talk only in July 1943; he probably regarded me as sympathetic to ELAS.

During our first session Zervas, Komnenos, Tom and I were present. Zervas behaved like an Englishman throughout, skating over the real issues and concealing his strong political feelings. It cost me another session and strong disapproval from Tom, before I got Zervas to talk like a Greek. I really wanted to know his ideas about the plans of ELAS when the Germans left, and these he finally gave to me. He was quite clear that ELAS would try to seize the cities and kill their opponents, while he himself would carry out Cairo's orders and attack the German forces. The result would be a blood-bath in the cities; and then if ELAS controlled the cities, they would attempt to hold them against the acknowledged Greek Government.

Originally Zervas had started his movement as a Republican, being opposed to the return of the King, and claiming as his political leader an elderly stateman, Plastiras, then living in Paris. But the civil war with ELAS had opened his eyes to the true situation, in which the real issue was not the King but the choice between Communism and freedom. He had therefore recognised the King's Government. Meanwhile, the King, under Allied pressure, had announced that he would not return, until and unless a plebiscite invited him to come back. Zervas was undoubtedly right about the real issue that faced us. The question was how could we prevent ELAS from entering the cities as the Germans left them. Zervas claimed that if he could attack ELAS now, he would defeat them, or at least weaken them in North and Central Greece. I felt that Zervas was over-optimistic. Even so, on the assumption that no Allied force came into Greece on the heels of the retreating Germans, it was difficult to see how ELAS could be stopped at all, or even delayed, if we did not let Zervas act as he wanted to act.

In these discussions Zervas and I ended by talking Greek entirely, and Tom withdrew. Tom said that I had brought out the worst in Zervas. He reckoned it would take him ten days' hard work to make Zervas reasonable again. For my part I had got what I wanted. Behind his great beard and belly, his genial personality and his military bravado, Zervas was a shrewd old fox who knew how to get the most out of Tom Barnes and the Allied backing, but he was also a patriotic Greek who had two aims, to expel the Germans and to keep the future of Greece open, so that men would be free to choose their own form of government. I admired Zervas, and I liked him. I judged him to be a very shrewd politician, and a loyal Greek, but I thought he was apt to over-estimate his own power and the power of his movement, EDES; indeed, he was EDES, in the sense that the best of his troops followed Zervas the man rather than a political line. We parted good friends and well-wishers of one another.

Later, during Noah's Ark, he and EDES carried out some fine
operations. When the country was liberated, many of his followers
went home. When ELAS attacked Athens in December 1944,
ELAS detached some of its forces, which drove Zervas into a
corner near Preveza, whence he and his men were evacuated
by our naval forces to Corfu. No doubt he blamed the Allies for
not having used EDES when it was at full strength to weaken
ELAS before the day of liberation.

While I was with Zervas, I met Colonel West, the American
commander who had succeeded Wines. A fine figure of a man,
West had been engaged at one time in business and politics in
South America, and he was much more alert on the political side
than Wines had been. On my advice he was seeing things for himself, and I was careful not to influence him by giving him my
own views at this stage. I went with him to visit an American
Support Group, analogous to our RSR troops. They were Americans
of Greek extraction, they looked business-like, and they had a
profound contempt for the Greek guerrilla, an attitude not uncom-
mon in the expatriate Greek towards the homebred Greek. One of
West's officers, Moses Hadas, was a classical scholar from an
American University; I arranged for him to join Mulgan, the most
enterprising of our commanders.

Another visitor at Dervisana was David Wallace. While West
had come in from the Cairo office of OSS, Wallace had come in
from the Foreign Office. I had seen him a year before at Pertouli,
when we had talked about ELAS (see p 76 above). On this occasion
I had only a short talk with him, but it was clear that he had
realised what the aims of ELAS and KKE were. He intended to
join me shortly at Mezilo and to study the ELAS situation there
before reporting to the Foreign Office. Most unfortunately he
joined in a raid which was being made on a German post at Minina
in the EDES area and was killed. His death had serious consequences. The lack of a report to the Foreign Office strengthened the hand of the Commander-in-Chief Middle East against
the Foreign Office in the critical decisions which had soon to be
made.

I was still at Dervisana when Cairo sent an urgent signal that a
Russian Mission had arrived at Neraidha on 26 July, and that
West and I were to hurry back to Mezilo and meet them. Our
orders were 'to be cordial and to say nothing about policy'. We
were told that Russia had been invited to send members to the

Allied Military Mission in 1943 and had refused. Subsequently an agreement was made between the three great powers, whereby Russia agreed to send a mission to Yugoslavia but not to Albania or Greece.*

The Russians had broken this agreement in a barefaced manner by getting a plane out of Italy under false pretences, flying to Tito's HQ and picking up their posse of Russians there, and depositing them on Greek soil. On the way south the plane dropped some officers in West Macedonia, from where they crossed the frontier into Albania. The remainder — three Russian colonels headed by Popov, and five others — landed at Neraidha, and attached themselves to ELAS GHQ.

I travelled fast, going ahead of West. Nikos and I took a short route along the spurs of Mount Tsoumerka which I knew from my travels before the war. It was glorious weather. Such walks as these gave one a rest from wireless signals and a relief from the tension of ELAS GHQ.

West and I opened the game with our Russian allies by inviting them to a lunch, for which our marquee was arrayed in festive style. There was an abundance of food and local wine, which our guests thoroughly enjoyed, after the sparse Andarte fare they had been having at ELAS GHQ. When all were replete, we five colonels withdrew to a room in the village school and drank coffee and ouzo. Popov spoke excellent English. He was a tall, fine-looking man, who carried himself with some hauteur and disliked any jokes at his expense. West was particularly good at pulling Popov's leg later on, as his oblique American humour often eluded the Russian.

The second colonel was the brains of the party. He spoke French well, and he did not say more than he had to. The third was a rough-neck. He had served in the Spanish Civil War as a demolition expert, and he prided himself on his three or four words of Spanish. In general he had no small opinion of himself.

When our social chatter began to run out, I asked Popov if we could talk business, and asked him what policy he and his officers had come to pursue. An uneasy silence ensued. Popov then said that he was not at liberty to discuss his plans. I asked him whether, for instance, he meant to visit EDES, from which we had just come, as our Allied Mission was accredited to all resistance movements.

* See *The Second World War*, VI, 64 f and 198.

Popov replied that he had not yet had instructions to do so. When Popov put similar questions to me, I made similar non-committal replies. It was apparent that we had had the same orders from our respective HQs: 'to be cordial and to say nothing about policy'.

I invented a covering gambit for such moments of awkwardness. Turning to Colonel Rough-neck, I used to model with my hands a bridge or a train entering a tunnel, lay an explosive charge in dumb-show, roar 'Boom! Bang!' and shout *'Buono, buono!'*, to which he would reply *'Buono, buono!'* This never failed to bring the house down. The only thing that we got out of Popov was that he thought ELAS was small beer (and we did nothing to disillusion him), and that he did not like escaped Russian P-o-Ws. In due course I sent him a present of all the remaining Russians who had accumulated since Molotov stopped their evacuation, but I doubt if Popov ever celebrated the anniversary of the Red Army's birthday with them. He told me later that he had given them a good dressing-down and sent them off to fight with ELAS.

Soon after our lunch-party Popov invited West and me to 'tea'. We were less dressy than the Russian colonels, who wore fine uniform and high boots, but we had two social assets; my enormous moustaches, which overshadowed those of Colonel Rough-neck, and West's capacity for strong liquor. The 'tea' consisted of a saucer of tomato slices, a bottle of whisky from Italy, a flask of vodka, another of brandy from Russia, and the *reserva*, a demijohn of ouzo.

Popov explained that it was the Russian practice to drink their tea 'bottoms up', at one gulp. We sat down and he poured out a small tumbler of whisky for me first, as I had been longest in the Greek mountains. Then he toasted, 'Long live Churchill!' We duly gulped it down. As I emerged from the shock, I heard 'Long live Roosevelt!', reached out to find my tumbler of vodka, and gulped that down. From very far off I heard the cry, 'Long live Stalin!', groped blindly for my tumbler, and downed it like the others.

I awoke in the grey light of dawn on a strange bed in a strange room. I went next door and there in the room of the tea-party lay the three Russians flat on the floor, fully dressed with their boots on. In another room I discovered West, who was lying fully clad on a bed with his boots off and his socks on. I had some difficulty in arousing him. He opened a bleary eye, re-marked, 'Say, bo, we said nothing', and went to sleep again.

At a late hour we all breakfasted together in a rather chastened mood. As we left, West remarked to Popov, 'Say, Popov, I'm sorry we stayed so long.' As we walked back from Vatinia to Mezilo, West told me that I had gone down like a ninepin after drinking Stalin's health, and that he had drunk on until the Russians fell out one by one. They too, it appeared, had said nothing.

Our main object was to parade our goodwill towards Russia, both to the Russian officers and to ELAS. I therefore laid on a reception for the Russians, the PEEA leaders and the ELAS High Command. It went off very happily. In the course of it Siantos pulled Popov, Svolos, West, and myself aside, said the Germans were starting a drive against ELAS, and demanded that I should obtain supplies from GHQ Middle East. I politely but firmly put off a decision until we met at ELAS GHQ.

Popov too, it transpired, was in need of help. His wireless set, operating probably to the Russian Mission with Tito in Yugoslavia, was not making regular contact properly. He was most grateful when I sent our W/T sergeant to put him on the air. We even lent him gold sovereigns; for the Russian currency and the American dollars which he had brought with him were almost worthless as compared with the sovereigns and the parachute-silk which we used as currency.

My main interest was in the effect of Popov's arrival on ELAS and PEEA. At first Siantos was very jubilant. But his face soon began to fall, especially when we suggested that he should ask not us but his great Russian allies for supplies. There was some cooling-off between Popov and ELAS GHQ. West and I suspected that Popov had made it clear to Siantos that no help was forthcoming for ELAS and PEEA, and that the Russian offensive would not come as far south as Greece; but we did not know. Neither did we know whether GHQ Middle East would send any troops into Greece when the Germans moved out; we had not been told (with good reason), and the slow progress of our forces in Italy made it seem unlikely that any troops, other than a few RSR troops, would come into Greece.

The question was becoming of acute concern to us in July 1944; was Greece going to be left to stew in her own juice, when the Germans moved out? If so, and if we marked time meanwhile, the initiative would still be with Siantos. He would be able to occupy Athens, Salonica, and every other city, except perhaps Ioannina, long before the forces of the Greek Government in exile could enter the field. Indeed, those forces had mutinied recently; they might not be serviceable at all in such an eventuality. The only dependable unit, the Greek Brigade under Tsigantis, was in action on the Italian front. In short, if Greece was left to the Greeks, Siantos would have it all his own way; ELAS would liquidate its opponents in the cities, and Greece would become a Communist state.

In my awareness of this danger, I asked Cairo for information and advice. I was given neither and had to think things out for myself. It seemed to me that at this time ELAS and PEEA were in the trough of a depression and that the morale of the leaders was lower at the moment than it had ever been. If Cairo drifted on, as it had tended to do, and took no initiative, this moment would pass. Moreover, each day was bringing closer the withdrawal of the Germans from Greece and the possibility of ELAS taking over the cities. I consulted West. He shared my fears but was unwilling to make any recommendation on a matter of policy.

I therefore sent a long report on my own to Cairo. In it I described the situation as I saw it. In my opinion it was important that we should try to make ELAS think, whether it was true or not, that large Allied forces would land when the Germans were leaving. If ELAS did believe this, then they would stay in the hills; for I was confident that ELAS would not oppose the landing and deployment of Allied troops and their entry into Athens; for Allied troops would be greeted with immense enthusiasm by the people as liberators. If it was intended to send a considerable Allied force, the main thing when they were coming into Greece was to employ EDES and ELAS against the retreating Germans and to take over the towns promptly. Thereafter the problem was beyond my view.

If it was not intended to send any considerable Allied force and if ELAS knew or suspected this was so,* then ELAS would achieve a coup d'état without much doubt. Geographically, they had a long start over EDES and they could forestall any forces which the Greek Government might send in. Once in the cities they would no doubt liquidate their political opponents; for nothing in the cities, neither the Greek police nor the Security Battalions, could oppose ELAS with any hope of success.

There were already some signs that ELAS was preparing for

---

*   We were aware that EAM-ELAS had their own good sources of information about the plans of GHQ Middle East; they had British as well as Greek sympathisers there.

a move into the cities. We had heard that in Athens ELAS assault squads were already fighting at night in the suburbs against the police and the Rallis Security Battalions, that they were killing their opponents, many of whom had fled there from the hills, and that the Germans had concentrated their troops in the inner part of the city and left the Greeks to kill one another. I had obtained this information from would-be recruits for PEEA who had come out from Athens.

Another source of information was Despotopoulos. In an unguarded moment, he told me that ELAS GHQ was starting a 'Free German Movement' on the Russian model. They were no longer killing any Germans they captured; instead, they were forming them into a small force which was to operate with ELAS. He mentioned also that ELAS had heard of German plans to evacuate Athens. He was embarassed when I asked him what means he had of recruiting 'free Germans', and what was his source of information about German plans.

His silence gave me good grounds for suspecting that ELAS was in secret contact with the German forces. An agreement with ELAS would suit the Germans very well and enable them to withdraw with a minimum of trouble. Was ELAS hoping on its side to come to some understanding, whereby they could secure supplies of German ammunition on the German withdrawal, even as they had secured Italian supplies after the Italian collapse?

The problem for GHQ Middle East, *if they were not sending Allied troops*, was how to avert such a coup d'état by ELAS. The only solution or chance of a solution in my opinion was to order ELAS to attack its targets on the eastern side of Greece, and to order EDES to attack its targets on the western side, when the date for Noah's Ark was approaching but had not yet come. If ELAS obeyed the order, it would be showing a real willingness to co-operate with the Allied Command, and things might improve; and EDES would be able to come out of the corner in which we and ELAS were keeping them under the Plaka agreement. If ELAS did not obey (and I thought that they would not agree to move off the area in Epirus which enabled them to pin EDES down), then GHQ Middle East would denounce them as mutinous, just as the Greek Government had denounced PEEA as rebellious. On the other hand, EDES would certainly obey the order, and GHQ Middle East would support EDES as a force loyal to the Allies and to the Greek Government.

To judge from past experience, a renewal of civil war might

ensue between EDES and ELAS in Northern Greece, a renewal
which GHQ Middle East could so time that it would coincide
with the German movement out of Greece. Such a civil war, if
publicised outside Greece, would disillusion those who thought
of EDES and ELAS simply as heroic patriotic movements, and it
would keep ELAS engaged in the mountains, while the Greek
Government took over the cities as the Germans withdrew. Zervas
was ready to face the danger of such a civil war, and the Mission
stations and RSR groups would be able to maintain themselves
and even move down to attack the Germans.

To recommend such a policy was a nerve-racking business. It
was of course entirely conditional upon GHQ Middle East *being
unable to send Allied troops into Greece* as the Germans withdrew. Even with this proviso it needed a cold-blooded resolution
on my part to propose it. Yet the logic of my past experience and
of impending events left me no reasonable alternative. I knew
that ELAS was out to seize power and that their partisans would
commit atrocities and massacres in the cities, as they had done in
the hills. In my opinion, a war between EDES and ELAS on the
eve of the liberation was a less disastrous thing in the long run
than giving carte-blanche to ELAS after the German withdrawal.

Cairo replied that an Allied force of undivulged size would
be sent and that in Greece I alone was to know this fact. This
reply was an enormous relief to me. In the light of later events
I think that the policy I recommended *if Allied troops were not
to be sent* was a sound one; for, as those later events showed,
ELAS did aim at a coup d'état and could be thwarted only by
fighting. In fact even if troops were to be sent (as indeed they
were) a civil war in August or September 1944 might have cost
Greece less in blood and misery than the civil war of 1945–1950.

At the time my sense of relief gave me a great impetus to put
pressure on ELAS and PEEA. The Germans had started a series
of drives against the guerrilla forces in late July and early August,
which were calculated to clear their lines of communication
before the withdrawal began. Our policy was not to offer strong
resistance but to conserve our strength and ammunition for the
time when the Germans began withdrawing and the Noah's Ark
operations were put into effect.

ELAS made a weak showing. Two German forces penetrated
far inland, one westwards from near Karpenisi, and the other
eastwards from Amphilochia, the two forces almost joining
hands. It was for these attacks that Siantos asked me for sup-

plies at the reception we gave for the Russians and the Greeks. My answer to him was that all supplies must be husbanded for the great attack on the Germans, when they were finally withdrawing from Greece. I knew too that ELAS still had dumps of ammunition, which they were reserving for their own purposes.

There was considerable gloom at ELAS GHQ. Popov and his colleagues were proving broken reeds as far as ELAS was concerned. The success of the German drives was depressing. The leaders of ELAS and PEEA were feeling the effects of Papandreou's strong line as head of the King's Greek Government. I did my best to make them believe that large Allied forces from Italy would enter Greece. My method was to tell them the truth as I understood it, namely that only a small force would be available. Siantos and his friends would assume this to be a lie; for to them the art of deception was much more sophisticated than just telling the truth. This small force, I said, would enter each city on the heels of the retreating Germans, and then join hands with ELAS, EDES and the RSR groups in attacking the Germans in Central and North Greece. Of course, if ELAS and PEEA stood aside as a separate 'state', they would find themselves isolated and powerless, and ELAS in particular would have no share in the glory of liberating Greece. The best policy for PEEA was to join Papandreou's 'Government of National Unity', and the best policy for ELAS was to gain the credit to which it was entitled by making a success of Noah's Ark under the command of GHQ Middle East.

At last, in the middle of August,* Siantos gave way. He agreed to abolish PEEA provided that six representatives of EAM and PEEA were admitted to the Government of Papandreou. After some haggling about offices, both sides agreed; Svolos, Tsirimokos, Porphyroyennis, Angelopoulos, Zevgoyannis, and Askoutsis, a mixed bag of Communists and fellow-travellers, were accepted for office in the Papandreou Government.

When I reported that Siantos accepted these terms, I warned Cairo that in my opinion this was simply a tactical step by Siantos and indicated no change of heart. But it did mean that for the time being Siantos had given up the hope of a coup d'état as the Germans withdrew, and that Greece could be liberated in the name at least of a united Government. Even with these provisos

---

* Churchill met Tito in Italy on 12 August and summoned Papandreou from Cairo (*Second World War*, VI, 78 f.); Siantos was probably informed of this by wireless and realised that he was becoming isolated.

the abdication of PEEA from the scene was a great success for the policy which we had been maintaining so consistently.*

The next task was to make our final disposition for Noah's Ark and to involve ELAS in it as far as possible. Since the departure of Chris I had been doing his job as acting commander of the Allied Mission and my own job as chief liaison with ELAS and commander of the Missions in ELAS areas. It still seemed to me that Chris would not return. As the direction of Noah's Ark would now take precedence, I should need to shed my second job. I therefore sent for Arthur Edmonds to act as my second-in-command and as chief liaison officer with ELAS GHQ. I appointed Ronald Prentice to take command in Macedonia in his place. The change was indeed advisable on other grounds; for Edmonds was at odds with ELAS in Macedonia, because he had not been firm enough in protecting his Greek interpreters, and then he had been unduly unaccommodating in other matters. I sent for John Mulgan at the same time, asking him to bring me details of his plans for Noah's Ark.

While Edmonds and Mulgan were on their way I sent to SOE Cairo a long signal. The draft of it (the only document I took out with me later on) is reproduced as Appendix B. In addition to summarising the lessons to be drawn from operations between 14 June and 20 August and the extent of co-operation between the resistance troops and the RSRs and OSS Groups, I proposed plans for bridging at once the gap between the Greek forces outside Greece and those within Greece, for instance by sending ELAS and EDES staff officers to join GHQ Middle East and Greek regular units to help in Noah's Ark operations; and for bringing war correspondents into Greece. The opportunity for putting these plans into action was provided by the fact that representatives of the resistance movements were about to enter the Papandreou Government of National Unity, and it seemed to me too good an opportunity to be missed. It was essential to follow up Siantos' concession at once and drive home our advantage before Noah's Ark began. Had my proposals been approved, we should in the event have had almost two months within which to implement them.

*   See *The Second World War*, VI, 100. 'On the evening of 12 August M. Papandreou said [to Churchill] that EAM had joined his Government because the British had been firm towards them, but the Greek State itself had no arms and no police. At present only the wrong people had arms, and they were a minority. I told him we could make no promise and enter into no obligations about sending British forces into Greece, and that even the possibility should not be talked about in public.'

CHAPTER TEN
A New Policy

At this juncture Cairo informed me that the brigadier who headed the Greek section of the Cairo office was coming in by aeroplane to Neraidha. He intended to visit me and call on ELAS GHQ. This was a surprising piece of news, because we had had no such visitor since John Stevens (see p 59 above) and this particular visitor was higher in rank than any of us in the field. Shortly before the brigadier and his aide, an Irishman called Major O'Toole, were due to arrive at Mezilo, we got a message by runner from John Cook that the brigadier had been enraged by the unmilitary bearing and turn-out of the officers and men at Neraidha. When the brigadier and the major rode up to my HQ on horseback, I had my men duly on parade. I doubt if he was much impressed. Their uniforms were fairly nondescript, and I was no model of military etiquette myself, as I had no cap and was wearing my original battledress top. It was perhaps not the occasion to explain that I kept wearing this old battledress because diamonds had been sewn in under the pips, in case I was ever caught.

Brigadier Barker-Benfield — known as B.B. by our wireless staff (they had been in the habit of exchanging ribald jokes with the Cairo girl cypherines, until B.B. heard one of them and stopped the fun by issuing a round-robin to all stations) — was a tall, genial officer of fifty or so, who wore immaculate uniform and put his faith in military etiquette. He reminded me of a delightful Master of Trinity Hall whom I had known in his friendliness and in his ready conversation, but not in his intelligence. We all chatted over a meal, and then he and I had a talk. He began by expressing his annoyance with John Cook for having failed to welcome him with sufficient ceremony. He added that the HQ house at Neraidha was dirty and untidy, and that he disliked the beards he had seen on some of the officers and other ranks there (we had a few at Mezilo too). I tried to mollify him by explaining that barrack-room cleanliness could not be maintained in these mobile stations, and that we had no trouble with the important side of discipline.

However, B.B. would have none of it. To him the hair or lack of it on the military face was important. He used my wireless set to send a long signal to Cairo in which he ordered all members of the Allied Military Mission to shave off their beards and to set their HQs in order. This no doubt caused some annoyance at the other stations. At this time I had direct internal communication by wireless with Tom Barnes. As he had a famous beard, he sent me a snappy message saying I must have let B.B. get out of control.

B.B. then discussed Noah's Ark with me. He expressed satisfaction with the arrangements I had made. He put up some suggestions about details, which showed that he had very little conception of our terrain and of our limitations, which was natural enough in one who seemed to me to be thinking only in terms of regular warfare and orthodox situations. I was a bit alarmed that, even when I had explained our situation, he still stuck to his suggestions with (I thought) unreasonable tenacity. However, all was very friendly.

We then turned to the subject of ELAS and PEEA. He regarded the entry of Svolos and the others into Papandreou's Government as evidence of a real change of heart. His line was that ELAS and its leaders, whatever they had done in the past, were now behaving like gentlemen and that, if we treated them as gentlemen, they would continue to behave as such. I pointed out that my signals had suggested exactly the contrary, and that my experience of ELAS and the experience of Chris were diametrically opposed to B.B.'s view. But B.B. said he would see ELAS and form his final opinion then.

B.B. had not invited West to this talk with me. I remarked on this omission and said that we had always treated our American opposite number with full confidence, and that we had found the result was a close co-operation. B.B. replied that in regard to the liberation of Greece we should not take West into our confidence, in particular not on any political issues. In fact throughout his stay B.B. more or less disregarded West, and in particular he did not take West along with him to see ELAS GHQ, whereas I had always asked West to accompany me and he had generally done so.

In the evening we played a friendly rubber of bridge. Several of us had played a good deal lately. Allen was an expert, and he and I had once beaten the local Mission champions, Worrall and Hartmeister. B.B. showed himself to be a stubborn but not a very clever player.

Next day B.B., O'Toole and I with Allen as our interpreter set off for ELAS GHQ. We rode over to Vatinia, and I remember telling O'Toole of my experience with brigadiers in the past which had ended in ructions. B.B. happened to overhear me and said that he hoped this would not happen with us. I had warned ELAS GHQ to expect B.B. and they had had wind of his preferences. So they all put on their best uniforms (B.B. was in his finery and he had lent me one of his military caps which, being much too large, sat on my ears). Even better, a guard of honour was mounted to receive him. Siantos, Sarafis, and Despotopoulos were geniality itself. They wisely left Sarafis, the regular soldier, to do the preliminary honours. B.B. used O'Toole as his interpreter. O'Toole's Greek was good and colloquial, and he tended to exaggerate the sense of some of B.B.'s remarks.

This opening visit was intended to be mainly a good-will visit, but B.B. went on to discuss the Noah's Ark plans. He complimented ELAS on their dispositions and he made some suggestions which ELAS glibly accepted, knowing, as I well knew, that they would not and indeed could not implement them. He and the ELAS officers then discussed the difficulty of defining the responsibilities of ELAS and EDES in some of the Noah's Ark operations. B.B. was most sympathetic to the complaints which ELAS lodged against Zervas, and O'Toole (exaggerating B.B's comments) said 'Zervas was an old fox'. Later in the day B.B. visited Svolos. I took him to the house and I proposed that I should go in with him, but B.B. asked me to wait outside (Svolos spoke fair English). That evening I told B.B. that ELAS was liable to abuse any concessions one might make, and that it was important to respect the Plaka Agreement and to be fair to Zervas. B.B. clearly disagreed. He expressed some disapproval of both Zervas and Barnes.

The next meeting with ELAS GHQ was a great deal worse from my point of view. B.B. cheerfully and genially granted to ELAS almost every request which I had been refusing them for months. He did this sometimes at the expense of EDES and sometimes at the expense of our control of the Noah's Ark operations, and he reversed the priorities of supplies on which we had hitherto insisted.

That evening B.B. concocted a long signal to Cairo, outlining his new policy. I told him that as he was using my WT set, and as I was in command of the Allied Military Mission in Greece, I wished to see his signal and to add my comments, which he was, of course, free to read. He handed over his signal. In effect, he wished to reverse the policy towards ELAS which I and West,

and Chris and Wines before us, had maintained. He recommended
making concessions to ELAS at the expense of Zervas in breach of
the Plaka Agreement, and he wanted to give ELAS more supplies
and more say than hitherto in the conduct of the Noah's Ark
operations, in particular allotting to ELAS some targets on the
Metsovo-Ioannina road. He also reported favourably on ELAS
GHQ and its co-operative spirit. I appended a short signal, stating
my complete disagreement with B.B.'s recommendations, and
basing it on my long experience with ELAS GHQ. I showed my
signal to B.B. He was most annoyed, but he permitted it to go
out with his.

Relations were now a bit strained. After our evening meal
B.B. wanted to have a game of bridge; so we sat down for a game,
and I drew B.B. as a partner. We were playing against Allen and
George, a strong partnership. Unfortunately B.B. and I did not
establish an understanding in our bidding. When we were vulnerable but in reach of the rubber, I bid up to a small slam, while
B.B. made no call and looked very huffy. When Allen doubled,
I redoubled. I made my contract and we won outright. B.B. was
highly incensed at my unorthodox bidding. I was diplomatic
at first, but when he pressed me for my reason for bidding so
high, I rather imprudently said that I had had to assume his
failure to disclose an ace, and that my assumption had turned
out to be correct. This was our last hand of bridge during his
stay.

Next morning I woke up with a bad bout of malaria which
laid me low. B.B. was very sympathetic. I got myself injected
with quinine and was soon on my feet again. The effect of such
bouts was lowering but short-lived, and I was able to attend B.B.'s
next and, as it proved, final session with ELAS GHQ. It was
clear that B.B. and O'Toole were going ahead with the policy
which B.B. had recommended in his signal to Cairo. There was
as yet no reply from Cairo, but as B.B. outranked me there was
nothing I could do to stop them. What interested me was the
reaction of ELAS GHQ. Siantos and his colleagues could hardly
believe their ears. They did not know whether B.B. was serious or
insane. They certainly suspected a trap, and they did not take
B.B. at his word at all.

When we returned to Mezilo, B.B. met Arthur Edmonds and
John Mulgan, who had just arrived. They reported on their plans
for Noah's Ark. B.B. thought that Edmonds had good military
ideas but was not much impressed with him otherwise. He admired

Mulgan's directness but did not like his low rating of the fighting qualities of ELAS. B.B. then told me that he realised that I disliked his policy with ELAS, that he knew I was in poor health and had asked for leave some months back, but that he nevertheless wanted me to stay in command of the Mission for the final stage up to the liberation of Greece.

We went on to discuss the command system of Noah's Ark. It was clear that our views differed on this matter also. B.B. wanted a more detailed plan to which area commanders would be committed, and a more centralised command at my HQ, whereas I intended to allow much more initiative to my area commanders and to leave the central control of operations to Cairo. Here, too, B.B. stuck his toes in. He dismissed my past experience and my arguments in a summary manner; he knew the answers both on policy and on military operations.

I then said that in view of my differences with B.B. I did not wish to continue in command of the Mission. B.B. agreed to my wishes with (I think) reluctance. He decided to ask Arthur Edmonds to take command, and he accepted. It was arranged that I should accompany B.B. and the EAM delegates (Svolos, etc.) when they left in a plane from Neraidha.

For a day or two I was a spectator. The staff at Mezilo expressed regret at my going, and the Greeks among them, especially Allen and Uncle Bill, were apprehensive about the future. ELAS GHQ asked me to a dinner which they were giving in honour of the delegates who were going out to join the Papandreou Government. It was an open-air dinner, held in good spirits, and Siantos made a speech in which he said nice things about my services to Greece and about my friendly personal relations with ELAS GHQ. On the way to Neraidha, I met Karayeoryis, the former EAM controller of Thessaly, who gave me a genial send-off. When we reached Neraidha, I found there were some spare places on the plane, and I arranged to take a few sick Italians who needed surgical operations. During the evening some senior Italian officers asked if they could go in place of the sick men. When I said no, one burst into tears and knelt before me.

It was a soft mild night with a clear sky on 29 August 1944. We heard the drone of a plane far off. It circled over us showing signals in response to ours; once the recognition was assured, we lit the flares and the plane landed smoothly between the flares, ran their length and turned back. It stopped short of its full return up the flare-path. We rushed over to greet those who landed, — among them John Clows, now fit again and posted by me to Triklinos in Amphilochia, and some other friends. The plane was slightly bogged. It was pushed out by some Elasites, we shouted goodbye, piled in and were off on our course to Bari in Italy. My stay in Greece was ended.

The aftermath takes little telling. I found Chris at the Allied HQ at Caserta; he was kicking his heels until the force under General Scobie was ready to enter Greece. He told me that B.B.'s attitude was symptomatic of a general swing which had taken place in the opinions of the high-up military command in the Middle East. They had ceased to support the policy which had been maintained by Eddie, Chris, and myself and they intended henceforth to trust ELAS rather than EDES, in the hope and indeed in the belief that ELAS would obey the commands of GHQ Middle East and would abandon their political aspirations. It was thought in military circles that Chris and I had become embittered by too long an experience in the field, and that our view of ELAS had grown distorted and biassed. Chris had fought against this attitude in the Middle East and in London but without success.

General Paget and his staff were already committed to the policy of what was in our view the appeasement of ELAS. On the other hand, the Foreign Office and especially Rex Leeper, the Ambassador attached to the Greek Government, subscribed to our interpretation of ELAS. However, the Foreign Office had been over-ruled by the War Office in this matter, partly because the Foreign Office lacked the full report denied them by the death of David Wallace (see p 160 above). There was therefore little that I could do except add to Chris's representations. Opportunities even for that were few with B.B. in immediate command of us. For example, when B.B., Chris and I visited the general who commanded the forces of SOE in the Balkans, it was B.B. who gave the report on the situation in Greece; I then expressed my dissent and my reasons, adding that B.B. had only seen one side of the picture, and that briefly, and that he had not visited EDES. The general was a tired man with little fight in him, and he made it clear that he adhered to B.B.'s views and to those of the higher command. It was arranged that we should see General Paget also, but that arrangement fell through.

I had an interview with General Scobie, who was concerned solely with the possibility of encountering resistance from ELAS during the entry of light forces into Greece. My advice was that

ELAS would not offer opposition. Among the reasons I gave was the concern of the leaders for the prestige of the movement and their belief that the Allied forces would be large; moreover, it would take a considerable time to move the heavier weapons of ELAS down from the hills along mule-tracks. I made it clear also that that was not the end of the story, and that ELAS would still be a dangerous force after the liberation. Scobie was an active-minded and intelligent man, quick to grasp an argument and to appraise a situation. It was a relief to find that he was to command the liberating troops. I then met his subordinate, General Hughes, under whom it was intended I should, after a spell of leave at home, act as Antiquities Officer, assisting the Greek Government in the preservation and recovery of monuments and antiquities. He was interested in the danger of armed opposition and consulted me also about the problem of giving relief and of starting the rehabilitation of Greece, because he was to command AML, the forerunner of UNRRA, in Greece. My most genial interview was with two American generals who were the opposite numbers to those of our section in Allied GHQ. Unlike the formal British generals, they slapped me on the back, said they knew nothing and asked for my story. But the Americans were to play no part in the liberation of Greece, and they exerted no influence on policy at all.

It had been intended that I should fly to Cairo to meet Rex Leeper and Street and others, but I was told suddenly that I was wanted at home to report on the situation in Greece. So off I went by air to London. My arrival coincided with a bout of malaria. At our London office the man in charge of the Greek section was the man who had been my boss in Athens in 1941. Then and later in Cairo in 1942–43, when I had last seen him, he had been much in favour of the left wing in general and of ELAS and EAM in particular. It was clear from the outset that he was not open to conversion or even argument about ELAS and EAM. One felt that one was talking not about realities at all but only about his vague memories of reported events. Then I went to see General Gubbins and Lord Selborne, respectively the military head of SOE and the civilian head of the Ministry of Economic Warfare. They were very kind in their praise of my work in Greece, but the problem of ELAS was not familiar to them. Their eyes, in any case, were turned to Western Europe, where Paris and Brussels had just been liberated. An interview was arranged at the Foreign Office at their request, but it was postponed because of some crisis there. Malaria and amoebic dysentery then intervened, and some months later, when I was again fit for service, I went not to Greece but to Germany.

Looking back in the light of after-knowledge, one can see that the change of attitude towards EAM-ELAS which I had first seen in B.B. was already at that time widespread in military circles and in SOE. It seems not to have stemmed at all from Churchill and the Foreign Office. They had no illusions about the aims of EAM and ELAS; indeed they intended to thwart those aims and to secure in a liberated Greece the free conditions under which the Greek people could make its own choice of government. The change seems rather to have originated in the military minds of GHQ Middle East and particularly in those of the Advanced HQ at Caserta; and B.B. both as head of the SOE section and as a military man himself fell into line with the new thinking. My impression at the time of B.B.'s visit was that he had come with his mind made up and did not evolve a new policy on the basis of the little he saw on the spot.

One reason for the change was that, as Greece was about to come again into the operational theatre of our regular forces, military circles had a greater say in the direction of affairs. Their interest was short-term. As I saw in my interview with General Scobie, he did not look beyond the military complications which might arise when he was treading on the heels of the retreating Germans. It was enough for him if he could avoid a conflict with the guerrilla movements.

It was fortunate that the change of attitude came too late to affect the conditions under which Greece was liberated. Before B.B. appeared on the scene, the vital decisions had already been taken by Siantos. These were to abolish PEEA, to participate in Papandreou's Government, and in consequence to confirm the dependence of ELAS on GHQ Middle East. When B.B. did appear, his behaviour was even more surprising to Siantos and his colleagues than it was to me; for I was familiar with such things as the Mad Hatter's Tea-Party, but they were obsessed with ideas of 'perfidious Albion'. They assumed with the tortuousness of the Greek mind that B.B. was playing a double game. If they had believed him, they would have stepped up their demands not only in regard to EDES, but, more importantly, in regard to Papandreou's Government. As it was, Siantos implemented the decisions he had taken prior to the appearance of B.B.

Accordingly Svolos and the others came out with us. They

entered the Greek Government and stayed in it until after the liberation of Greece. With the disappearance of PEEA the armed forces of ELAS could no longer claim allegiance to a government in 'Free Greece'. From a military point of view they agreed, as EDES had done, to carry out the Noah's Ark operations under the orders of GHQ Middle East; and from a political point of view, when the choice was seen to lie between isolation and adoption into the Greek Government, Siantos swallowed the pill. On 26 September Sarafis and Zervas signed an agreement in Caserta, placing the forces of ELAS and EDES under the directional orders of General Scobie. Thus the military and political objectives of the Allied Mission were achieved.

In the military field the liberation of Greece depended solely on the Germans. In mid-September they began withdrawing from the Peloponnese, and on 1 November the last of them left Macedonia. As the withdrawal progressed, light British forces entered southern Greece unopposed; they reached Athens in mid-October, where the Greek Government of National Unity was soon established. Meanwhile the Mission was carrying out the operations known as Noah's Ark against the withdrawing Germans. In these they were supported by the RSR groups, by the American assault groups, and by some forces detailed for the purpose by ELAS and EDES. In general, however, the two resistance movements were more concerned to get into the towns of the vicinity than to harass the Germans. As the mass of the withdrawal was on the eastern side of Greece where ELAS had a monopoly, there is no doubt that large amounts of German supplies fell into the hands of ELAS, and that the military control which Germany surrendered was taken up at once by ELAS in eastern Greece north of Athens.

The danger in the post-liberation period was the belief, so simply expressed by B.B., that EAM and ELAS would behave like gentlemen. Anyone who had had the opportunity of studying EAM and ELAS at close quarters for any length of time would have said, as I had said in my signal to Cairo, that they had not undergone a change of heart but had merely adopted a change of tactics. In other words, their strategy was still a coup d'état, and it would be attempted as soon as opportunity offered. Nor had ELAS sacrificed any of its real power. Its members were still bound by their original oath to stay under arms and in the field, until a plebiscite on the return of the King was held. In the hills it had a monopoly of weapons; moreover, its control of the means of disseminating news was as strong after the liberation as before it. Indeed ELAS became less restrained in its use of power, because it was less open to observation, now that the Mission stations and the accompanying troops were gradually departing.

While the western press sang the praises of EAM-ELAS in harmony with the earlier military tune, ELAS was moving its armaments down from the hills and preparing to launch its sudden and generally unforeseen attack on the small British and Greek forces in Athens. The coup d'état came within an inch of a success which Yugoslavia and Albania would then have been eager to support. The bloodshed and the suffering which ensued for several years fell once again upon the unfortunate villagers in the mountains of Northern Greece.

Retrospect

Since 1944—45, when I wrote down these memories, the evaluation of the Greek resistance movements and of the Allies' part in their affairs has become an increasingly controversial matter. It is, therefore, desirable to mention some relevant points which have been increasingly forgotten. The first is that these movements on the Greek mainland started of their own volition. In this respect Greece was different from Yugoslavia. In 1941, when I served in SOE in Athens, we sent from there a considerable quantity of military supplies to General Mihailovitz, whom SOE had contacted before the change of government in Yugoslavia and had instigated to mount a resistance movement. This he did in that very year. But on the Greek mainland the policy of SOE was to train wireless operators and saboteurs (see p 13 above), and the only idea of setting up a resistance group in the mountains in spring 1941 was still-born because it was far too late in the day. I knew of it because Peter Fleming invited me in Athens to join him in developing a plan which I regarded as impractical at that date.

On the other hand, in Crete a British officer, the archaeologist John Pendlebury, from summer 1940 onwards was organising a resistance group of his own choice (I met some of his chosen men at the time of the Cretan campaign), but he was captured on his way from Heraklion to the mountains and was later killed by German parachutists. Without his leadership the group disintegrated.

It was the German invasion of Russia that kindled the first organisation for resistance on the Greek mainland in autumn 1941. It soon took the name of EAM with a Central Committee in Athens and a system of cells there and in other cities. The next stage, that of sending armed men into the mountains with the name ELAS, came only in summer 1942. By then another group had formed in Athens, calling itself EDES, and its armed forces took the field in north-west Greece under the command of General Napoleon Zervas also in summer 1942. Thus ELAS and EDES were already in action before the first British troops returned to Greece in October 1942 in order to carry out a single commando operation, in conjunction in the event with troops of ELAS and EDES. These two resistance movements sprang from the Greek spirit of resistance and were indigenous and autonomous creations of that spirit.

Armed resistance in the open countryside is something rarely undertaken. Only men of extreme, even fanatical enthusiasm will undertake the initiation and the leadership of such resistance, because it invites terrible reprisals on one's family, friends and fellow-countrymen from an occupying power as ruthless as Germany was in 1942. The object of such an enthusiasm may be freedom from oppression, expressed so admirably in the Rigas song, or it may be power over others in the wartime period and political power in the ensuing period when the occupying army has withdrawn. Of course some men may combine the two objects; and admirers of Enver Hoxha and Tito will claim that they did so. Such men cannot succeed unless they find a large number of recruits who are ready not only to face the same dangers but also to tolerate the prospect of such reprisals. In Greece these recruits were found at first in the experienced men of the un-defeated army which had fought in Albania. Their aim was pre-dominantly to fight to the death against the occupying powers.

This fierce spirit of fighting in the cause of independence was what united Britain and Greece in the winter and spring of 1940—41 and them alone. Other nations then looked on, and the defeated nations such as France did not then or later put armed forces of resistance into the mountains. When Italy and Germany occupied Greece, most Greeks thought of the comparable occupation by the Turks and drew inspiration from the spirit of resistance which had freed one part of Greece after another from 1830 to 1912. So now, in 1942—43, the resistance movements endowed themselves, and were endowed by most of the population, with the glorious and glamorous tradition of the great freedom fighters of the past. They were a symbol then of Greece's undying spirit, and on 25 October 1981 this was recognised for the first time since the war by the laying of wreaths in honour of the Andartes who gave their lives in the cause of freedom.

The Russian connection appeared later when Siantos, Hoxha and Tito became known as the actual leaders of their resistance movements. For it then transpired that they and some of their immediate supporters had been trained in Moscow during the prewar period, and that they had returned to their countries with a shared technique and a common aim: the seizure of power and the conversion of their states to a Stalinist form of Communism. The aim of Russia in training these agents was not to fight Germany (for the training was prior to the outbreak of war and Russia came into the war only because she was attacked) but to gain control of the Balkan states by revolutionary methods. It was part and parcel of that Russian expansionism which has created so much conflict in the postwar world. This, however, is to be wise after the event. At the time the attention of the Allies was on Russia's invasion of Poland and then of Finland and her continuing pact with Germany; Russian plans in the Balkans were unknown or underestimated.

In 1941 SOE Athens was training Communists in wireless communication and sabotage techniques, and early in 1943 SOE Cairo seemed to be more in favour of building up ELAS than EDES. The first proof of the dominant role of the Greek Communist Party (KKE) in the affairs of EAM was sent to SOE Cairo by Chris, who went into Athens and met six members of EAM's Central Committee in January and February 1943. 'At the two conferences,' he wrote later, 'only two men altogether spoke. Their names were Andhreas Tzimas and Yioryios Siantos; and both were members of KKE.' This information was not passed on to the missions in the field, for instance to Rufus Sheppard or to me.

The first proof of the co-ordination and the co-operation of the Communist parties of Albania, Greece and Yugoslavia and of their armed forces was sent by me to SOE Cairo in May 1943. This too was not made known to missions in the field, and it is uncertain how far it went beyond SOE in London. The fact that Russia and Germany were locked in conflict and that there was apparently no means of communication between Russia and any agents she might have in the Balkans may have made these matters seem unimportant.

On the British side, when it became known that there was some form of armed resistance in the mountains of Greece, it was decided to use it as a springboard for a purely military operation, the destruction of the Gorgopotamos bridge. Success there led SOE Cairo to probe further. Chris went into Athens to investigate the nature of EAM, and Rufus Sheppard and I were sent into the field to find out about ELAS in January and February 1943. Chris presumably and Rufus certainly were to report on the political as well as the military situation; but I was told only to report on the military potential of ELAS, and all subsequent officers were ordered to keep to military matters and avoid political issues. Next came the decision by GHQ Middle East, to create the British Military Mission to the resistance movements and to build up the strength of those movements for military purposes, which soon crystallised into the operations of June and early July 1943. Those who are critical of that decision should not forget the desperate situation in what had become a global war and the overriding need to force an entry into Europe, whether in the region of Salonica or in Sicily. And the decision seemed to be justified, even though the cost in arms, equipment, gold and aircraft was high, by the success of the resistance movements and the British Mission in drawing the attention of the Germans and easing the invasion of Sicily, which began on 10 July. Within Greece it fuelled the spirit of resistance and enabled the movements to hold their own against the enemy; indeed, it even brought those movements together and provided in the Joint GHQ a means of achieving a common policy which had hitherto been lacking.

Once Sicily and Italy were invaded, resistance in Greece became a matter of minor importance to the military planners. What attracted attention now was the political aspect. In mid-July David Wallace was sent from the Foreign Office to ascertain the political colours and aims of the resistance movements (p 76 above); he was able to meet many leading personalities of the movements at the Joint GHQ and he talked with the senior BLOs at the conference at Pertouli. In mid-August he accompanied Eddie Myers and a deputation from the resistance movements which was flown out from the landing strip at Neraidha to Egypt. The aim of the British was to bridge the gap between the two parts of the Greek world: 'Free Greece' dominated by EAM-ELAS, a fierce opponent of monarchy and of the monarch's government, and 'The King and his Government' with his armed forces, the official representative of Greece in the Grand Alliance. The result was a deadlock which was not to be resolved for almost a year. Wallace and Myers went on to London to report and did not return. The deputation was flown back to Neraidha in mid-September. As it was accompanied by the first American officers, the Mission was re-named the Allied Military Mission; and Chris continued to be the acting Commander, as he had been since Eddie's departure. What had happened in Egypt was not revealed to the members of the Mission at the time or subsequently; and it did not much concern them because things had moved fast in 'Free Greece'.

The belief that Greece might be liberated in the latter part of 1943 was widespread, partly because the British bluff had been successful and partly because the Germans deliberately encouraged it by their movements of troops. What EAM-ELAS wanted on the eve of this expected liberation was a monopoly of armed power in the mountains, and they set out to obtain it with as much parade of justification as possible. The first example was PAO. At the second meeting in Salonica (p. 67 above), at first at Elafina and later at Joint GHQ the representatives of EAM-ELAS were conciliatory and appeared willing to compromise; but in fact ELAS destroyed the band of PAO guerrillas outside Elafina in the latter part of August and made sure that important messages did not reach PAO in Salonica, even imprisoning the unfortunate Colonel Mousterakis. While the PAO incident was still under consideration, the Pinerolo Division moved from the plain of Thessaly into ELAS territory on 12 September and was for the most part persuaded to hand over its weapons, ammunition and stores to ELAS in the following weeks. ELAS now had far greater resources than its rivals. In the second week of October units of ELAS attacked units of EDES in several places. Although ELAS GHQ tried to justify these attacks, the BLOs on the spot provided evidence that ELAS was the aggressor. Its aim was clearly to destroy EDES and control the diminutive movement, EKKA.

The attacks by ELAS on PAO and then on EDES with the consequent sufferings of so many villagers in northern Greece in a period of enemy occupation were acts of military madness from the point of view of the Allied Military Mission. The only sanction we had was to cut off all military supplies and money from ELAS as the instigator of civil war. This was done in Macedonia from late August onwards, and in all areas from mid-October onwards. On the other hand we continued to deliver supplies to EDES and EKKA which had carried out the orders of GHQ Middle East, and continued to do so.

Was this course worthwhile? Would it not be better to withdraw the Allied Military Mission? This question was put by GHQ Middle East, to all senior BLOs in command of areas in the latter part of October, and in the light of their answers the decision was taken to stay. As the wisdom of the decision has been questioned, it is worth considering the alternative. If the Allied Military

Mission had been withdrawn, there would have been no mechanism
for supplying any Movement or for maintaining contact. ELAS
would certainly have destroyed EDES in the end, established
its own government and brought its own forces down to occupy
the cities as the Germans withdrew. Siantos would have concerted
his plans with Enver Hoxha in Albania and Tito in Yugoslavia,
and the aim of all three was certainly to keep the Western Allies
out of the Balkans. It is difficult to see how those Allies, with
their forces committed in Italy and France, could have forced
their way into Greece; and it is probable that they would not even
have attempted to prevent the entire Balkans falling into the
sphere of Russia.

While Hoxha and Tito eliminated or neutralised their rivals,
Siantos failed to do so. But his policy remained the same. He
knocked out EKKA, and he was ready to attack EDES if a favourable opportunity should offer. He moved on to the next part of
his programme, the establishment of a government inside 'Free
Greece', and this ensured the continuation of the deadlock with
the Greek Government in Egypt and its forces. Meanwhile the
Allied Military Mission persisted in staying in Greece and in
pursuing its policy of concentrating on military objectives. It
persuaded EDES and ELAS to admit British RSR and American
OSS groups into Greece and to help them to reach their military
targets. Although ELAS was condemned for destroying EKKA
and was again deprived of supplies, it was made clear that supplies
would be renewed if ELAS would take its part in attacking the
Germans in accordance with the orders of GHQ, Middle East.

It required constant pressure and persuasion from the British
end and the bleak message of the Russian colonels to push EAM-
ELAS over the hump and end the deadlock. The Eamite government PEEA was disbanded, delegates of EAM-ELAS entered the
government of Papandreou and the claim that a plebiscite should
be held to determine whether or not the King would return was
met. Late in September the guerrilla forces commanded respectively by Zervas and Sarafis placed themselves under the Greek
Government and were allocated by that Government to operations
under the command of General Scobie. The Government entered
Athens on 18 October, and the last Germans left the mainland on
1 November. The days of the Allied Military Mission were at an
end.

The future lay with the Greeks themselves. But it was a future
that was sadly compromised by the past. The dictatorship of

Metaxas left a terrible legacy in the division of Greek society. If you were against the regime, you were deprived of your job or at least lost any chance of promotion; and if you supported the regime, you obtained the better paid posts. Almost every walk of life was affected in this way (officers, civil servants, teachers etc). Then the suppression of free speech and the ban on political expression were contrary to all Greek standards of democracy. The great mass of the people hated the regime. I was in Athens in 1939 on 4 August, the anniversary of Metaxas-day. Leaving the city at dawn to avoid witnessing the Hitler-like displays I found myself in good company: almost the entire population was heading for the countryside and the islands. The King, George II, was stamped with the brand of Metaxas. The Royalist cause was brought into longlasting disrepute by the association of George II and Metaxas.

One extremism fostered another extremism. The Communist Party, banned by Metaxas, received many adherents, who worked clandestinely in Greece or were trained in the techniques of international Stalinist Communism abroad, especially in Moscow. The neighbours of Greece — Albania, Yugoslavia and Bulgaria — were ruled by monarchies which did not commend themselves to the majority of their people in the late 1930s; and there too the Communist Parties were gaining ground. The general swing to the left was strengthened when these countries were occupied by the forces of the great dictators and the ruthlessness of their methods was felt, for instance, in the German blockade of Athens in winter 1941—42.

It was this swing, together with the wonderful Greek spirit of resistance, that was harnessed by KKE to create ELAS as the army at first simply of central and leftist opinion. But when KKE showed its teeth in savaging EDES and killing PAO and EKKA its own extremism bred another extremism: rightist elements joined EDES and even the Greek security forces of Rallis Government under the German occupation were regarded in some quarters as bulwarks against a Communist attack which might be launched with the co-operation of the Communist parties of the Balkan states.

Thus as Greece emerged from the occupation in October 1944 it was caught in the cross-currents of the extremisms of the right and the left. What added to the confusion was the lack of information (almost unimaginable in peace-time). Before the liberation the occupying powers had not only banned all news from outside their area but also disseminated false propaganda within it; and that was true not only of the Germans and the Rallis Government but also of EAM/ELAS in Central and Northern Greece. After the liberation ELAS stayed in the mountains and maintained the ban on news from outside. What were its intentions? Perhaps to strengthen the hands of the EAM/ELAS representatives in the Papandreou Government of National Unity; perhaps something more sinister.

The messages which I had sent as acting Commander of the AMM from Mezilo in July/August and my conversation with General Scobie thereafter might have forewarned the British command that there was danger in the air. But the eleventh-hour conversion of SOE Cairo and GHQ Middle East to the belief that the ELAS leopard had changed its spots seems to have prevailed up to the last moment of November. Meanwhile ELAS forces and supplies were being moved secretly over a period of some weeks from the mountains to within close reach of Athens. At the beginning of December, when the first ELAS troops moved into Athens for the coup d'état, General Scobie, in the name of GHQ Middle East to which they had pledged their allegiance, ordered them to withdraw. The order was not obeyed. The battle of Athens ensued, in which British troops maintained the position of the Allied Greek Government and kept open the possibility of free and democratic decision by the Greek people.

This final act by ELAS has to be included in this retrospect because it grew from the period of occupation. The policy of Siantos as Secretary-General of KKE had always been to create a dominant military power in Greece and then to seize political power by whatever means. It is arguable that he would have succeeded if he had waited for the postwar elections. But he decided to use revolutionary force. In taking this decision he and his colleagues will certainly have conferred with their Communist neighbours to the north and with their own centre of allegiance as represented by the three Russian colonels. The attack on Athens was the final item in a preconcerted programme to which Siantos as a sincere Communist of the Stalinist persuasion was irretrievably committed. If it had succeeded, Siantos' seizure of power would not have been reversed either from within since ELAS alone had military resources and militant allies, or from without, since, as it was, the British action in Athens was criticised in Parliament and was regarded with open disfavour by the

Government of the USA. As it happened, Greece was saved at a further cost in British lives. Even so the struggle was not yet over, and the Greeks themselves fought to preserve their freedom in what was called 'the civil war' until 1950.

The objective historian in the future may draw attention to a strange disparity in effort and consequence. Russia provided nothing except the concept of Communism and the training of some émigrés in revolutionary techniques. Britain expended on Greek soil what some have regarded as a disproportionate amount of men, material and gold. The consequence was by the narrowest of margins a victory for Britain in the sense that Greece remained in the free world and had a chance to decide her own future. And the lesson for the historian is that the potency of this form of Communism should never be underrated.

APPENDICES
AND INDEX

Appendix A

As C.M. Woodhouse pointed out in his *Apple of Discord*, p. 295 f, 'The use of forged documents to discredit political opponents' was a commonplace in the war of propaganda between the rival groups during and after the occupation. I give here in translation one example which concerns relations between PAO and ELAS:

Protocol of Collaboration

Today at Elafina, 22 August 1943, we the undersigned — namely the English Lt-Colonel Eggs, representing Allied GHQ in dealing with EAM-ELAS, Colonel of Infantry K. Kleos (Ioannes Mousterakis) representative of the Organisation PAO, and George Kikitsas (Sarandis Protopapas) representative of the Organisation EAM, —we, having approved each of the Organisations, have agreed as follows for the time being:

1) The Organisation PAO and its guerrilla groups of the E.S. (Hellenic Army) is recognised as a national Organisation designed to act against the occupying powers in Greece and on behalf of the Allies.
2) The representative of the Allied GHQ has the obligation, in accordance with the Eddy Protocol, to undertake the supplying of the units of the E.S. with arms and ammunition by air-drops.
3) To prevent misunderstandings each commander of an armed unit should inform all armed units of either Organisation in advance of his presence or of his passage.
4) From the signing of the present agreement, every commander of an armed unit bears the fullest responsibility if a clash should occur on his initiative.
5) From the acceptance of the present Protocol, without delay, prisoners of either Organisation are to be set free.
6) Every commander of an armed Andartic unit is under the obligation to make known to any Andartic unit of either Organisation in writing or by word of mouth the present Protocol of Collaboration.

7) Andartic groups of E.S. and ELAS accept the obligation to give mutual support in the event of clashes with the Germano-Italians and the Bulgarians.

8) The sphere of action of the Andartic army of the Organisation PAO (E.S.) is defined as Mount Vermion and precisely south of the understood line 'Ano Vermion (03-44-Naoussa-0 14–48)'.

Signed by Eggs, Kleos, Kikitsas.'

Another such 'document', printed in the newspaper *Athena* of 12 November 1975, is said to be 'an unpublished letter by Lord Hammond of the Staff of the BMM to Psarros', dated 12.3.44 and signed by 'N.G.L. Hammond Lord'. (This elevation to the peerage alone shows the forged nature of the document.) The letter concerns itself with the disputes between 5/42 Regiment (EKKA) and ELAS, and the adverse effects of these disputes upon 'Ark', and it contains an offer to transfer responsibility for the targets in this area C to EKKA and have ELAS 5th Division released from any co-operation in the area, because 'GHQ ME has full confidence in EKKA'. The letter went on to define the duties of Geof (Gordon-Creed) and John (Ponder). This was intended to encourage EKKA and stake a claim to full responsibility for the disputed area. It was a cleverer forgery than the one quoted above.

Appendix B

Draft of a Wireless Message of 20/21 August 1944 (not verbatim).

Report on AMM and Greek Situation 14 June — 20 August Military situation:

1) *AMM.* The infiltration and transportation of RSR and OGs into areas B, 1, 2 and 3 was successfully achieved during this period. Interim operations by the AMM were maintained at a high level in Area 3, where railway traffic by night was almost completely suspended; in Areas 2, D and Tingewick sporadic operations were carried out; Area 1 was subjected to two German drives (on Vermion and North Pindus) and failed to conduct interim ops. Area 4 (EDES) was banned from ops. in the interest of the naval base; when this ban was lifted, highly successful ops. against batteries (Preveza area) and L of C. followed.

It is not sufficiently realised that the infiltration and transportation of RSR and OG, each involving journeys of a month or more, imposed a considerable strain on AMM resources of personnel; this was aggravated by the absence of Col Chris [Monty Woodhouse], Lt-Col Barnes, Major Power, Major Nevill and Major Worrall.

Thus while interim ops were less extensive than we had wished, the scale was good in relation to our resources.

2) *Rebels* [the English term for Andartes]. The quality of ELAS units varied with that of local commanders. Thus 9 Division in Area 1 almost collapsed during the German drive; 5 Brigade in Area C beat off three or more German attacks based on Amphissa; 10 Division in Area 2 raided on MT and L of C. In general ELAS GHQ policy was to raid towns especially in July, where the Greek opposition to EAM was a target; otherwise to stay on the defensive and withdraw in face of German drives.

EDES units fought well in Epirus, getting to close grips with the Germans and capturing battery positions; this

showed an offensive spirit and high morale which are generally lacking in ELAS areas.

The Germans in populated centres appear to have concentrated German troops in fortified buildings on the defensive and to have left ELAS to overrun the Greek opposition.
The German drives on Vermion and North Pindus disorganised
the rebels and liberated German L of C from danger of
attack; the drives on Karpenisi from Lamia and Agrinion
were calculated to maintain German morale and blood the
German troops. In neither drive did the Germans meet with
serious resistance (for instance in the drive from Lamia on
Karpenisi Major Mulgan estimates German losses at 150 in
all; in the drive from Agrinion to Karpenisi Lt Philpot reported
only 1 hour's action by rebels during the advance of the
German force).

3)   *Co-operation of rebels with AMM.* After some initial difficulties with ELAS GHQ we obtained full co-op from ELAS
local units for transporting RSR and OGs, whose arrival was a
great stimulant to rebel morale. In early June a rebel commando group of 40 began training for close co-operation
with RSR and OGs in Area 3; when the OG arrived in July
and RSR in August, this commando co-operated well in
action. Accordingly the system was extended in early August,
ELAS GHQ allocating 200 rebels in Area 1, 160 in Area 2
and 120 in Area 3 for this purpose.

So long as interim ops were limited to small raids on L
of C, rebel co-op was good; but all attempts to launch combined attacks against major targets failed — e.g. Kaloneri in
Area 1, Koutsoufliani bridge in Area 2, Kaitsa station in
Area 3. The main causes of failure were the incapacity of
ELAS senior officers and the inability to keep the operation
secret. There were many contributing factors such as in-
sufficient liaison, lack of combined training, inadequate
reconnaissance and intelligence; these may be overcome, but
the main causes of failure are likely to persist, unless ELAS
command and methods are changed radically.

In EDES area co-operation with AMM and OG was good,
and major ops against batteries and Paramythia were successfully carried out in a manner not yet paralleled in ELAS
areas.

4)   *Prospects for phase 3 Ark.* (a) ELAS area. The above summary indicates that operations for phase 3 are not likely in

ELAS areas to exceed the scale of interim ops but are likely to be more numerous. The present plan of co-operation envisages (1) rebel commando groups for assault purposes, who will train and fight with our troops and are likely to give a good account of themselves. (2) Picked ELAS units of battalion strength who were allocated by ELAS GHQ in January for co-op in Ark and have been chosen specifically by Area Commanders. (3) Other ELAS troops allocated by ELAS GHQ in January who will be used mainly as harbour area troops.

(b) EDES area. Although Area 4 has no RSR, EDES rebels have shown themselves capable of attacking major targets, and they are likely to raise the scale of phase 3 above that of interim ops.

Recommendations for improving the prospects in phase 3 are made later. It should be noted in the case of ELAS areas that co-operation is greatest with small units and decreases as one rises to larger units and higher commands.

Rebel policy. (1) ELAS GHQ adhere firmly to the idea that ELAS is a regular army organisation with centralised command and a strategy of defence; once this defence is broken, ELAS divisions evade action or casualties. This was clear in the Area 1 drive, of which Lt-Col Edmonds sent a full report; in the August drive on Karpenisi a limited defence was put up in the Spercheiada valley but the subsequent penetration of the Germans into the mountainous hinterland seems to have been little contested. Lt Philpot reported that 7 Bde held a defensive position on the W side of Achelous, and as a result never contacted the German drive which lay east of the river; this although the officers and men were anxious to attack.

Neither centralised command nor a strategy of defence are suitable to the conditions of guerrilla warfare in Greece; lack of communication and lack of heavy equipment for defence are among the most obvious militants against such concepts. This has been recognised by AMM and had been proved time and again; equally ELAS in the early part of 1943 achieved better results despite smaller numbers, because it neither centralised its command nor based its strategy on defence.

There can be little doubt that ELAS higher command is aware of the situation but chooses this policy for political reasons; in order to conserve their forces and stake claims on liberated territories. The price of this policy is shown in the low morale of ELAS rebels e.g. in Area 1 and in the civilian opposition to ELAS. With regard to Allied troops and AMM, ELAS GHQ is endeavouring to centralise command under itself for phase 3. For instance, it wishes all plans for phase 3 including present interim ops to be passed by ELAS GHQ before being executed; and it would like to see a corresponding centralisation of command at AMM HQ. At the same time for reasons of prestige ELAS GHQ is agreeable to some rebel commando groups sharing in allied ops.

(2) Zervas' policy is, I believe, sincerely to execute the orders of GHQ ME to the full against the Germans; he is prepared to accept such orders from Lt-Col Barnes without question or evasion. At the same time he requires the protection of his limited harbour area against ELAS or German attack which pins down some of his best troops in a defensive role.

Policy for German surrender or collapse. ELAS GHQ admit to a change of policy in June when they began to take POWs and to issue propaganda to German units for surrender. At present they have a 'Free Germany' committee in contact with that of Moscow and maintain contact with German circles in Athens. They have also been pushing their claims to considering all POWs taken by ELAS as their exclusive property. It seems probable that EAM-ELAS plans for repeating their policy with the Italians in the case of the Germans are well advanced and aim to exclude the AMM and GHQ ME.

EDES agree to evacuate all German POWs as desired by GHQ ME; it is probable that Zervas does so also for reasons of propaganda, hoping to forestall ELAS in the event of a German collapse in Epirus.

ELAS–EDES relations. The 24 Regt episode and the ELAS raids on towns have exacerbated feeling between the two organisations and account for the increase in frontier incidents. The 24 Regt episode revealed that a balance of power has now been created and this leads to a corresponding stalemate between the two organisations. ELAS aim to exploit this by raising the Plaka pact from the status of an armistice pact to that of a guarantee of the status quo irrespective of the operational needs of Noah's Ark for which the secret clause provided. As ELAS cannot now hope to eliminate EDES, it aims to keep it pinned to a small area and to blacken it by propaganda. EDES on the other hand awaits an order from GHQ ME to expand, if necessary by armed conflict with ELAS. There are no doubt elements in EDES which put hatred of EAM-ELAS before hatred of the Germans. To help Zervas to hold such elements in check, Zervas must be able to direct them against the Germans.

Political situation. As the past has shown ELAS to be controlled by a political group, it is unwise to regard the military problem in Greece apart from its political background. The inclusion of EAM in the Cairo government has been achieved by pressure, and it seems probable that its participation will not be sincere. For instance, the controlling power in PEEA and EAM-KKE, Siantos and his colleagues such as Gavrielides, Roussos, Bakertzis and Partsalides, are not going to Cairo; the delegates are mainly from the moderate party (Svolos, Askoutsis and Tsirimokos), which carries little weight inside PEEA-EAM-KKE. Moreover, participation in the Cairo government may be reckoned to have come too late to change the status quo of armed power within Greece. Neither the use of terrorism in 'Free Greece' nor the control by EAM of ELAS higher commands has been abated recently; it appears, if anything, to have increased. For instance, Kalabalikis, OC Mac Corps, is being replaced by Bakertzis.

Beneath the superstructure which Siantos controls there are many signs of disruptive forces. The dislike of ELAS and its works was apparent in West Macedonia after the German drive; it was apparent in Area C after the dissolution of EKKA; apart from the hatred aroused by acts of terrorism, the war-weariness of the civil population is very marked and the dissolution of ELAS is as heartily desired as the end of the German occupation.

Inside ELAS the same forces are active; I consider that more than 60% of ELAS rank and file are eager to leave ELAS, if they can do so with any chance of safety, and are eager to co-operate with our troops against the Germans. The bulk of ELAS joined for patriotic motives; they have been misled and know it but can see no way of escape.

Military policy recommended for phase 3 Ark:
1) The participation of PEEA-EAM-KKE even if only nominal in the Cairo government should be exploited at once by endeavouring to bring ELAS and EDES under direct command of GHQ ME.

Judging purely from the basis of internal conditions I recommend the following methods:

(a) Representatives of ELAS and EDES higher command be instructed to join the Greek General Staff ME. The Greek General Staff in close collaboration with GHQ ME should direct phase 3 operations from ME.

(b) ELAS and EDES become part of the Greek National Forces in name. Greek senior officers from ME be infiltrated as soon as possible to sit on ELAS and EDES GHQs and Divisional and Bde HQs.

(c) AMM officers be accredited as military representatives of GHQ ME on ELAS and EDES HQs down to Bde HQs inclusive. They also retain command of allied non-Greek troops in each area.

(d) Picked units of Greek National Army in ME be infiltrated or dropped into ELAS and EDES areas to co-operate in operations with the Allied units and rebel commandos, thus stiffening our strength in target areas.

The above recommendations are put forward on the assumption that time does not allow for any serious re-organisation of rebel forces or the infiltration of many troops from ME. The main value of mixed HQs will be to form a bridge between ME and the rebels and so stress a larger loyalty. The infiltration of even small cadres of troops will raise the rebel morale and increase our chances for Ark phase 3. ELAS GHQ in its modified form would be administrative, not operational.

It is most important in my opinion that accredited military press correspondents go into Greece at this stage under cover of the political unification — without reference to consent by ELAS or EDES organisations — in order that the shroud of secrecy over Greek affairs may be lifted.

Index